The War of Art

The War of Art

A History of Artists' Protest in America

Lauren O'Neill-Butler

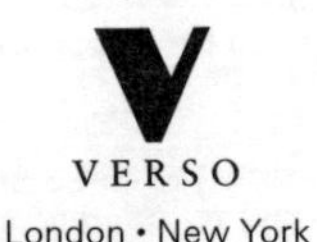

VERSO
London • New York

This paperback edition first published by Verso 2026
First published by Verso 2025

Chapters 1 and 10 were previously published by Pioneer Works (November 11, 2020, and January 25, 2022, respectively). Chapter 2 was previously published by Bookforum (March 4, 2021). Chapters 4, 5, and 6 were previously published by Artforum (August 24, 2020, October 2019, and February 2019).

The manufacturer's authorized representative in the EU for product safety (GPSR) is LOGOS EUROPE, 9 rue Nicolas Poussin, 17000, La Rochelle, France, contact@logoseurope.eu

1 3 5 7 9 10 8 6 4 2

Verso
UK: 6 Meard Street, London W1F 0EG
US: 207 East 32nd Street, New York, NY 10016
versobooks.com

Verso is the imprint of New Left Books

ISBN-13: 978-1-80429-636-3
ISBN-13: 978-1-80429-635-6 (US EBK)
ISBN-13: 978-1-80429-634-9 (UK EBK)

British Library Cataloguing in Publication Data
A catalogue record for this book is available from the British Library

Library of Congress Cataloging-in-Publication Data
A catalog record for the hardback edition of this book is available from the Library of Congress

Typeset in Sabon by MJ & N Gavan, Truro, Cornwall
Printed and bound by CPI Group (UK) Ltd, Croydon CR0 4YY

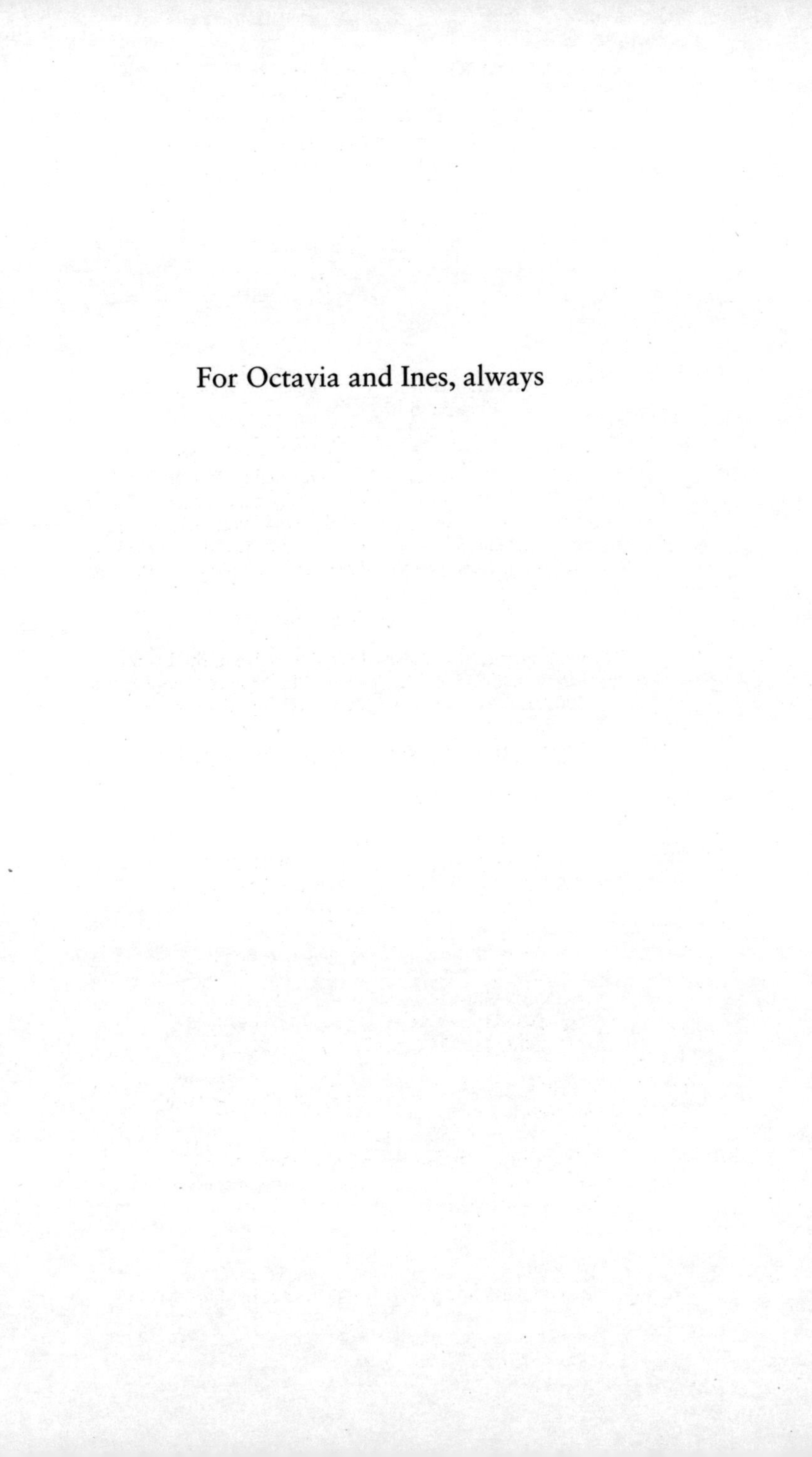

For Octavia and Ines, always

Contents

Acknowledgments

As a non-native settler living in what is presently known as the United States, I want to first offer my profound respect for all Indigenous peoples, creators, scholars, artists, and cultural knowledge keepers.

I am beyond grateful to the students who took my classes at Hunter College and the School of Visual Arts. You are too many to name individually, but I thank you for all your incisive comments and questions. Thanks as well to the editors who originally commissioned some of these essays: Brendan Embser, Michael Famighetti, Zack Hatfield, David Everett Howe, David O'Neill (for a borrowed title!), Elizabeth Schambelan, and David Velasco. This book also benefited from critical feedback given by Lisa Darms, Nicole Miller, and Michael Massnig. Leo Hollis, thank you for being an ideal editor and collaborator.

I'm also indebted to the friends, artists, writers, critics, editors, curators, art historians, and art workers who have provided key support, research assistance, and interviews for this book: Marshella Abrams, Katie Anania, Jennifer Ashton, Catherine D. Anspon, Anneliis Beadnell, Walter Benn Michaels, Skip Blumberg, Julia Bryan-Wilson, Miriam Campos Quinn, Mary Ellen Carroll, Michael Chisolm, Katie Cicatelli-Kuc, Harry Cullen, Chad Dawkins, Agnes Denes, Eva Díaz, Trisha Donnelly, Amelia Farley, fierce pussy (Nancy Brooks Brody, Joy Episalla, Zoe Leonard, Carrie Yamaoka), Marc Furi, Nan Goldin, Nancy Goldring, Andrea Greer, Clayton Guthrie, Edgar Heap of Birds, Shanna Ketchum-Heap of Birds, Nicole Haroutunian, Laura Hoffmann, Nene Humphrey, Jodie Jacobson, Poppy Johnson, Alex Jovanovich, Joyce Kozloff, Jennifer

Krasinski, Lucy Lippard, Rick Lowe, Israel McCloud (thank you so much for allowing your work to grace the cover), Brenda Miller, Carrie Moyer, Yxta Maya Murray, John Melick (and everyone who made the Beverley Art Writers Grant possible for me—I never thought I'd finish this book while traveling in Australia, but I am so glad I did), Lucas Michael, René Mogensen (and the haven of Wassard Elea where I wrote some of the first few chapters), Jenny Moore (and Tinworks staff), Sabra Moore, Margot Norton, Amy O'Neill, Adam Putnam, Melissa Ragain, Ethel Renia, Jocelyn Rodriguez, Sue Schaffner, Olivia Shao, Brian Sholis, Katy Siegel, Howard Singerman, Jacqueline Skiles, Martha Tenney, Leslie Tonkonow, Libby Viera-Bland, Nick Walther, Megan Williams, Kyle Williams, Katherine Wolkoff, Willie Jamaal Wright, Rachel Valinsky, Eero Yli-Vakkuri, and anyone I missed.

Thank you to the staff at the research institutions that made this work possible: Adobe Krow Archives and Ryan Lee Gallery, Barnard Archives and Special Collections at Barnard College, the Benny Andrews Foundation, the Berkeley Art Museum and Pacific Film Archive, University of California, the David Wojnarowicz Foundation, the Fales Library and Special Collections at New York University, Manuscripts and Archives Division at the New York Public Library, the Museum of Modern Art Archives and Library, the Schomburg Center for Research in Black Culture at the New York Public Library, and the Whitney Museum of American Art Archives. The New School Professional Development Fund provided a stipend to travel to Oklahoma City and Houston, for which I am grateful.

To the teachers of my children: thank you so much. Finally, huge thanks to my family for enduring and encouraging me along the way. This book is dedicated to Ines and Octavia, but it couldn't have happened without Colleen. And above all, I thank Arthur Ou, for everything.

Introduction

On November 10, 1971, the artist, educator, and Black Emergency Cultural Coalition (BECC) cofounder Benny Andrews entered the Manhattan House of Detention for Men, aka the Tombs, to give a two-hour drawing demonstration to about thirty inmates. In the eleventh-floor auditorium, he presented a lesson on how to sketch a face from three different angles, and then instructed the group to give it a go. "Don't try too hard," he advised, "The rhythm comes from your head; you're just using your hands."[1] Andrews brought along a reporter from the *New York Times*, to ensure media coverage. This became a BECC strategy from then on.

The successful workshop marked the beginning of the coalition's engagement with the incarcerated, through its Prison Arts Program, which lasted until 1982, when it lost crucial funding from the National Endowment for the Arts (the same year Andrews was appointed director of the endowment's Visual Arts Program). The eleven-year effort became an inspiration to later endeavors, and, as I'll argue here, broadened the critical activism that originated with the BECC's protest of the Metropolitan Museum's *Harlem on My Mind* exhibition in 1969 and subsequent demonstrations at the Whitney Museum of American Art.

In 1971, Andrews was also working on his "Bicentennial" series of paintings, which offers a biting critique of American racism and sexism through a blend of social realism, collage, surrealism, autobiography, and Southern folk art. He was questioning some old ideas he'd learned back in art school, namely that art should not be instrumentalized.

Art is not a means to an end, so the story goes, and therefore it should not have any utility. To seek that would mean to sacrifice art's unique nature as discrete, timeless, porous, and boundary-defying. Many artists follow this edict today—they do not expect their output to cause any profound changes in the world. They work in their studios, often alone, and do not intend their art to "do" anything, particularly within a society that they feel is already overly instrumentalized and prone to evaluation and assessment. But, increasingly, artists are tired of these ideas. Andrews was one such painter who decided to start working collectively for social change by using his voice, and art, to speak truth to power. Sometimes it meant putting his own body on the line.

This is a book about artists and their activisms, which span a range of methods—from protesting to philanthropy, and from wheat pasting to planting a field of wheat. There are many forms that a protest can take. What binds them is that they had a desire for social justice—though specific outcomes could never be controlled. The motivating factor was always anger, rage at the unjust. But also at the social perception of *who* is allowed to be angry, and *who* can be punished, gaslit, or shunned for their ire. "My anger," Audre Lorde reminds us, "has meant pain to me but it has also meant survival, and before I give it up, I'm going to be sure that there is something at least as powerful to replace it on the road to clarity."[2]

Anger leads to action. Action leads to tactics. And each era demands its own, though some strategies remain key. When these approaches are studied together, the successes and failures become clear, offering lessons and encouragement for younger generations tackling some of the same structural issues today, including racism and sexism. Perhaps by looking closely at the past, artists today will not feel as though they are taking the first step, but rather that they are building on previous accomplishments while expanding definitions of artist-led activism. In the same way, the artists discussed in this book stand on the shoulders of activists from the civil rights movement and the feminist movement.

The pressure to act can feel like a heavy load, and the expectation that artists should change the world is, for some, understandably too much to bear. To be sure, my argument is *not* that artists are the solution. They certainly don't have the money nor the means it takes to fix the various ills of society. What I aim to show, however, is that they have motivated change and left a major mark.

This is a journey through that history, centering on tactics and strategies across a fifty-year timespan and within a single country—the United States. Why? This focus certainly doesn't stem from an idea of American exceptionalism, but rather because it's an efficient organizing principle, and the United States is where I have the most experience as an arts writer. The widening field of activism looks entirely different across the globe, and my objective is not to offer a comparative survey as that falls outside my knowledge.

The word *war* in the title of this volume refers to how artists have fought for change. By using the word, I want to also acknowledge, more broadly, the ongoing war around the globe. This constant war creates expropriation, violence, death, and other barbaric outcomes, and, as Silvia Federici notes, it produces new forms of war. The chapters in this book offer alternative new forms—of solidarity, autonomy, and ways to de-commodify life. Each detailed case study is an examination of how artists and collectives resisted exploited artistic labor under capitalism and took it upon themselves to create solutions.

While the book doesn't follow a strictly linear timeline, to instead observe overlapping activisms, it could be said to begin in the late 1960s, when the strategies artists used to protest inequality in museums replicated the primary functions of the institutions themselves: publicity, distribution, display, and publications. An early chapter takes up the world's first feminist artists' collective, Women Artists in Revolution (WAR), which originated in May 1969 in New York City and was soon followed by several more brief but highly effective groups. The late 1960s was, of course, a critical moment for radical activism in the US, and while artists were somewhat late to join in, one radical cadre, the Art Workers' Coalition (AWC), tried to make political and economic changes in the art world. It was very male, however, and many women in the group felt alienated. Though it did initially put forward demands to help Black and Latinx artists, the AWC wasn't concerned that women were largely not invited to show their works at galleries and museums.

The members of WAR argued, correctly, that what was readily available to a male artist, such as exhibitions and press, was typically denied to women. My research for the chapter involved conducting interviews while poring over primary materials—largely printed matter. Not everything could be found or remembered; too much time had passed, and, sadly, too many people had passed away. But this is a story that needed to be finally told—in a more focused way than before—about a group of intergenerational women striving against sexism, racism, a lack of institutional support, and ultimately against a structural process of disenfranchisement. They organized and tried to change museums but couldn't. Some moved on to build their own infrastructures, including galleries and studios, leaving "permanent revolution" behind.[3]

The subsequent chapter moves to the BECC, which was established on January 9, 1969, by Benny Andrews, Romare Bearden, Vivian Browne, Cliff Joseph, and Norman Lewis. These artists first organized in response to the Whitney Museum of American Art's 1968 exhibition *The 1930s: Painting and Sculpture in America*, which omitted the contributions of Black artists. Faith Ringgold—perhaps this book's patron saint—spearheaded the protest on November 17, 1968, at the museum. A crowd of about thirty showed up outside. "On the picket line I met the artists Tom Lloyd, William T. Williams, and Benny Andrews for the first time," Ringgold recalled, and it's clear that this protest was instrumental to the formation of the BECC.[4]

The BECC then famously protested the Metropolitan Museum of Art's 1969 show *Harlem on My Mind: Cultural Capital of Black America, 1900–1968*, which also neglected to include Black painters and sculptors. As noted, in 1971, the group's focus grew to include the creation of the Prison Arts Program—encompassing slide lectures on art history, workshops in painting, drawing, and sculpture, and exhibitions—in jails, prisons, juvenile detention centers, and mental health facilities throughout the United States.

By the time I began researching and teaching the BECC's tactics and pedagogy, its primary members had also passed away. Thanks to Michael Chisolm, the BECC's administrator for many years, its archive is held at the Schomburg Center for Research in Black Culture in New York. Andrews's studio notebooks are also a fount of BECC information, and reading them at his estate in Brooklyn was helpful, as was listening to interviews conducted by Camille Billops and James Hatch for their oral history series, which are archived at City College of New York, CUNY.

While the BECC was skilled at writing press releases and speaking to journalists, in the 1970s artist-led groups in the guerilla media movement took the means of reporting into their own hands by using newly available, portable video equipment such as the Sony Portapak. They soon began to bypass mainstream media, making their own television programs, art films, and documentaries. Perhaps the most pioneering group of the time, the Top Value Television collective, or TVTV (the subject of chapter 4), was formed in San Francisco in 1972.

Its finest activism occurred right at the beginning, when it invaded the presidential nominating conventions in Miami

Beach that year and produced two fascinating documentaries that challenged the networks' at-a-distance coverage of the same events, through content and production. For a few decades, much of this footage languished, until, almost twenty years ago, hundreds of hours of TVTV footage were gifted to the Berkeley Art Museum and Pacific Film Archive. In 2019, the institution launched a major restoration and digitization project, with help from a National Endowment for the Humanities grant. An accompanying website presents a bounty of raw footage, interviews, and TVTV's paper archives.[5]

WAR, the BECC, and TVTV's approaches were taken up by artists in later decades—from the beginning of the AIDS epidemic in the 1980s to the opioid epidemic that began in the 1990s. Of course, artists have historically participated in protests—from partaking in the French Revolution to later rebellions in Russia, Mexico, and China, to fighting in the civil rights and women's liberation movements. They have long used activism as a tool for undoing abuses of power. Many were part of the avant-garde or members of marginalized communities who organized because there was a need to see and be seen. At the time of this writing, artists are involved in social movements ranging from climate justice to Palestinian liberation to prison abolition. Increasingly, artists describe themselves as activists, but has the term become normalized? Instrumentalized? Some veteran activists have abandoned the term altogether and prefer to be called community organizers. Meanwhile, activism seems to mean multiple things, from signing petitions and clicktivism on social media to risking arrest in direct action. Artist-led activism is the subject of classes (some that I've taught); it's a concentration in some art schools; and it's an ongoing presence in numerous museum and gallery exhibitions. In short, "it's timely," to cite the most common refrain. But when is it not?

All of this was on my mind when artists led the way to effective change in US art institutions in 2019: including the New Museum's unionization of staff, the resignation of Warren B. Kanders as vice chairman of the Whitney Museum of American Art's board, and the rejection of donations from the Sackler family after Nan Goldin led a series of protests broadcasting their connections to the opioid crisis. In spring 2020, when the art market was momentarily suspended during the beginning of the Covid pandemic, a break occurred.

Artists near me in New York began to quickly organize—from collaborating on fundraisers for hospitals to organizing anti-racism campaigns to establishing mutual aid groups to collect and distribute PPE. At the time, I was teaching an art history seminar on activist collectives that emerged in the late 1960s, including WAR and the BECC. I began noticing some similarities between these newer groups—a sense of necessity, urgency, and community—and those of the past. There was an echo and it seemed that the changes could last, that the art market could cease operating as such a controlling presence over the way contemporary art is made, exhibited, and written about, and that perhaps art institutions would become less conservative.

Unfortunately, business as usual recrudesced not long after. By the end of 2020, it became clear that while there had been an explosion of artist-activists, there had also not been enough study to link the past to the present in a comprehensive way. To fill that gap and to resist further cultural amnesia, I sensed we needed a detailed account of an enduring, interconnected struggle of artistic activism—one that could connect untold stories and pay attention to their various disconnections.

What constitutes artist-led activism? How is it different from political art? The best way to answer these questions is not through theory or evaluative tools, but through case studies, which can show the relation of activism to politics in each instance. This book also makes an activist argument for a few more well-known artworks, particularly those that are still evolving. For example, Agnes Denes, a pioneer of environmental art and the subject of chapter 5, has always been concerned with renewal even while predicting oncoming climate catastrophe, and that is one reason why it felt so urgent to discuss her work in this book.

Beginning in the 1980s, her activism was ignited through her iconic large-scale, pre-social practice artworks that often require a living, organic format and several hundred volunteers. *Wheatfield: A Confrontation*, 1982, which was planted in Lower Manhattan and *Tree Mountain—A Living Time Capsule—11,000 Trees, 11,000 People, 400 Years*, 1992–96, which is still active in rural Finland, are two prime examples of Denes's activist works that had clear objectives, such as durable land reclamation and restoration. They are complex and, as I'll argue, not perfect projects. In June 2024, I presented selections from this chapter at Tinworks in Bozeman, Montana, while Denes's new iteration of her most famous work was rising in the nonprofit's field. It was the first time Denes had accepted an invitation to reposition the work in another US context, and it took a more specific approach than the 1982 version, addressing the role of wheat in the history and economy of Montana, including the loss of farmland there.

I have learned while teaching and writing that it is generally not helpful to offer strict definitions of activism aside from that it is always a means to an end. Activist art is *always* political, though not all political art is activist art. The fine line between them collapses often, and that's a good thing. There have been many contemporary artists who have productively blurred this boundary. The legendary jacket that David Wojnarowicz made and wore to an AIDS Coalition to Unleash Power (ACT UP) protest in 1988 at the Food and Drug Administration (FDA) headquarters became a meme in later years because of the urgency of the pithy text he wrote on it, and because

Wojnarowicz is regarded as one of—if not *the*—best-known artist-activists worldwide. (It read: "IF I DIE OF AIDS—FORGET BURIAL—JUST DROP MY BODY ON THE STEPS OF THE FDA.") His near martyrdom in contemporary times speaks to who is allowed to be a canonical dissenter, and who is not. While Wojnarowicz is central to the book's first chapter, the following pages aim to expand that canon.

Hock E Aye Vi Edgar Heap of Birds, the subject of chapter 8, has created numerous text-based political works. He is an enrolled citizen of the Cheyenne and Arapaho Nation, well known for his prolific engagement with multiple media—paintings, drawings, prints, and public art—and has been based on tribal land in Oklahoma since the 1980s. Since 2021, he has focused his activism as philanthropy at public universities and has, in turn, created opportunities including residencies and exhibitions for Indigenous artists from the United States.

Ringgold likewise toed the line between political and activist art. She participated in many protests over her long life, urging museums to show work by more Black women artists. "The main thing is that I didn't let things just pass," Ringgold once told me about her many years of activism, adding, "There could be a lot more change, and I think there will be more change. There's room for a lot more. There's got to be more consistent opposition to hatred and contempt in the world, and not adding more evil."[6]

Some of her most famous artworks directly refer to America—to symbols such as its flag, but also to its people. She was acutely aware of the American penchant for dissent and created paintings and posters about the civil rights movement and civil disobedience. She was a member of several collectives to be discussed early in this book that proposed the idea of intersectionality before it was coined as a term, including Women Students and Artists for Black Art Liberation (WSABAL) and the Ad Hoc Women Artists' Committee (AHWAC).

It has long been said that Nan Goldin makes political art, but in 2017, she also began to be an activist. She was prompted, in part, to spearhead Prescription Addiction Intervention Now (PAIN) the focus of chapter 10, after reading Margaret Talbot argue in the *New Yorker* that "no group of activists quite as angry and eloquent as ACT UP has emerged" to make the opioid crisis an "urgent priority."[7] The collective has focused on the toxic philanthropy of the billionaire Sackler family, who kindled the epidemic with their drug, OxyContin.

From the beginning, PAIN exposed the institutions that had accepted the Sackler's donations and through direct action, the collective successfully compelled many museums and universities to refuse Sackler funding and cut ties with the family. PAIN's work has also expanded to fight the stigma that surrounds drug use and advocates for models of treatment grounded in harm reduction. It advocates for legislation that can provide life-saving treatment for people who use drugs. PAIN's demands include accessible naloxone (the lifesaving medication that reverses overdose), overdose prevention centers, and medicated, assisted, effective, and compassionate treatment.

Not long after Wojnarowicz wore his famed jacket to a protest at the FDA headquarters, he wrote an essay for a catalog accompanying *Witnesses: Against Our Vanishing*, the pivotal New York exhibition about AIDS, which Goldin organized at Artists Space in 1989. In his piece, Wojnarowicz excoriated politicians who were cruelly obstructing AIDS education and treatment. The National Endowment for the Arts had also callously defunded *Witnesses*, but the resulting controversy attracted the press and raised the exhibition into the national conversation. In an interview at the time, Wojnarowicz pointed out that for decades, if not centuries, art had had no clout at all, as it was always competing with other media and the news. But, as he said: "If images and words have such power to create this storm of controversy, isn't that great? It means the control of information has a crack in its wall."[8]

I asked Goldin if she finds a connection between *Witnesses* and her more recent protests, which similarly have shown that the control of information has a crack in its wall—that artists can and do influence the news cycle, increase awareness, and prompt changes. "There's a lot of direct links," she said, adding, "The opioid crisis is the epidemic of our times, like AIDS was, and it's also related to government malfunction and to the lack of medical practices and lack of prescriptions that are used to help people. They also share the same stigma, and so a lot of our work is to try to de-stigmatize addiction, and to educate people on that. Our battles are similar."[9]

While PAIN's protests have been well documented, the group's understanding of tactics, such as the mediagenic die-in, was sharpened by studying earlier activist groups in the late 1980s and 1990s, including ACT UP. But what's also important is that ACT UP had derived that very tactic from environmental rights activists in the 1960s. One can trace a genealogy of these protest images, which were largely taken by news reporters. (And clearing rights for such imagery is a costly endeavor, as I've learned.) ACT UP also enacted other strategies employed earlier by the BECC, such as forming strong relationships with the press, tipping off journalists to their actions, and staging press conferences to publicize their position, which the BECC, in turn, learned from the civil rights movement.

It's no surprise that one of the most effective forms of activism is media attention, and such "hits" are always a means to an end—as getting people to talk and to think is one of the best ways to create an impact. Occasionally, the campaigns with the most press attention have been the most successful.

But many activists today are seeking larger frameworks beyond the media. They are looking for more integrative, coalitional ways of working. There is a need for greater coordination across groups, to expose the always underlying connections between gender, race, and class. This is not a new idea: the suffrage and abolition movements formed nearly simultaneously and sometimes shared ideas; the civil rights movement and the New Left informed one another, and due to some of their sexist shortcomings, drove women to kick off the second wave of feminism. To some degree, some of the groups in this book collaborated. While researching WAR, I discovered a statement by artist Tom Lloyd, of the Black and Puerto Rican Committee of the Art Workers' Coalition: "I would like it clearly understood that the Black artists wholeheartedly support the demands of the women's group of AWC," he wrote, adding, "We see their demands as paralleling ours. We will work with them to see aims realized. I urge all art workers to support them."[10]

The AWC and WAR met at the same artist-run space, simply called "Museum," for regular meetings. Similarly, during the 1980s and '90s, several AIDS activist groups met at "The Center"—or, The Lesbian, Gay, Bisexual & Transgender Community Center. These "third places," or community hubs of power, have been historically crucial for activist organizing—they were the backbone of the civil rights movement. Such spaces are particularly important for working-class artists and collectives who could not afford a studio to work in, let alone rent spaces in which to meet. Some of the direct-action groups that met at the Center include ACT UP (founded in 1987), Gran Fury (the propaganda arm of ACT UP, founded in 1988), and Queer Nation (founded in 1990). Many artists were involved in these collectives, united by friendship and an urgent desire to draw awareness to the political nature of the epidemic. Collectives that emerged from these groups include fierce pussy (chapter 6) and Dyke Action Machine! or DAM! (chapter 7). While fierce pussy embraced low-fi, rough-and-ready aesthetics, DAM! preferred glossy advertising graphics that took months to create—sometimes completed at their corporate day jobs. Both collectives created acts of graphic subversion that ultimately countered consumer advertising and exposed the deficiency of lesbian visual representation in mainstream culture.

Much of this book is about activism begun in the 1990s—perhaps that's because as a teenager I closely followed the anti-globalization movement against the International Monetary Fund and the World Bank. I watched protests unfold from Seattle to Prague and participated in a few in Florida. At the same time, I studied second-wave feminism, which argued for more educational and professional access for women, legal protections against rape, harassment, and workplace discrimination, and, as a third waver, I absorbed those fights.

With a group of friends in the mid-1990s, I became involved with a local Food Not Bombs group and participated in protests for animal rights and against the School of the Americas in Georgia. We set up "distros" in front of shows and distributed zines and photocopied essays by the likes of Emma Goldman and Howard Zinn. A few years later, as an undergraduate at New College of Florida, I studied Richard Rorty's then-current takes on pragmatism and feminism, and his ideas remained with me for decades, and even appear in the chapter on fierce pussy (which, it's worth noting, was the spark for this book, and comes out of a feature essay I wrote on the group in 2019).

An important example of grassroots artist-led activism in the Southern United States (one that I first learned of while at New College) is Project Row Houses (PRH). Founded in 1994 in the Third Ward area of Houston, Texas, by seven local artists, PRH began as a community-engaged effort to restore a row of eight shotgun houses and has moved far beyond social practice art, into a robust nonprofit that presents exhibitions, events, workshops, and perhaps most intriguingly, affordable housing. A guiding principle of PRH—which recalls Edgar Heap of Birds's commitment to living in Oklahoma—is that change, stability, and growth depend on the artists who stay in their community. This is an approach that requires different kinds of tactics, which are meant to make change in the long run.

While there is much to say about PRH's inspiring history, chapter 9 spotlights how the organization has confronted the affordable housing crisis in Houston. At the time of this writing, PRH encompasses five city blocks and thirty-nine structures, including fifty-four low-income apartment units. I visited PRH in March 2024 to interview its founders and staff about development in the neighborhood and to join its exuberant thirtieth anniversary celebrations. Across from nearly every PRH site, I noticed a new, high-rent townhome going up, which provided a strong contrast to the work of Project Row Houses to preserve the character, culture, and affordability of the neighborhood as it transitions.

In 2020, when I began conceptualizing this book, I was collaborating with DYKWTCA? (Do you know where the children are?), a direct response to the Trump administration's detaining and separation of immigrant families. In 2019, artists Mary Ellen Carroll and Lucas Michael began to conceive of a traveling benefit exhibition by artists taking a stand against the US government's internment of nearly 5,550 unaccompanied children seeking asylum in the country. After putting out a call to action in December, Carroll and Michael received over one hundred new works, in various media. Each piece incorporates an account, in whole or in part, from a child who was separated from their family and detained by the government.

Their narratives come from interviews conducted in June 2019 by legal, medical, and mental health experts, working under the 1997 Flores Settlement Agreement, which provides protections for minors detained in immigration custody. These experts decided to go public with the interviews, which spoke to the torturous and illegal conditions of the detainment centers. The nonprofit Project Amplify shared the transcripts with the organizers, who then made them available to the participating artists.

The show's first iteration, *When We First Arrived . . .* was held at The Corner at Whitman-Walker, a community health center in Washington, DC, from January to March 2020. Each work was made available at a set price/donation of five hundred dollars and was distributed through a random selection process to buyers, with private foundations matching the sales. All proceeds were donated to immigrant rights organizations: Innovation Law Lab, Team Brownsville, Terra Firma, and the Safe Passage Project. The digital registry Artory and the art advisory and appraisal firm Winston Art Group registered the works using blockchain technology to permanently log the Flores interviews with their associated artworks. Additionally, DYKWTCA specified that if the initial donor/owner holds the work of art for less than five years, the proceeds of any sales would be split equally between the seller, the artist, and one of the organizations.

Inspired by the project's focus, urgency, and long-term political goals, I assisted Carroll and Michael with various needs: from the micro (press release editing) to the macro (brainstorming meetings). It was striking to see it all come together so pragmatically. One way that happened was through a constant focus on having the Flores interviews continue to be read and circulated in the public sphere. It was a simple yet practical plan that worked.

It wasn't lost on me that the show in DC stood in a long lineage of artist-organized exhibitions—including *Witnesses*—that have pushed back against state-sponsored oppression. Some thirty years later, the last line of Goldin's bracing essay accompanying her exhibition continues to reverberate, sounding an alarm to all artists: "We will not vanish."

1

The Jacket

March 11, 2016: Hillary Clinton apologized today, saying she "misspoke" in an interview on MSNBC. The former secretary of state had stated that Nancy Reagan, who died on Sunday, March 6, and her husband, President Ronald Reagan, "started a national conversation" on AIDS that "penetrated the public conscience." But the former president didn't deliver a major speech on the epidemic until 1987, six years after the Centers for Disease Control and Prevention (CDC) first reported on the disease, and after more than 47,993 people had already died of AIDS in the United States.

After Clinton "misspoke," I kept thinking about an odd episode from Nancy Reagan's real history: her cover story in the December 1981 issue of Andy Warhol's *Interview* magazine. Editor Bob Colacello and his assistant Doria Reagan (Ron Jr.'s new wife) had arranged the chat, the first lady's debut in-depth conversation after occupying the White House. Warhol reluctantly agreed to go down to Washington to conduct the discussion. The same issue featured erotic pictures of men by Herbert List, George Platt Lynes, and Edward Steichen. There were also photographs by Robert Mapplethorpe, staff photographer for the magazine, of various glamorous people partying around New York.

It's strange to think that Nancy Reagan could have been an ally of queer communities, that perhaps the homophobic culture wars of the 1980s could have been avoided. Was this what Clinton imagined? Probably not. Right after her statement was published, a fierce outcry broke out across social media. Many people were particularly enraged that the truth surrounding the Reagans and AIDS—the administration notoriously saw the disease as only afflicting gay men and, to a lesser extent, intravenous drug users—continued to be forgotten, ignored, and, even worse, fabricated.[1] The redrafting of the past had to stop.

Clinton wasn't the only presidential candidate putting out fires that day. Donald Trump's campaign canceled his Chicago rally moments before it was to begin, citing security concerns. Hundreds of anti-Trump protesters had breached the rally's University of Illinois venue, and police arrested five people as violent clashes broke out. Trump called for "peace" in a statement. While I wasn't sure what was going on with Clinton's bizarre misremembering, I knew Trump's words amounted to irony.

Meanwhile, an iconic image of the artist David Wojnarowicz began to circulate on Instagram, from a protest that took place in another, not too far away world. It pictured him

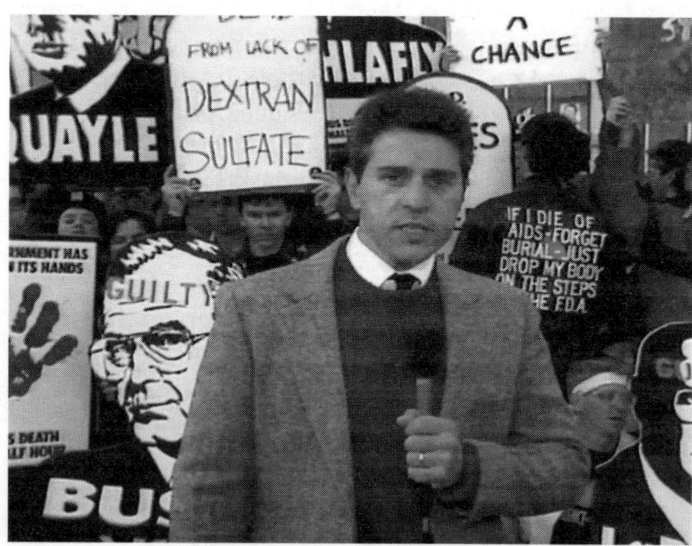

Still from Chris McKim's *Wojnarowicz*, 2020, color, sound, 108 minutes.

from the back, wearing a bespoke denim jacket during a 1988 demonstration at the US Food and Drug Administration (FDA) headquarters. The image was taken by the activist and lawyer William Dobbs. Over a painted pink triangle (a reclaimed LGBTQ symbol, made in response to the upside-down version used by the Nazis), Wojnarowicz meticulously scripted a rageful text in white letters on his jacket:

IF I DIE OF AIDS—FORGET BURIAL—JUST DROP MY BODY ON THE STEPS OF THE FDA.

In 1988, Wojnarowicz was thirty-four years old. He had been diagnosed with HIV the year before and had a deep sense of parrhesia: an obligation to speak out, even at personal risk. The ancient Greek tragedian Euripides, who coined the term, would have loved Wojnarowicz's capacity for refusing silencing and the production of false histories. (Tragic theater, particularly its tradition of showing violent wounds, and activism are uniquely interlinked. The tragic plays were one of the earliest forms of activism, but that's a story for another time.) In 1987, after the death of Peter Hujar, his longtime friend/mentor/lover, Wojnarowicz became more politically active, crafting works about AIDS and the political conflicts in El Salvador. Before this, one of his main outlets for expressing his political views was his East Village band, 3 Teens Kill 4, which he was primarily involved with from 1980 to 1983.

Wojnarowicz's parrhesia found a home in his jacket. He was aware of the logic of activist art—take, copy, distribute—a trio that prefigures the self-propagating digital meme. At the time there were other incubating statements, namely the Silence=Death Project's 1987 poster of another pink triangle and General Idea's *Imagevirus*, 1987–1994.[2] Wojnarowicz may have had those in mind when he wrote the text on his jacket; it's also possible he was crafting his 1989 catalog essay for the Nan Goldin–curated exhibition *Witnesses: Against Our Vanishing*. In "Postcards from America: X-Rays from Hell" he wrote:

> I imagine what it would be like if friends had a demonstration each time a lover or friend or stranger died of AIDS. I imagine what it would be like if, each time a lover, friend, or stranger died of this disease, their friends, lovers, or neighbors would take their dead body and drive with it in a car a hundred miles to Washington, DC, and blast through the gates of the White House and come to a screeching halt before the entrance and then dump their lifeless forms on the front steps. It would be comforting to see those friends, neighbors, lovers, and strangers mark time and place and history in such a public way.[3]

Vulnerability, abandonment, and communal decline are central to his art, as evident in his stark and somber untitled photograph of buffalos falling over a cliff—later the cover of U2's single *One*. Wojnarowicz took the picture at the Natural History Museum in Washington, DC, in a diorama showing the mighty bison being hunted. The image still circulates widely on social media, but the picture of him in the jacket has been gaining traction since at least 2016 and may have eclipsed it. What's more, its text has turned into its own image "virus" and has mutated, as variations on a meme. Adopted by different people in different cataclysmic circumstances, the transmuted text in each case has condemned a government that didn't operate under conditions of maximum public transparency, nor communicate the real scope of a threat to endangered populations, nor implement measures of mass testing and preventive care. In the face of a public health emergency and a rising death toll, the people circulated their own infection.

William Burroughs's idea of language as a virus from outer space—of humanity as infected by a language virus that is really a medium for social control—is relevant here as a foil, though I don't purport to totally understand what he meant by it, and likely he didn't want it to be understood, anyway.[4] But it helps to show the flipside of this coin: that take, copy, and distribute is a tactic embraced by most political campaigns.

This is an ancient and nonpartisan strategy: meme (a word modeled on gene), which derives from *mimeme* (or the ancient Greek μίμημα): an imitated thing.

Another word derived from ancient Greek: metaphor. The original Greek is μεταφορά (metaphorá), or "transfer." Today in Greece you can still see the word emblazoned on certain trucks and vans carrying boxes and furniture, as the modern Greek equivalent, *metaphores*, means "movers," or those that transfer stuff from one place to another. Metaphors and illnesses often function as bedfellows, which is something we should always be wary of, per Susan Sontag. "My point is that illness is *not* a metaphor," she wrote in 1978, "and that the most truthful way of regarding illness—and the healthiest way of being ill—is one most purified of, most resistant to, metaphoric thinking."

In a series of three essays first published in the *New York Review of Books* and collected as the book *Illness as Metaphor*, Sontag famously tracked the influence of metaphors linked to diseases such as tuberculosis and cancer, and how these comparisons were applied to ill people so persistently that they obscured the facts of the illnesses. For example, it was said at the turn of the last century that people contracted tuberculosis due to "too much passion." Fifty years later, cancer stemmed from "psychological repression" and "insufficient passion."

In 1989, Sontag applied her same ethical analysis in a follow-up book, *AIDS and Its Metaphors*. Throughout the 1980s, the Reagan administration and the conservative Christian right held that those with HIV contracted it because they were prone to moral laxity or turpitude. Some even believed the disease was a divine punishment, and so, as Sontag writes, "With this illness," as with others, "the effort to detach it from loaded meanings and misleading metaphors seems particularly liberating, even consoling."

Wojnarowicz's "If I Die . . ." statement is resistant to metaphoric thinking, and could be read as a response to Sontag's book, which is why I bring her up. The subsequent variations on his jacket are also not metaphors. They are not clicktivism. They do not delay nor thwart the treatment of a problem or disease; rather they are urgent calls for change. I want to be clear on this because I'm afraid that in the endlessly contextless context of the internet, these images may seem as such.

Under the sign of Sontag (and Wojnarowicz), my intention here is to push back against the idea that diseases, illnesses, and pandemics are political metaphors because, more often than not, such representations are only used to further marginalize and target underprivileged and vulnerable communities. They are made to create more endless war: on February 10, 2020, the Chinese leader Xi Jinping vowed to win the people's *war* against the novel coronavirus. One month later, in his address to the nation, President Emmanuel Macron repeated "Nous sommes en *guerre*" ("We are at war") six times and was soon followed by British Prime Minister Boris Johnson and of course by Trump, who presented themselves as *wartime* leaders. As I wrote this in 2020, I feared that the constant metaphorization of the novel coronavirus would enable new surveillance technologies beyond contact tracing. I still worry that the creation of metaphors is a way of distancing, forgetting, and spinning false narratives rather than challenging and overcoming. But most of all, I fear that metaphors being invented and deployed are a way of avoiding a confrontation with those who are truly responsible for mass destruction. (Using the word *war* in the title of this book became a way for me to keep all of this in mind.)

July 18, 2015: A viral hashtag once again exposed the deep distrust between African Americans and US police. The hashtag #IfIDieInPoliceCustody emerged after the death of Sandra Bland. Bland was pulled over by a Texas police officer for failing to signal before changing lanes, and cops detained her after, they claim, she assaulted an officer. Three days later she was found dead in her jail cell. Police say the twenty-eight-year-old Black woman killed herself, but family, friends, and people on social media do not believe the story—in large part because Bland had just moved to Texas to start a job as a college outreach officer.

While #IfIDieinPoliceCustody is not directly linked to Wojnarowicz's "If I Die . . ." statement, it resonates because police brutality against Black communities continues to be one of our most pervasive public health emergencies. Just as #BlackLivesMatter (BLM) became a unifying narrative frame connecting anti-Black racism to the history of slavery, debt bondage, segregation, and a punishment system geared toward the degradation of Black lives, #SayHerName and #IfIDiein PoliceCustody have also amplified the BLM movement.

In June 2020, during the first wave of the novel coronavirus pandemic and worldwide BLM protests following the police killing of George Floyd, several professors of public health and officials in major cities in America began to declare racism as a public health emergency. They argued that racism is built into institutional and structural mechanisms, such as residential segregation: "Where you live, for most Americans, determines where you go to school and the quality of education you receive," scholar David R. Williams noted. "Where you live determines the quality of your neighborhood environment. Where you live determines even the quality of city services that you have access to. So, in many profound ways, your zip code is a powerful predictor of the factors that drive health." From birth rates to death rates to places of residency and everything in between, racism impacts all levels of public health. As Williams concluded, "We have gotten to the point where we can no longer tolerate such behavior that is literally killing people."[5] Enough is enough.

March 14, 2018: During today's national student walkout to advocate for gun policy change, a protester carried a sign that read: IF I DIE IN A SCHOOL SHOOTING DROP MY BODY ON THE STEPS OF

THE CDC. #IfIDieInASchoolShooting circulated widely on social media in the following weeks, after other school shootings. In another direct reference to Wojnarowicz, Leah Ogdon wrote on Twitter, "The news will talk about me for a while and then forget about me. I will never get to graduate college, become CEO of a company, or start a loving family. If I die, I want my body to be thrown on the steps of the capitol building."

The parallels between the FDA's lack of AIDS research in the 1980s and the CDC's ongoing inaction to prevent yet another ongoing public health crisis—gun violence—is striking. We can fault the Reagan administration for the former and Arkansas congressman Jay Dickey for the latter. In 1996, the Dickey Amendment passed in Congress and effectively ordered the CDC never to fund research that could be seen as advocacy work for gun control.

By and large, the amendment passed because of the National Rifle Association's lobbying efforts—the notorious organization claimed it discovered anti-gun bias in previous CDC-funded studies. And then, in an inexplicable turn of events, Congress members took the exact same amount allocated to gun-violence research ($2.6 million) and reserved the funds for researching traumatic brain injury.

Since 1996, the American Medical Association and the American Public Health Association have shown again and again that gun violence is a public health problem. After the Sandy Hook shooting in 2012, President Obama signed an executive order commanding the National Institutes of Health to take up the study of gun violence. It never happened. A bill that passed in May 2018 now allows the CDC to study gun violence, yet it doesn't reverse the Dickey Amendment and there's a debate about proper funding behind it.

Essentially, this means that it's still up to lawmakers to balance Second Amendment rights with scientific data. In the spring of 2020, there were frequent news reports and

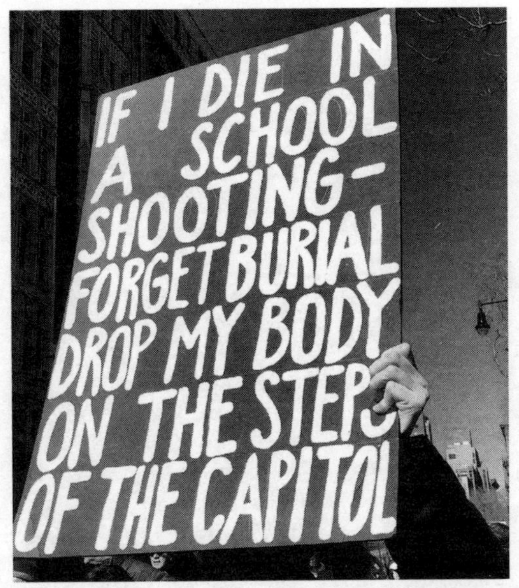

Beth Caron, March for Our Lives Protest in New York City, March 24, 2018.

commentaries on the spikes in gun sales all over the United States. A June 2020 study found that gun owners were nearly four times as likely to die by suicide than people without guns, even when controlling for gender, age, race, and neighborhood. In 2021, after a nearly twenty-five-year hiatus imposed by Congress, the CDC finally began funding research into gun violence.

December 1, 2019: IF TRANSPHOBIA KILLS ME—FORGET BURIAL —DROP MY BODY ON THE STEPS OF CONGRESS. *Via Instagram at the Nashville airport.*

One thing the CDC considers a public health issue: suicide. According to a 2015 report, nearly one-third of lesbian, gay, and bisexual high school students had attempted suicide at least once in the prior year compared to 6 percent of

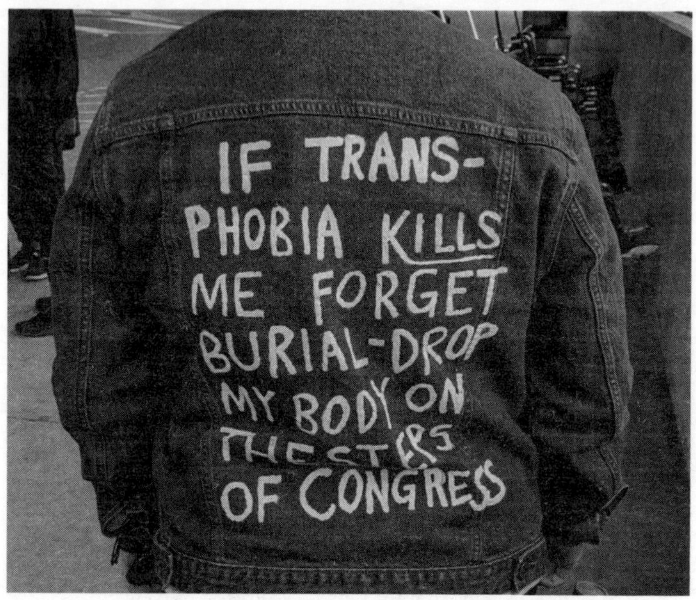

@evren_7 Twitter account, December 1, 2019.

heterosexual youth. A study published in 2018 found that gender-nonconforming youths are at even greater risk, with more than half of the transgender male teenagers attempting suicide over the three years they were followed.

Despite these reports and the rising rates of violence against trans individuals in the United States, states continue to introduce transphobic measures to chip away at transgender rights, including criminalizing medical professionals who prescribe hormone treatments to minors. Other proposed and recent measures include prohibiting transgender people from changing their birth certificates to match their gender identities; banning transgender athletes from playing on sports teams that do not correspond to their sex assigned at birth; and making it illegal to perform gender-affirming surgery.

March 24, 2020: The New York chapter of ACT UP and Housing Works collaborated on a face mask: IF I DIE OF COVID-19—FORGET BURIAL—DROP MY BODY ON THE STEPS OF MAR-A-LAGO.

I'd been waiting for the Wojnarowicz text to pop up again, but I didn't think the comparison of AIDS to the coronavirus would be so controversial. In an April 2020 op-ed for the *Washington Post*, Professor Paul Renfro commented on the ACT UP/ Housing Works mask: "While the novel coronavirus and HIV/ AIDS should certainly be placed in conversation with one another, the notion that the former closely mirrors the latter is overly simplistic and problematic," he wrote. "Yet the gap between the two can always shrink if the president and others continue to couch the coronavirus pandemic in racist and xenophobic terms—and if rich and famous Americans continue to obtain testing and treatment while others go undiagnosed and untreated."

Unfortunately, by then the gap had already shriveled. Trump repeatedly linked Covid-19 to Chinese and East Asian societies (in calling it the "Chinese virus" and "Kung flu"), which has, in turn, stoked violence and harassment in the United States. Through that othering, fearmongering, and stigmatization, the coronavirus and AIDS share some, and probably many more, similarities.

Avram Finkelstein, an artist and founding member of the Silence=Death and Gran Fury collectives, wrote:

> The question of whether AIDS and Covid-19 are comparable, is a question with many answers. Placing aside differences in rapidity of transmission and universality, both pandemics have been molded by institutional lies, intentional neglect, and political subtext. The American agencies responsible for disease surveillance and drug research and approval remain institutionally entrenched.[6]

I wonder if, decades from now, when we look back at 2020, we'll say that the connections between Covid-19 and AIDS seemed almost formal in the beginning—lies, neglect, subtext—but in the end they had nothing in common. As artist Robert Gober put it: "Nobody was banging on pots and pans at seven o'clock during the AIDS crisis."[7]

October 11, 1988: "Our takeover of the FDA was unquestionably the most significant demonstration of the AIDS activist movement's first two years. Organized nationally by ACT NOW to take place on the anniversary of the March on Washington for Lesbian and Gay Rights and just following the second Washington Showing of the Names Project quilt, the protest began with a Columbus Day rally at the Department of Health and Human Services under the banner HEALTH CARE IS A RIGHT and proceeded the following morning to a siege of FDA headquarters in a Washington suburb."—Douglas Crimp[8]

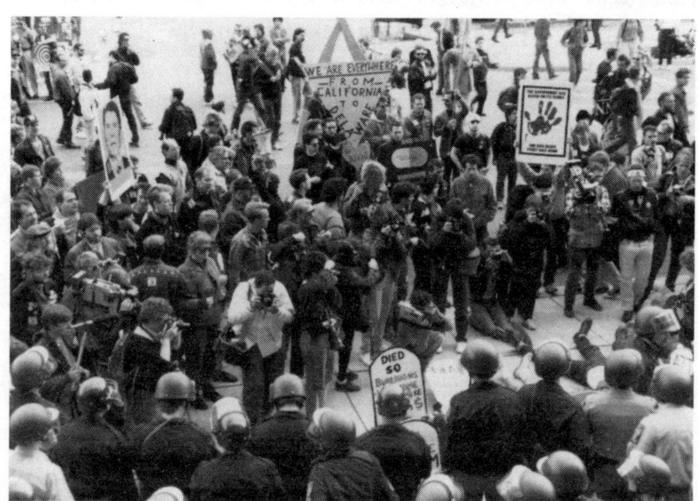

The press capturing an ACT UP die-in at the FDA, Rockville, Maryland, October 11, 1988.

Nearly a thousand people attended "Seize Control of the FDA" in Rockville, Maryland, on October 11, 1988. ACT UP, formed in 1987, had been conducting teach-ins for the rally in the months before. "I think they did them at P.S. 122 . . . I remember these big fat handbooks and all this research," recalled the artist Zoe Leonard, adding, "I basically walked in and then within like two weeks or three weeks was actually understanding the landscape of AIDS in a way that I'd never understood it before."[9]

Wojnarowicz drove down from New York with his partner Tom Rauffenbart and Leonard, who was then twenty-seven years old. Leonard had met Wojnarowicz when they were both working at Danceteria in 1980. By 1988, they had formed the Candelabras, an ACT UP affinity group. Each group—comprising five to fifteen people—was tasked with coming up with its own action and making its own props for the FDA protest. ACT UP had already held a few die-ins, wherein protesters would lay down on the ground; accordingly, the Candelabras came up with foam-core and painted tombstones for protesters to hold. Slogans written on them included "AZT wasn't enough" and "I got the placebo."[10]

In her brilliant Wojnarowicz biography, *Fire in the Belly*, Cynthia Carr notes that he and Tom were arrested that day along with 176 others—one person was charged with assaulting a police officer and the other 175 were charged with loitering. According to a *Washington Post* article, "A glass door and two windows were shattered, and organizers said six activists managed to sneak inside the building for a brief period. The only reported injury was a police officer's scraped nose."[11]

The art historian and critic Douglas Crimp, who certainly knew of Wojnarowicz's art though they were not friends, observed that the protest's success "can perhaps best be measured by what ensued in the year following the action. Government agencies dealing with AIDS, particularly the FDA and

NIH, began to listen to us, to include us in decision-making, even to ask for our input."[12] As I stated in the beginning of this chapter, by 1987 more than 47,000 people in the United States had already died of AIDS. Many of the protesters wore T-shirts that day designed by ACT UP's Majority Actions Committee that read: WE DIE—THEY DO NOTHING.

In smaller text *they* were listed: Ronald Reagan, George Bush, Michael Dukakis, the NIH, the FDA, the US Congress, the Congressional Black and Hispanic Caucus, our national media, and our national minority leaders.

Wojnarowicz died at age thirty-seven on July 22, 1992, in New York. One week later, an ACT UP affinity group called The Marys, who were known for organizing bold actions, prepared a demonstration for him in the East Village. (The Marys included, among others, Joy Episalla and Carrie Yamaoka, also of the lesbian art collective fierce pussy, the subject of chapter 6.) This was the first "political funeral" in a series that came out of the crisis. In the years following Wojnarowicz's death, Rauffenbart scattered his ashes in several meaningful places, including on the lawn of the White House: on October 13, 1996, during ACT UP's second Ashes Action, Rauffenbart climbed the fence in front of the presidential palace and threw some of Wojnarowicz's remains over.

As for the jacket, Wojnarowicz was not known to wear it after the FDA protest, and it's never turned up since 1992. According to sources, Rauffenbart—who passed away in 2019—did not know of its whereabouts.

December 6, 2023: Postscript

Today, the Palestinian writer and professor Refaat Alareer was killed in an airstrike by the Israeli military, along with his brother, his brother's son, his sister, and her three children. His final poem, "If I Must Die," is being shared widely around the world. Israel's ongoing siege of Gaza continues. I am reminded that governmental neglect in the United States takes many forms, including funding genocidal campaigns instead of healthcare and societal wellbeing. Here is Alareer's poem in full:

> If I must die,
> you must live
> to tell my story
> to sell my things
> to buy a piece of cloth
> and some strings,
> (make it white with a long tail)
> so that a child, somewhere in Gaza
> while looking heaven in the eye
> awaiting his dad who left in a blaze—
> and bid no one farewell
> not even to his flesh
> not even to himself—
> sees the kite, my kite you made, flying up above
> and thinks for a moment an angel is there
> bringing back love
> If I must die
> let it bring hope
> let it be a tale

2

Women Artists in Revolution, 1969–71

Though Women Artists in Revolution (WAR) was short-lived, it burned bright for three years and emerged with several lessons of effective activism: how to promote a sense of necessity, setting a solid foundation, and sustaining a strong community. WAR regulars included second-wave feminists Muriel Castanis, Silvia Goldsmith, Juliette Gordon, Doloris Holmes, Janet McDevitt, Doloris O'Kane, Sara Saporta, Jacqueline Skiles, and Nancy Spero. This group of mostly artists—which didn't care that its acronym was militaristic, even while the United States pushed its imperialistic agenda in Vietnam—grew out of the iconic Art Workers' Coalition (AWC). WAR was significant because it also took on issues beyond the arts affecting women, such as reproductive rights. But, as the art critic Lucy Lippard asserted, "Because most of the individuals involved were too young or too unknown to be recognizable, WAR's immediate impact on the art world was minimal, although its long-term breakthrough was immensely important."[1]

Many of the women in WAR were working-class artists without gallery representation—hence "too unknown to be recognizable"—but they drew inspiration from groups such as New York Radical Women, who had already begun to organize in the fall of 1967, and their activist solutions to the problem of easy dismissal were often bold and brilliant. Nonetheless, the art historical canon often leaves out many of these artists, preferring instead to focus on middle-class, white, feminist art and its emphasis on the female body, and on a few leading artists, such as Judy Chicago. Unfortunately, that reading fails to capture the spirit of the women's movement, which was driven by many individuals yearning for change. In their studios, the women of WAR worked diligently, patiently: Sabra Moore was trying to reconfigure quilt making and create a connection to her working-class roots in Texas. Muriel Castanis was making large sculptures of fluidly draped figures. Nancy Spero was painting her *War* series, 1966–70, which challenged both the political orthodoxies of the era and the horrors of the Vietnam War.

1970 was a prime year for feminism. Thriving groups in New York City at the time included Redstockings, WITCH (Women's International Terrorist Conspiracy from Hell), New York Radical Feminists, and countless consciousness-raising groups. This was also a year when feminist books became available, such as Kate Millet's *Sexual Politics*, Shulamith Firestone's *The Dialectic of Sex*, and Robin Morgan's anthology *Sisterhood Is Powerful*. In fall 1970, Lippard started visiting women's studios and founded her own group with artists and AWC members Poppy Johnson, Brenda Miller, and Faith Ringgold. They called it the Ad Hoc Women Artists' Committee (AHWAC), and collaborated with Women Artists in Revolution, and with Women Students and Artists for Black Art Liberation (WSABAL). The latter was a collective led by Ringgold and Michele Wallace that sought to unsettle the simultaneous narratives of second-wave feminism—which primarily benefited white middle-class women. The group also addressed the Black power movement of the time, which had dominant tones of patriarchal authority.[2] While the artists came from different racial and class backgrounds, and worked in different mediums and styles, they were connected by a city, a time, and the drive to demand recognition.

Lines soon started to blur between these splinter groups. Intersectional feminist brain trusts were formed, and they quickly became focused on the interconnected politics of race, class, and gender.

❧

The Art Workers' Coalition has a storied past in art history, but the important role of women in it is not well known.[3] It was formed during the first few months of 1969, not long after the Greek sculptor Takis (Vassilakis) and several friends famously removed his *Tele-Sculpture* (1960) from *The Machine, as Seen at the End of the Mechanical Age* at the Museum of Modern Art (MoMA), on January 3, 1969. Takis no longer wanted to be represented by the piece and felt the museum should have consulted him when choosing a work for the show. He calmly took his work into the institution's sculpture garden and remained there until he received written confirmation from museum staff that it would be withdrawn from the survey, even though the sculpture was no longer technically his: MoMA had acquired it in 1963 for its permanent collection. While in the garden, Takis and his supporters handed out leaflets regarding "artists' control over their works," stating that this was "just the first in a series of acts against the stagnant policies of art museums all over the world."[4]

The incident was certainly an omen of more to come. Aside from the formation of the Black Emergency Cultural Coalition, which I discuss in the next chapter, Takis's protest led to the formation of a small group that held a series of meetings at the Hotel Chelsea to discuss issues relating to the political and social responsibility of museums to artists. In addition to Takis, the gatherings included an international array of artists including Wen-Ying Tsai, Hans Haacke, and Len Lye; *Avalanche* magazine cofounders Liza Béar and Willoughby Sharp; and *Village Voice* art critic John Perreault. This was a group that soon grew exponentially and became known as the Art Workers' Coalition.

They began a dialogue with MoMA director Bates Lowry on January 28, 1969, and presented him with a list of thirteen demands to reform the museum. Opening with a call for the museum to hold a public hearing in February on "The Museum's Relationship to Artists and to Society," they then stated that "a section of the Museum, under the direction of Black artists, should be devoted to showing the accomplishments of Black artists, and that the museum's activities should be extended into the Black, Spanish, and other communities." The list also makes a working-class-focused claim for artist's fees, that admission to the museum should be free, and that the museum should recognize an artist's right to refuse showing a work owned by the museum, among other ideas. Conspicuously absent are any demands regarding women. However, there does seem to be an allusion to the lack of women's representation in the call for a space in the museum "permanently devoted to showing the works of artists without galleries."

MoMA was not an arbitrary target. As Lippard explained in 1970, the museum was then considered the "seat of power," "qualified by its rank in the art world, its Rockefeller-studded board of trustees." There just weren't enough people to tackle all the museums at once and MoMA was especially of interest to the AWC because of its "dependence on galleries and collectors, its maintenance of a safe, blue-chip collection," and, as Lippard notes, in particular, "its lack of contact with the art community and recent art, its disdain for the advice and desires of the artists who fill its void."[5]

While there were always artists in the AWC who disagreed with the museum as an adversary, a majority agreed that such public institutions should be held morally accountable, and perhaps even seen as paradigms of equity. During the first half of 1969, the AWC grew to include hundreds of artists, filmmakers, writers, critics, museum workers, who began to hold demonstrations at MoMA to dramatize its demands. They convened weekly chaotic meetings every Monday night at 8:00 p.m. at Museum: A Project of Living Artists, which was located at 729 Broadway, a few blocks from Washington Square Park. "Robert's Rules of Order had no place" in the meetings, as WAR member Jacqueline Skiles has written. "At worst they sometimes degenerated into shouting matches between competing factions over policy, tactics, and personalities."[6]

A "third place" for coalition building, Museum was initially intended as a community center for artists and was spearheaded by Arthur Hughes, Gary Smith, Sharon Brant, and Robert Resnick, among others. It had a membership of more than 300 artists by 1970, yet as Julie Ault writes, it "was beset by considerable philosophical disagreement. Some members wanted formal exhibition and administrative structures; others wanted a looser art association with exhibitions, events, forums, and services; and still others wanted a completely unrestricted artists' space."[7] Crossover between the AWC and Museum membership ran deep—and political disputes were extensive in both groups.

In response to the AWC's demands, Lowry proposed to establish a Committee on Artists Relations at MoMA to deliberate the issues over a series of meetings; however, he resigned from his job before that group was established. Since MoMA did not agree to the AWC's first demand, the coalition held its own evening forum, the awkwardly titled "An Open Public Hearing on the Subject: What Should Be the Program of the Art Workers Regarding Museum Reform, and to Establish the Program of an Open Art Workers' Coalition," on April 10, 1969, at the School of Visual Arts' auditorium at 209 East Twenty-Third Street. More than 300 people attended and galvanized a subgroup that updated the Art Workers' Coalition demands by June 1969 into a new list of eleven for "modern art museums in general and the New York Museum of Modern Art in particular."

New to this list was the demand that "the Museum should encourage female artists to overcome the centuries of damage done to the image of the female as an artist by establishing equal representation of the sexes in shows, museum purchases and on selection committees." In April 1970, the AWC also created a list of demands for galleries. As if aware of its own posterity, in 1969 the AWC published the papers presented in the open hearing as a Xeroxed book and produced *Documents I*—another photocopied compendium—that gathered the group's early activities, including correspondence, flyers, internal documents, and press coverage.

Though the AWC ended its activities in 1971, it created lasting change. For example, it successfully pressured MoMA into implementing free admission, although sponsored by a corporation (currently the Japanese retailer Uniqlo), and only on one night a week. "For one demonstration," Lippard recalled, "we advertised a free day at the Modern . . . [The artist Scott Burton] did a performance piece that consisted of handing out dimes as the elite entered for an opening, an ironic emulation of John D. Rockefeller's habit of distributing dimes to workers while making millions off them."[8]

Perhaps a more constructive outcome of the AWC was its pressuring of museums into taking a moral stance on the Vietnam War and the related creation of its *And babies* poster (1970), which the AWC used during a protest at MoMA in January 1970 with members of the Guerilla Art Action Group

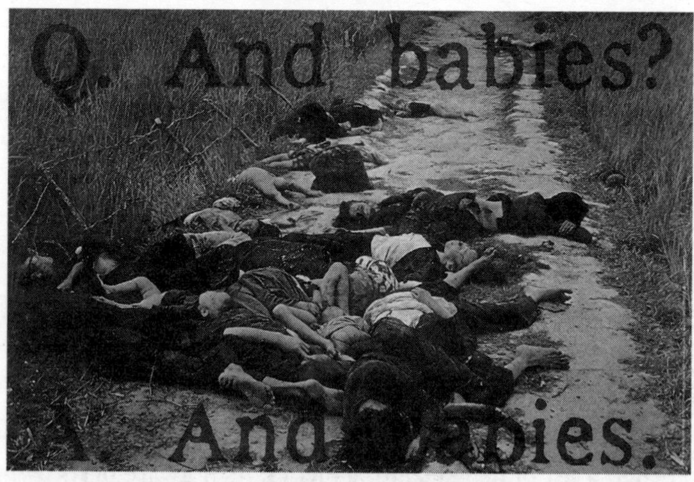

Art Workers' Coalition, *Q. And babies? A. And babies.*, 1970, offset lithograph on paper, overall: 25 × 38 in. (63.5 × 96.5 cm), Smithsonian American Art Museum, Gift of Jon Hendricks, 2017.10, © 1970 Irving Petlin, Jon Hendricks, and Frazer Dougherty.

(GAAG) in front of Pablo Picasso's *Guernica*. The poster replicates a color image taken by US combat photographer Ronald L. Haeberle on March 16, 1968, after the My Lai Massacre, documenting the fact that American soldiers had killed babies in Vietnam. The picture is overlaid in semi-transparent blood-red lettering that asks, along the top, "Q. And babies?" while the bottom answers, "A. And babies." The quote is from a Mike Wallace CBS News television interview with the American soldier Paul Meadlo, who participated in the massacre. The lettering was sourced from the *New York Times*, which printed a transcript of the Meadlo interview the day after.

Under the sole sponsorship of the AWC—MoMA initially said it would fund and circulate the poster, but it pulled financing at the last minute—the New York City lithographers union printed 50,000 posters, which became a vehicle for artists and others to vent their outrage at the Nixon-led government that allowed these atrocities to happen. The work has since been included in several MoMA exhibitions, beginning with the historic 1970 *Information* show of conceptual art curated by Kynaston McShine. Many scholars have noted that it is easily the most successful poster to vent the outrage that so many felt about the conflict in Southeast Asia.

The AWC also urged museums to close on October 15, 1969, as part of the Moratorium to End the War in Vietnam—a day of thousands of mass demonstrations and teach-ins across the United States, which bolstered the anti-war movement at a critical juncture. MoMA, the Whitney Museum of American Art, and the Jewish Museum acquiesced to the AWC's demands and many commercial art galleries also closed for the day. Although the Metropolitan Museum and the Guggenheim Museum did not comply, under pressure from the AWC, the Met postponed the opening of its American painting and sculpture show scheduled for that day, and the Guggenheim was picketed.

The most important facet of the AWC—getting back to the subject of this chapter—was that it served as a springboard for many subgroups, the strongest of which were feminist and action-oriented. These groups—WAR, the Ad Hoc Women Artists' Committee, and WSABAL—paved the path for museums to begin to seriously consider race, class, *and* gender. The feminists didn't just want to be included or have their voices heard, they wanted visibility—which meant both seeing and being seen. While the AWC's efforts have been nostalgically canonized, and its influence on contemporary arts activism is clear, much less has been written about these groups' insurgent feminist politics and the generative connections—and disconnections—between now and then.

What were the conditions of the day for most women artists? Menial jobs that barely covered rent and meals, small artist-run galleries in which to show your work, and, if you had children, a constant need to carve out time for oneself. There was an "unstated need among women," as WAR member Juliette Gordon wrote in 1970, to create a splinter group—to take the AWC's focus on economic and political reforms in the arts and put a much more precise point on it. Non-white, non-male artists needed representation in museums, and they needed to be remunerated on the same scale as those with more privilege.

WAR started "with small meetings in various lofts," as Gordon recalled, and then began to gather at Museum on Mondays at 6:30 p.m., as advertised in their declaration from January 1970, which argues: "We began to crack the traditional record of no hits in the art world during the last half century, but the female is still encased in a basically restricted image which needs to be changed both within the self and in society as both are mutually interdependent."[9]

The feminism adopted by WAR at times seems to embrace essentialism—an innate femaleness. For example, Gordon argues in the flier mentioned above that "women should be able to be wives and creative beings," without an analysis of how women's inequity in the public domain was related to

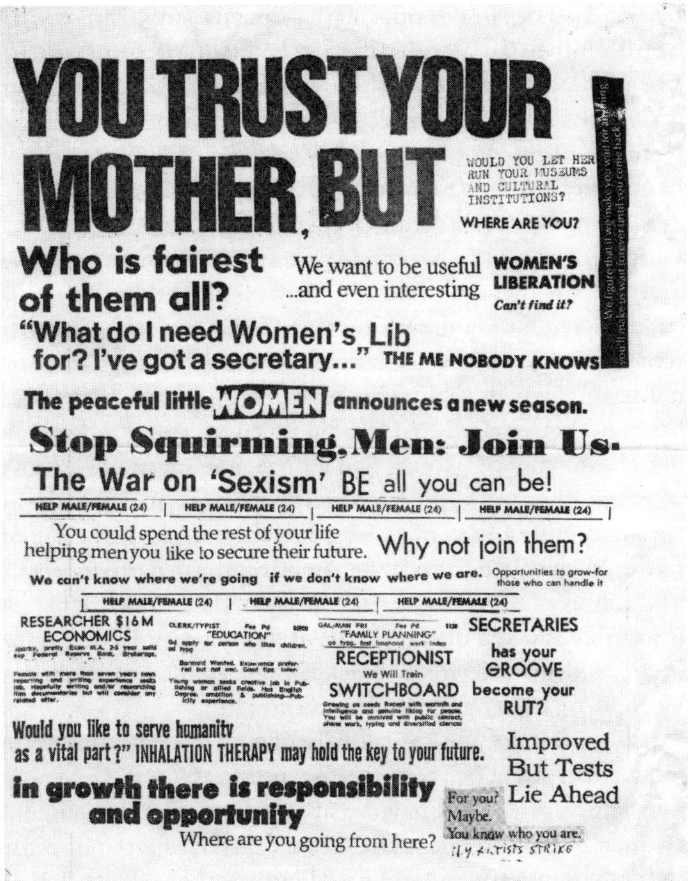

YOU TRUST YOUR
MOTHER, BUT

WOULD YOU LET HER
RUN YOUR MUSEUMS
AND CULTURAL
INSTITUTIONS?

WHERE ARE YOU?

Who is fairest
of them all?

We want to be useful
...and even interesting

WOMEN'S
LIBERATION
Can't find it?

"What do I need Women's Lib
for? I've got a secretary..."

THE ME NOBODY KNOWS

The peaceful little WOMEN announces a new season.

Stop Squirming, Men: Join Us·

The War on 'Sexism' BE all you can be!

HELP MALE/FEMALE (24) | HELP MALE/FEMALE (24) | HELP MALE/FEMALE (24) | HELP MALE/FEMALE (24)

You could spend the rest of your life
helping men you like to secure their future.

Why not join them?

We can't know where we're going if we don't know where we are.

Opportunities to grow-for
those who can handle it

HELP MALE/FEMALE (24) | HELP MALE/FEMALE (24) | HELP MALE/FEMALE (24)

RESEARCHER $16M
ECONOMICS

CLERK/TYPIST
"EDUCATION"

"FAMILY PLANNING"
RECEPTIONIST
We Will Train
SWITCHBOARD

SECRETARIES
has your
GROOVE
become your
RUT?

Would you like to serve humanity
as a vital part?" INHALATION THERAPY may hold the key to your future.

Improved
But Tests
Lie Ahead

in growth there is responsibility
and opportunity

For you?
Maybe.
You know who you are.

Where are you going from here?

N.Y. ARTISTS STRIKE

WAR, "You Trust Your Mother But . . . ," ca. 1970, photocopy, 8 ½" x 11". Sabra Moore NYC Women's Art Movement Collection, 1969–1996; Box 1 and Folder 1; Barnard Archives and Special Collections, Barnard College.

their subordination in the private sphere and family life. This is different from the radical, anti-capitalist, and more social-constructivist views held by other feminists at the time that rendered gender irrelevant, and that aimed to mobilize women based on their similarities to men and not their differences. The Ad Hoc Women Artists' Committee and Women Students and Artists for Black Art Liberation were closer to the radical feminists of the day, because they recognized there could not be equality within a racist and class-stratified system.

WAR initiated visits with "several renowned women artists," Gordon recalled, "to hear their personal experiences firsthand and to show them our interest. They spoke of things we, too, had suffered, as we drew closer."[10] Muriel Castanis similarly remarked that "out of isolation, we came together to communicate. First to each other, then to other women artists." Sabra Moore remembered that the meetings were "mostly fun but also intense . . . We all had a huge amount of energy and we were discovering how oppression wasn't individual but social."[11] What began by talking evolved into the gathering of statistics which reinforced "the sum of our related experiences," as Castanis said, "and as a result demands were made."[12] Here is just one statistic offered by WAR in February 1970: "65% of art students are women but only 3% of the artists shown by New York City galleries are women."[13]

As their first act, WAR issued a list of ten items titled "Program for Woman Artist Revolutionaries" to MoMA. On December 23, 1969, several WAR members had a meeting at the museum to discuss this document with John Szarkowski, the director of the museum's photography department, and Betsy Jones, a curator in the painting and sculpture department. Rather than making "demands," as the Art Workers' Coalition had in January that year, the program put forward by WAR comes off more as suggestions. Take, for example, the third point: "a. retrospective of Georgia O'Keefe, b. exhibition of famous women artists since 1850, c. exhibit of Black women artists."

The most interesting idea calls for the "creation of a women artist advisory board," with "one salaried female consultant."

Still, within Women Artists in Revolution, the "program" was controversial. "A huge conflict arose over this aggressive plan as several women said we would not be presenting the proper feminine image," Gordon explained, adding, "They tried to prevent us with words."[14] Some members were afraid of confronting curators, Moore recalled, and "that often depended on how much access one had already to them."[15] Despite internal tensions in WAR, the meeting at the museum resulted in a detailed, three-page report written by the staffers for MoMA's executive committee. Though Szarkowski and Jones disagreed with several of WAR's points, they concluded that the museum "should make an organized and extra effort to search out the work of quality by women artists," and that "an exhibition of women's art be given serious consideration."[16]

The statement is included in WAR's *A Documentary Her-Story of Women Artists in Revolution*, the only archive of the group's manifestos, statements, correspondence, and press—which it published in 1971, and then again in 1973. The book is a product of its era—typewritten text, grainy images, xeroxed black-and-white printed matter. It features pages of flyers and newspaper clippings from the International Artists Demonstration on October 20, 1970, in the great hall—the majestic main entry—of the Metropolitan Museum of Art, which was organized by a coalition of groups, including WAR. (It seems to have been a more peaceful version of the larger Art Strike Against Racism, Sexism, Repression, and War on May 22, 1970, also at the Met.)

A photocopied flier that WAR distributed at the protest declared, "Museums are sexist!" and "Women are tired of being 'shown' by men what the world is like. Women have eyes of their own." A collage of women's eyes float across the page and underscore the idea that after centuries of being watched, surveilled, and scrutinized, feminists were now acting

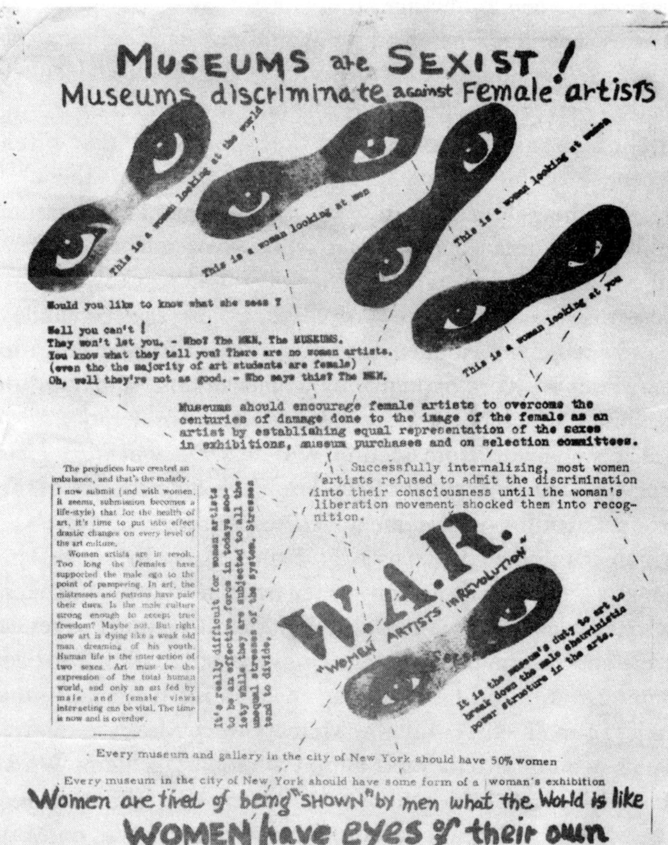

WAR, "Museums Are Sexist . . . ," ca. 1970, photocopy, 8 ½" x 11". Sabra Moore NYC Women's Art Movement Collection, 1969–1996; Box 1 and Folder 1; Barnard Archives and Special Collections, Barnard College.

as sentinels against such sexism. Writing for the *New York Element*, Therese Schwartz noted that WAR "had the most immediate cause of the day. They cited specific discrimination against women in museums."[17]

Crucially, however, WAR didn't restrict itself to art-world reforms. It fought for structural change against capitalism and patriarchy, including abortion rights. Gordon recalled, "We found a commune workshop which let us use some of their graphics equipment, and we scrounged up paper and inks and anything else we needed. Collectively, we silkscreened hundreds of red death's hand posters and tea aprons with the words: "Is this uterus the property of N.Y. State?"[18] WAR then participated in a pro-choice demonstration on March 28, 1970, and wore their screen-printed aprons and signs. That April, New York became one of the first states to legalize abortion, and, three years later, the Supreme Court decided *Roe v. Wade*. (Some WAR members such as Sabra Moore, went on to work at an abortion clinic that opened under the sponsorship of Judson Memorial Church and the Clergy Consultation Service on Abortion.[19])

While some of these designs seem dated today—essentialist and too invested in securing abortion rights through the state—the archive presented in *HerStory* charts a number of tactics that led to positive change. The most insightful part of the book documents feminist activism against the Whitney Museum in fall 1970. The goal of this agitation was equal representation of women in the museum's 1970 Sculpture Annual exhibition. (Before the Whitney switched to Biennials, it held Annuals.) Women made up over half of the population, so, they argued, 50 percent of any art exhibition should feature women.

WAR kicked things off in a meeting with the Whitney Museum in the spring of that year. According to a letter from Stephen E. Weil, the museum's administrator, to Dolores Holmes, dated June 18: "Following the meeting with you, we reviewed the Museum's holdings of work by women artists and concluded that they could serve as the basis for an exhibition which would trace the accomplishment of contemporary women artists."[20] In the letter, Weil also mentions their conversation as to "whether our curators give equal attention to the work of men and women artists in selecting the Annual and other group exhibitions." "I can only repeat," he says, "that it has long been, and continues to be, the Museum's policy to give such equal attention."[21]

Yet, clearly equal attention was not being paid. The 1969 Annual counted 143 artists; just eight were women. On September 28, 1970, during an Art Workers' Coalition meeting, artists Poppy Johnson and Brenda Miller added to the AWC's agenda the demand that 50 percent of the artists included in the Whitney Annual be women. According to Castanis:

> First, one male artist said, "Well, wasn't the position too strong? Couldn't you ask for maybe 10 percent and work it up gradually?" Another said, "Why not demand an open show for everybody?" My calculation of what he was saying was, if you're going to include women it might just as well be an open circus. And then (I still don't believe it), another male artist said, "But you realize how many artists you would be cutting out?" Other artists being male, meaning art is male, meaning the women included were not artists? Again! So convinced were they in terms of the male pecking order of women's valueless contribution, that they saw it, narrowly, as giving up a piece of the pie, rather than in the larger view, as diversity and enrichment.[22]

Johnson recalled that, "Those meetings were very exhausting and riotous. There were no rules of order or anything like that. It was just people talking—and the people who talked loudest and the most were noticed more. But I think Brenda and I stood up for ourselves pretty well."[23] The women carried the conversation over to Remington's, a nearby bar, and thus the Ad Hoc Women Artists' Committee was born.

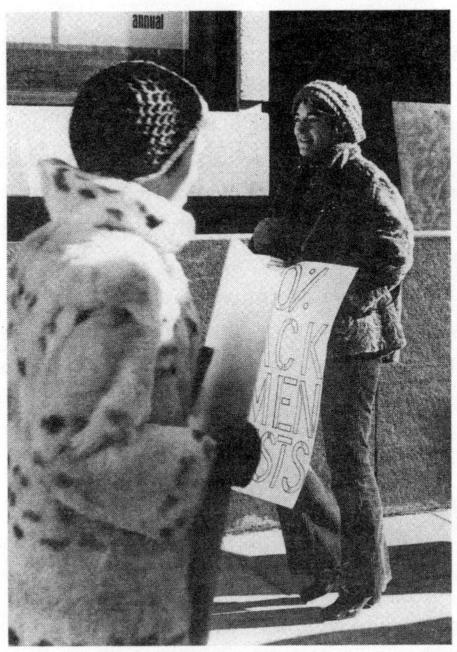

Lucy Lippard protesting in front of the Whitney Museum of American Art, September 1970. Photo: Ann Arlen.

On October 9 they met at Johnson's loft and decided to draft a letter to the four Whitney curators at the time, asking for a meeting within a week. This plan, while akin to WAR's earlier and more formal meeting with MoMA staff, was more forceful and showed that the Ad Hoc group was willing to take things a bit farther than WAR. According to Therese Schwartz, "They also planned a preliminary action to support their demand—telephone calls to the curators by all interested people, and they began gathering names of all women sculptors so that they could give this list to the museum in counter-action to a possible objection that there were not enough women."[24] It was further decided to ask male artists to telegraph their support of this plan, and, as a last resort to ask these men to take their work out of the Annual. According to Schwartz, fifteen men sent wires in solidarity.

By mid-October, the feminists received a letter from Weil stating that the museum would not meet with them to discuss quotas at the Annual, that doing so would "inflict a deliberate injustice on those artists whose work we think it important to show but who do not fall within the quotas which you and other groups seek to impose."[25] Weil particularly objected to a demand put forward by WSABAL, that 25 percent of the artists in the forthcoming Annual should be Black women, and asserted, "You cannot be unaware of the impossible situation to which these proliferating demands, if met, would lead."[26]

The group decided to cease their letter writing campaign and instead perform small rebellious actions inside the museum, all designed to exasperate the Whitney but not to damage any of its art. "There was some desire to have a unified plan of attack," as Johnson told me, "And then there was the idea that everybody should do what they want." In the end, each activist did her own thing. As Ringgold said:

> The corridors and galleries of the Whitney Museum became the focus of our attention. We went there often to deposit eggs. Unsuspecting male curatorial staff would pick up the eggs and experience the shock of having raw eggs slide down the pants of their tailor-made suits. I made hard-boiled eggs, painted them black, and wrote "50%" on them in red paint. I didn't want to waste food. They could eat my black eggs.[27]

The actions also included on-the-spot interviews with museum visitors about the protesters' demands and sanitary napkins and tampons labeled "50%" scattered around the floors and halls. In addition, the group commenced picketing outside of the museum every weekend—blowing police whistles and wearing placards, through the run of the show. "The museum loved the attention," Brenda Miller remembered: "They let us keep our signs there."[28]

Photographer Jan van Raay took invaluable photos of these protests and many others. "If she couldn't come, there were

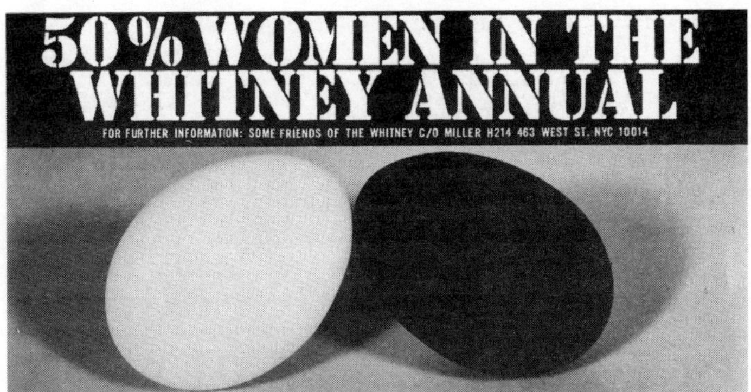

Ad Hoc Women Artists' Committee, advertisement in *Artforum*, December 1970.

no pictures!" Miller remarked, while noting that at the time "cameras were heavy and Xerox machines were expensive and scarce." Van Raay took many of these pictures while she was pregnant. "I went to the meetings every Monday," she told me. "So, I knew where the protests were going to be. Nobody ever asked me to take pictures of anything. I just felt the need to document."[29]

On November 9, 1970, the feminists wrote a terse letter back to Weil, stating, "At this point, some of us agree that further discussion is useless, that hard-boiled black eggs are preferable to more cafeteria tea and cookies."[30] The friction produced in these heated correspondences—between the museum's stern responses and the artists' uncompromising consistency—makes clear the kinds of critical negotiations that are always part of any kind of organizing.

The riskiest but most effective Whitney-related action was the group's distribution to the media of a cleverly written forged press release on museum letterhead stating that half the artists in the exhibition would indeed be women. When I asked who had this brilliant idea, Johnson responded that "Lucy was a big part of all of this, she understood the power of the word and came up with a lot of ideas that involved getting the press

WHITNEY MUSEUM OF AMERICAN ART

945 Madison Avenue at Seventy-Fifth Street New York, New York 10021 (212) 249-4100

Fake

For Release
On receipt
11/9/70

WHITNEY SCULPTURE ANNUAL TO BE 50% WOMEN

John I.H. Baur, Director of the Whitney Museum, with curators Robert Doty, James Monte and Marcia Tucker, announced today that the 1970 Annual Exhibition of Contemporary American Sculpture has been selected on the basis of fifty percent representation by women and 50% by men, equally divided between whites and non-whites. The Annual opens December 12 and continues to February 7, 1971.

For many years the policy of the Whitney Museum has been directed towards advancing the interests of women artists. Founded by a women artist, its board headed by a women, it has organized more one-man shows by women artists than any other New York museum, and a substantial part of its permenent collection is comprised of work by women. It is, therefore, only natural that the Whitney be the first museum in the United States to acknowledge the justice of equal representation for women as a means of responding most fully to the needs and aspirations of a major portion of the art world's.

The Whitney Annual, New York's only regular survey of the current scene, presents the ideal opportunity to offer women artists a greater role in directing the nature of American art today.

In a statement issued jointly with the Museum's Board of Trustees and the curators who selected the exhibition, Mr. Baur stressed that fact that "while percentages are not to become a museum policy for all exhibitions, increasing awareness of the achievements of special interest groups has led us to feel that an equal male/female representation at this time is a salutary and necessary step."

The Whitney Museum's schedule for the next six months also includes two shows by women artists (LOUISE NEVELSON and LEE LOZANO, opening November 10 and December 2, respectively), a selection of women's art from the permenent collection (Dec. 7 - Jan. 19), and BLACK ARTISTS IN AMERICA (April 6 - May 16).

For further information: Stephen Weil
Leon Levine
Ronni Roland

Fake

Ad Hoc Women Artists' Committee, Fake Press Release, November 9, 1970.

to cover various things."[31] Dated November 9, 1970 (the same day as their letter to Weil), it declares: "The Whitney Annual, New York's only regular survey of the current scene, presents the ideal opportunity to offer women artists a greater role in directing the nature of American art today." Today, the document can be found in the museum's library, X'ed out with the word *fake* written in the margins.

The press release read and looked credible enough that the museum decided to issue a rebuttal, addressed from its director, John Baur, which stated that the release was a complete forgery. Lippard had been told it was not libelous, but in fact it was "if the director's and other proper names appeared," she recalled. "As a result, the FBI visited the organizers, starting with Poppy, the youngest at nineteen. She asked them if she had to talk to them; they said no, and she warned us. Nothing scared us."[32]

On October 22, Whitney curators Marcia Tucker and Elke Solomon, and MoMA curator Jennifer Licht attended a meeting with the feminist groups. According to Schwartz, "There were about forty women artists there—a historic event, the first such meeting in New York art history, the first time that a group of women artists had met for action."[33] Though the gathering was tense, it seems that it had an effect: when the Whitney announced the 1970 exhibition, it had more women than any past Annual—20.2 percent (twenty women in a group of ninety-nine). Nevertheless, the feminist coalition persisted, asking for 50 percent women, and 25 percent Black women.

Before the opening of the show on December 11, 1970, the committee printed fake tickets and distributed them outside of the museum to anyone who wanted to demonstrate. Grace Glueck reported in the *New York Times*, "Ten policemen were stationed in the lobby and plainclothesmen moved among the guests on the upper floors," and that museum guards used ultraviolet light to determine the real tickets from the replicas, but "most of those rejected gained entrance anyway, with the aid of tickets slipped to them by invited guests."[34] With the help of artists Kes Zapkus and Mark di Suvero, the feminists projected slides of women's art on the museum façade—until, as Lippard has written, "it rained and we were afraid we'd be electrocuted by the generator, which I'd managed to plug in at a gallery next door, to the bewilderment of its staff."[35]

Faith Ringgold wrote about the scene as well:

> Although they supplied us with tickets to enter the museum, the white men in the show did not join our demonstration. (There were no black men in there I could approach.) However, the fashionable Whitney art-going crowd was eager to witness our action. They had heard of "sit-ins" and now they were going to see one for themselves. At a predetermined time, Lucy Lippard and I began to blow our whistles. The women came toward the center of the gallery on the second floor. We continued to blow. The people gathered around us, and we formed a big circle on the floor. Then we got up and walked around chanting, "Fifty percent women, fifty percent women." We pulled it off. The crowd was sympathetic, and the event satisfied our need to protest.[36]

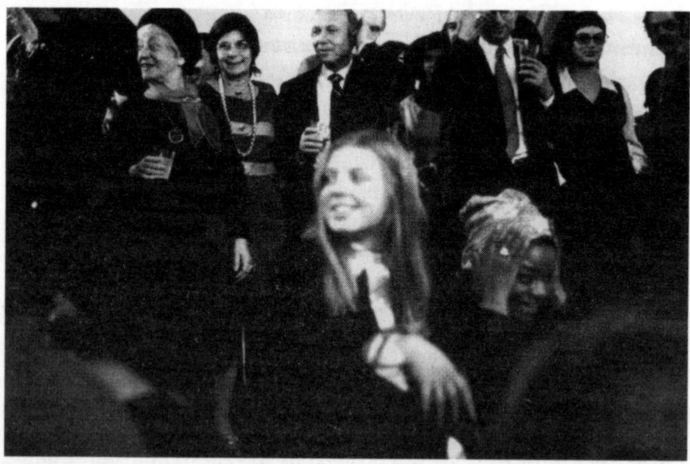

Center: Poppy Johnson and Faith Ringgold at a sit-in by the Ad Hoc Women Artists' Committee at the Whitney Annual opening, December 11, 1970. Photo: Amy Stromsten.

A lone photograph from this event conveys the warmth, showing Johnson and Ringgold smiling among an amicable crowd. Glueck concluded her article with a quote from sage exhibiting artist Louise Bourgeois, "who was sporting a red arm band," in solidarity with the protesting women, and said: "Since we've been discriminated against for so long, we need special privileges."[37]

Aside from all their Whitney-focused work, in 1970 the committee started the Women's Art Registry. This collection of slides and ephemera served as a means for gathering and disseminating information about art made by more than 600 women. It became a model for other activist initiatives and was an important resource for curators, educators, students, and more in a pre-internet age. For years it was housed at the co-op galleries 55 Mercer and A.I.R., then subsequently at Artists Space. Since 1994, it has been maintained in the Special Collections and University Archives at Rutgers University and is now known as the Lucy Lippard Women's Art Registry.

The committee stopped its direct-action activities in early 1971 at the end of the Annual. In January 1971, there was an exchange of letters between the artist Agnes Denes—on behalf of Women Artists in Revolution, the Ad Hoc Committee, and Women Students and Artists for Black Art Liberation—and Weil, which pointed to the possibility of a meeting between the groups and the museum that month, but it did not occur. Perhaps because the museum wanted certain "conditions," such as only four representatives from the feminist groups to be present.

By then, the AWC was also falling apart, due to the successes of actions by its splinter groups. As Lippard maintained, "The women became politicized and the men went back to their careers."[39] "We were the bulwark of the AWC," Miller told me, "We had more skin in the game than the men."[40]

In 1973 the Ad Hoc group also created the *Rip-Off File*, which gathered tales of discrimination from around the country. The artist Joyce Kozloff, co-editor of the 1973 dossier with Nancy Spero, recalled that after sending out a postcard to women—asking for their stories of put-downs in the art world and schools—"many responded. We put it into tabloid form very cheaply and distributed it as widely as we could."[38] The newspaper-like result included forty-one appalling stories that read as a predigital precursor to anti-sexual harassment campaigns such as #MeToo.

WAR continued to flourish, holding workshops in a former firehouse turned community center on East Eleventh Street where participants "presented or performed a body of work and opened it up to discussion."[41] There was a silk-screen workshop there, which Jacqueline Skiles supervised; she told me that "it was where we printed all our fliers and books."[42] WAR decided to raise grant money for a permanent location—the first women's art center and community space in New York—and received a modest $5,000 grant (1/5 of what they asked for to meet their minimum goals) from the New York State Council of the Arts (NYSCA) to open the Women's Interart Center (aka WIC, Interart, or most commonly, the Center)—only after WAR members Castanis, Nancy Edelstein, Jan McDevitt, and Skiles protested in person at the council's offices on October 27, 1970, that their proposal was being ignored.

The Center was eventually awarded more funds and moved into two floors of an abandoned city-owned building at 549 West Fifty-Second Street in July 1971. "It had a giant elevator that was used to move cars up and down," Skiles recalled: "It took a lot of effort just to get that space. There was one artist involved in WAR who happened to work for the city who knew about its donation of space to different groups—as the city had taken over so many buildings because of people's inability to pay taxes."[43] In October 1971, the Center registered with New York State as a nonprofit corporation with a mission to "encourage and advance the development and expression of women's skills and creativity in all areas of the arts." A more

WOMEN'S OPEN ART SHOW

WOMEN'S INTERART CENTER

549 WEST 52ND STREET

JANUARY 21,1972 - 7:30 PM

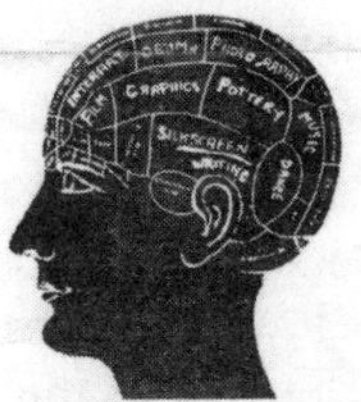

Women artists are invited to bring their work from January 15 to January 20, 10:00 to 2:00 pm. A space four feet in any direction is available for a rental fee of $2.50. The fee covers the full run of the show. (If more space is needed for a large work please call the center) Insurance will be made available for those who wish to insure their work. For further information about this or any other aspect of the show please call between 2:00 and 10:00 pm Wednesdays through Sundays.

If your are interested in helping to set up the show please contact us immediately.

Work can be picked up Sunday, February 20, between 2:00 and 10:00 pm.

11:30

246-6570

Women's Interart Center, *Women's Open Show*, January 21, 1972, black-and-white offset, 8 ½" x 11". Sabra Moore NYC Women's Art Movement Collection, 1969–1996; Box 1 and Folder 1; Barnard Archives and Special Collections, Barnard College.

substantial $35,000 NYSCA grant the following year helped the group, which by then had over a hundred artist-members, to expand operations.[44]

By 1972, as the Center had become the primary project for some members, WAR had officially disbanded. In a handwritten postscript to the 1973 edition of *HerStory*, Skiles offered this sanguine takeaway: "We have realized many of our goals. The Women's Interart Center is a place where women not only create in our many workshops but also present their work to the public . . . Things are slowly getting better!"

And they were: that year, the Center opened the Interart Theater, and its productions won numerous awards. Although it was women-oriented, the Center did not always explore feminist issues. It offered numerous shows, screenings, lectures, workshops, and technical guidance. Among some of its standout exhibitions was 1976's Sojourner Truth Festival of the Arts, organized by Ringgold, filmmaker Monica Freeman, poet Patricia Spears Jones, and critics Margo Jefferson and Michelle Wallace, recognized as the "first ever Black women's film festival." The Center had an illustrious history until it was essentially shuttered due to gentrification and neglect from the city in 2016, despite its decades-long activism and efforts to remain.[45]

While the Center will be remembered as a trailblazing space, the sweeping move by feminists toward forging rooms of their own in the 1970s left behind regular protests—another fundamental to effective activism. The creation of women-only spaces often became, as Adrienne Rich has pointed out, "valued over risk taking" and ultimately "a place of emigration, an end in itself."[46] Larger demands to transform society, and to challenge the male domination of it, gave way to personal and/or group transformation. Perhaps feeling as though things weren't going to change, some feminists began to care more about the creation of a women's-only counterculture, and so the focus was taken off direct-action campaigns and put more on building community support.

In the end, the Whitney and MoMA failed to meet the demands of the Ad Hoc Committee, and New York's museum directors became increasingly intolerant of artists speaking up. Intersectional values were also deserted by some feminist groups,

ATTENTION !

WOMEN ARTISTS

AND FEMINISTS !

Now is the time to end discrimination against women in museums, galleries and art schools . . .

Join WOMEN IN THE ARTS!

Rally and Celebration . . .

Help make public our demand to six New York Museums for a massive show of woman artists . . .

TIME: 10 A.M. - 1:00 P.M.

PLACE: 53rd Street in front of the Museum of Modern Art.

DATE: Wednesday, APRIL 12, 1972

Rain Date: April 19, 1972

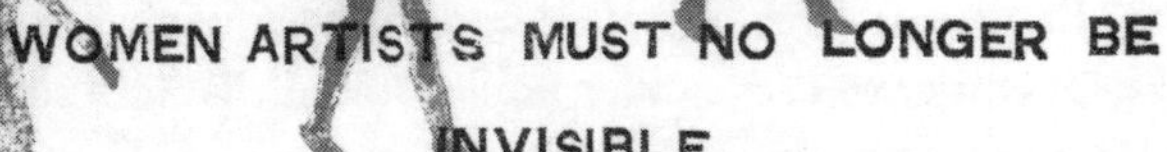

INVISIBLE

Poster for demonstration on April 12, 1972, in front of the Museum of Modern Art, 8 ½" x 14". Sabra Moore NYC Women's Art Movement Collection, 1969–1996; Box 1 and Folder 1; Barnard Archives and Special Collections, Barnard College.

another abandoned value. Howardena Pindell, a cofounder of A.I.R. Gallery—the nonprofit women's cooperative art space founded in 1972—recalled how the majority-white group had "no empathy for issues of race."[47]

"We didn't end racism, and we haven't ended sexism," Johnson echoed. "But it felt good to be part of something and to try—and we tried in different ways. On some level, there was also lots of posturing and there were weird things too; it turned out that some people were maybe FBI agents."[48] By 1969, the FBI had begun to infiltrate the women's movement, in addition to the Black Power movement, and it is reasonable to assume that agents were involved with making more tension in the various feminist groups. Still, the protests left an indelible mark. As Michele Wallace points out, "For a long time, whenever we would walk in any of these museums, the employees would call security. The guards would surround us because they'd think we were trying to start a demonstration of some sort."[49]

Eventually, museums began to examine their holdings by women and produce more solo shows of their work. MoMA's Modern Women's Fund, for example, founded by the philanthropist Sarah Peter, has been engaged since 2005 in a cross-departmental curatorial project to examine the museum's permanent collection from a feminist perspective, and this has led to several shows and a book. It may seem odd that the effort needs to be supported by a patron but that is often the case.

In 2007, the Brooklyn Museum opened the Elizabeth A. Sackler Center for Feminist Art, with Judy Chicago's *The Dinner Party*, 1974–79, installed on long-term view. (In 2018, this key member of the Sackler family stated that she admired Nan Goldin's activism with PAIN, the subject of chapter 10.) Throughout the 2000s, it seemed that even while museums were becoming more supportive of women artists, such recognition wasn't happening in a grassroots way across the nation (or the world), but rather as independent initiatives dependent on museum board members and donors, which leads to a much larger question regarding whether museums today have become de facto plutocratic organizations.

Yet, there was one effort that drifted from the course. In 2020, the Feminist Art Coalition successfully launched its program, which served 118 institutions in the United States. But even the need for its short-term organizing shows there's still so much more that can be done today. WAR and the Ad Hoc Committee were interested in equality with men, or 50 percent representation. Many feminists now have wisely abandoned the idea of equality, noting that it was always a false hope. Rather, they are interested in dismantling any system—from the macro, such as patriarchy, to the micro, such as a museum—that has been built on exploitation and violence. These goals and visions are much larger than artists in the 1970s could have dreamed of, and yet the question remains for feminist activists: What's attainable?

3

The Black Emergency Cultural Coalition, 1969–82

The Attica Prison uprising of September 9–13, 1971, was a wakeup call for many people. America's jails were becoming increasingly violent places, and could not be ignored any longer. It is often said that this turn began with the "tough on crime" policies advocated by Republicans and Southern Democrats beginning in the late 1960s, which sought longer prison sentences, more frequent use of the death penalty, and the explicit or implicit targeting of politically marginalized people, which has resulted in the racial transformation of the prison population from mostly white at mid-century to 65 percent Black and Latino today.

Attica's severe overcrowding—in September 1971 the prison held nearly 2,250 prisoners even though it had been designed for only 1,600—increased the likelihood of an incident. Racial tensions were also a major factor in the revolt; the inmate population was nearly 55 percent Black and 10 percent Hispanic, while all the guards were white. As Heather Ann Thompson has described, "In the summer of 1971, Attica's prisoners weren't just frustrated, they were . . . becoming much more politically aware. Not only had these men been developing a powerful critique of poor prison conditions, but they also had begun to discuss how they might reform their institution—what they might do, concretely, to get the state to treat them as human beings who were serving their time, not as monsters deserving of abuse and neglect."[1]

During the ensuing revolt, inmates seized control of the prison and took staff members hostage, insisting on improved living conditions. Their "Manifesto of Demands" included educational opportunities, vocational training, access to books and media, an end to racial segregation, and an end to incarcerated people being persecuted for their political beliefs, peaceful dissent, or race.[2] After four days of negotiations, state police officers stormed the prison, killing twenty-nine inmates and ten of the captive correctional staff. The McKay Commission, which provided the official report on the events at Attica, noted that "the state police assault which ended the four-day prison uprising was the bloodiest one-day encounter between Americans since the Civil War." The repercussions have been vast: after Attica, prison administrators expanded punitive measures such as isolation units and supermax facilities, to prevent inmates from organizing.

Artists Benny Andrews and Cliff Joseph of the Black Emergency Cultural Coalition (BECC) immediately responded to the prisoner's manifesto of demands, by taking the guerrilla tactics they had been developing while protesting art museums and putting them to a new use: the development of prison arts programs. Andrews and Joseph were key members of the Black Arts Movement that had emerged in the wake of the Black Power movement following the 1965 establishment of poet Amiri Baraka's Black Arts Repertory Theater in Harlem, New York, as a place for artistic expression. The BECC grew out of this moment, as Black people around the world engaged in struggles for liberation and equality to promote Black self-determination through cultural production.

Andrews was the BECC's de facto leader. He was born into a sharecropping family in rural Plainview, Georgia, in 1930, and studied at Fort Valley State University before serving in the Air Force and going on to earn his BFA in painting from the School of the Art Institute of Chicago in 1958. A decade later, Andrews began teaching at Queens College, City University of New York, where he stayed for over thirty years. By 1969, Andrews was focusing the coalition's efforts to agitate for greater representation of Black artists and the hiring of Black curators in New York City museums.[3] To do so, the group often appealed directly to the press, by sending BECC announcements to newspapers and holding press conferences. As a group with no money or influence, and "no entrée into the white museum structure," as Andrews put it, media influence was really all the BECC had. Moreover, as Aruna D'Souza has pointed out, the BECC's members, "were canny about leveraging media attention—especially when it came to taking advantage of the police's fear of Black protest and the media's (racist) hunger for images of Black militancy, a common sight on nightly news broadcast at the time."[4]

Grace Glueck, who reported on most of the artist-led protests at museums for the *New York Times*, publicly announced the BECC's five proposals to the Whitney Museum on June 15, 1969, which included a show of Black artists at the Whitney during the 1970–71 art season; more Black artists in the then Annual painting and sculpture shows; and finally, the hiring of a Black curator.[5]

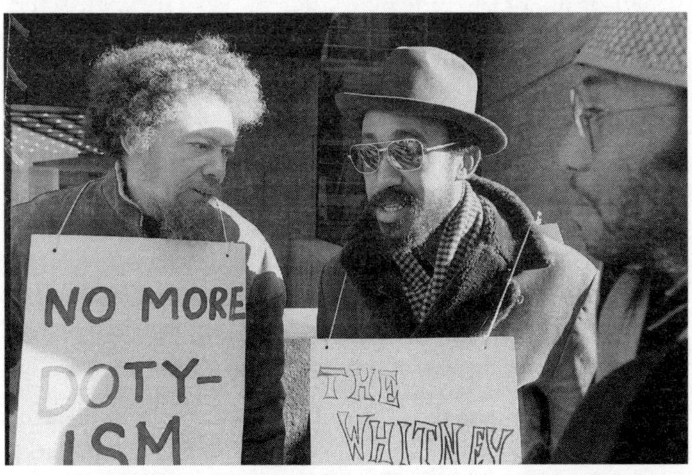

Benny Andrews (left) and Art Coppedge (center) at a BECC protest at the Whitney Museum, New York, January 31, 1971. Photo: Jan van Raay.

These goals were partially met, but six months of negotiations broke down when the Whitney refused to hire a Black curator for its upcoming "Contemporary Black Artists in America" exhibition. This "would prove to be the greatest sticking point between the BECC and the Whitney," the art historian Howard Singerman has noted, as a "site of particular mischaracterization and misrepresentation."[6] In a press release the BECC asserted, "As to the selections for the show, our fellow artists across the nation have reported being subjected to such humiliating experiences as having Mr. Robert Doty, apparently the museum's lone selector, enter their studios and demand to see only this or that piece of which he had heard or with which he was previously familiar, at the exclusion of all others. Many Black artists of outstanding ability have reported being bypassed altogether, and no Black curatorial assistance has to our knowledge been drawn upon to date."[7] In 1971, after the Whitney rejected any further talks with the group, the BECC shifted gears. It could have collapsed, but it didn't.

On October 6, 1971, Andrews and Joseph sent a letter on behalf of the BECC to the governor of New York, Nelson A. Rockefeller, condemning his hasty determination to forcefully end the Attica rebellion:

> Expressed in their several demands was the prisoners' need for a program of cultural relevance and freedom—one that would allow them greater opportunities for the discovery, utilization, and development of creative social skills. Sensing that their potential in this area has too long been stifled by the oppressiveness of forced isolation, we consider this to be a most reasonable demand made upon an institution supposedly responsible for the social rehabilitation of the people in its charge.[8]

Andrews and Joseph then offered proposals for improvements in US prisons, including a "culturally orientated, rehabilitation program" including classes and exhibitions, and suggested their services in its implementation. "Whether justly or unjustly convicted and detained for acts of social deviation, it is a cruel and unnecessary punishment to deny them the right to full and uncensored release of their creative abilities," they concluded.

This letter marked the beginnings of the BECC's Prison Cultural Exchange Program, which flourished until 1982. In a note to "fellow artists" (likely BECC colleagues and affiliates) written the next day, Andrews and Joseph argue, "In response to the Attica incident, the Black Emergency Cultural Coalition calls for a cultural revolution in this nation's prisons, as a necessary precursor to the ultimate liberation of its brothers and sisters in bondage."[9] They continue, "We must pledge ourselves to go into the prisons of America, as it is our right to do so . . . we must secure our right to share our art, our skills, our thoughts." Andrews and Joseph also cited the recent death of the artist James Lightbourne in this letter, who passed away in August 1971, at age twenty-seven, after spending nearly five years of his life wrongfully imprisoned. The BECC never received a response from Rockefeller, but it created a program nonetheless and placed a focus on the need for collaboration and exchange.

On November 10, 1971, Benny Andrews entered the Manhattan House of Detention for Men (aka the Tombs) to give a two-hour drawing demonstration to about thirty inmates. Notably, detainees had rioted at the Tombs one year earlier than Attica, taking guards hostage to negotiate for improvements to their conditions. The workshop had been arranged with financial assistance from the Junior Art Council of the Museum of Modern Art (MoMA). In a 1973 radio interview with Mimi Poser, host of the Guggenheim Museum's WNYC radio show *Round and About the Guggenheim*, Junior Art Council members Mary Bardsley, Catherine Colin, and Barbara Jakobson explained how they approached Andrews and Joseph. As Colin described:

> The Junior Council's original involvement came in the spring of 1971. We found that the Junior League had been doing a lot of work in the Tombs library and thought we might be able to donate some art supplies to the Tombs, which we did—that was in about May of 1971 and that was our original involvement. Then in the fall of 1971, Herman Green, a correctional officer at the Tombs, called and asked us if we couldn't possibly get a teacher to come into the Tombs and give classes.[10]

After the incident at Attica, some administrators, such as Green, responded to the demands of the incarcerated protesters by allowing more cultural programs. Jakobson then called Andrews, whose work was featured in the collection of MoMA. "It was just one of those fortuitous circumstances because Benny, Cliff, and some other artists involved in the BECC had been very anxious to begin this kind of work themselves," Colin pointed out.[11] The workshops commenced with volunteered time by the BECC's teachers and donated art supplies (or the money to purchase them) solicited by the Junior Council.

As with their previous actions, the BECC knew how to create publicity. An article in the *New York Times* appeared less than a week after Andrews's first visit to the Tombs. "I find that having an arts group can alleviate some of the pent-up emotions that sometimes cause unrest in a prison," remarks Green in the report, underscoring what is often true about prison arts programs: that prison administrators are more interested in the management of the prisoners, and keeping calm, whereas arts educators are more interested in collaboration and rehabilitation. Dated November 16, 1971, a photograph in the article shows Andrews in the Tombs's library and chapel teaching how to draw a face and profile on a chalkboard behind him. Andrews states that "he hoped to return for another class in a week or so," and that the BECC "was trying to get commitments from galleries and museums for art and artists to appear in prisons and, conversely, to exhibit prisoner's art and possibly sell it."[12]

According to his studio journal, Andrews returned on November 24 to give a second class, which was followed in 1972 by at least ten more visits to the Tombs, six visits to teach at the Bronx Men's House of Detention, and one class at the Queens House of Detention. (These are just Andrews's visits; there were, of course, more by other BECC teachers). An article published in January 1972 followed Joseph, Jakobson, and BECC co-director Camille Billops into the Tombs along with artist Rudolf Baranik and noted that while the "bad jazz trio"—a group that the teaching artists shared space with—played Duke Ellington's "Things Ain't What They Used to Be," the inmates "sketched a fellow inmate posed as Muhammad Ali, a pitcher warming up to the mound, and then whatever their heads passed on to their hands."[13]

The artist May Stevens (Baranik's wife) recalled that "Camille would bring in things like incense and all kinds of wonderful things to make treats for the prisoners, to make their lives more livable and make prison a less sense-deprived environment for them. She'd have to fight with the guards who didn't want her to take in anything special. One guard asked, 'What's the incense for?' And she said, 'For mood, man.' Camille was unstoppable."[14]

The BECC was incorporated in 1972 as a nonprofit organization, co-chaired by Andrews and Joseph. Billops, Russell Thompson, and Vivian Browne were also directors, while Michael Chisolm served as the program's administrator. It was not the only, nor the first, artist-led group to develop prison arts programs. Black feminists, such as the cultural critic Michele Wallace, who had cofounded WSABAL (as discussed in the previous chapter), had noticed that many arts programs were only being offered to male inmates and sought to correct that. In 1972, Wallace and Faith Ringgold founded Art Without

Walls with several other writers and artists. They received a ten-thousand-dollar grant from the New York Foundation for the Arts and began offering workshops at the Women's House of Detention in New York City once a month on mask making, theater, career counseling, and drug addiction prevention.[15]

In 2016, Wallace recalled that the BECC was "a very male-dominated group and were only interested in male artists and peaceful demonstrations in order to get people into shows . . . they were very effective at it."[16] It's true that feminism was not a priority to the BECC, even though it shared many activist tactics with concurrent radical groups led by feminist artists, such as picketing, protesting, holding meetings with museum officials, and speaking directly to the press about their goals. There was also an educational component: akin to the Ad Hoc Women Artists' Committee's slide registry, the BECC maintained a large slide registry documenting Black artists and organizations, and this was largely maintained by Billops.[17]

It is ultimately hard to know if the BECC was dismissive of feminism. In an interview from March 1972, Browne mentions that as a woman she was appointed secretary of the nonprofit: "I was a token," she exhales—but then so was Billops.[18] Yet in September 1972, Joseph and Browne participated in a two-person show at the Countee Cullen branch of the New York Public Library on West 136th Street titled "Beginnings in Unity," which they hoped might evoke a sense of equality between the sexes. In a 1973 interview, Billops said, "When you go within the Black art world, you find that the Black male artist is doing the same to you that the white just did to him —and yet you joined that picket line and everything with him to help him get in there."[19]

In a telling entry from Andrews's studio journal dated June 28, 1970, he writes that, "The BECC met at 25 East Fourth St, NYC, with Tom Lloyd, Faith Ringgold, Art [Arthur] Coppedge, Michael Chisolm, and James Sneed to discuss our differences. Well Faith Ringgold put us all down over our supposed

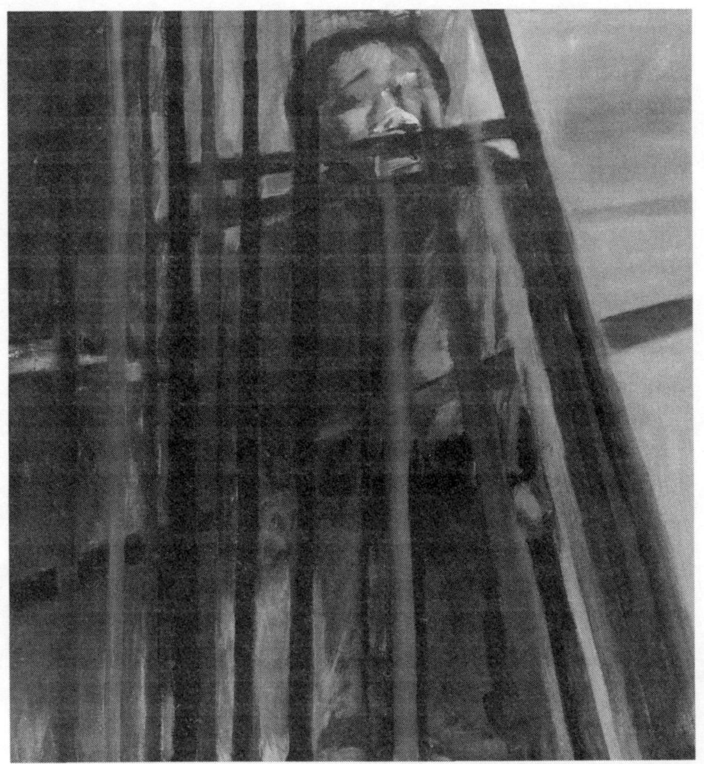

Vivian Browne, *The Prisoner*, 1972. Courtesy of Adobe Krow Archives, CA and RYAN LEE Gallery, New York.

anti-feminist attitudes."[20] Billops and Browne did not attend this meeting, though Browne became active within feminist groups in the 1970s and '80s, including the SOHO20 gallery and the journal *Heresies: A Feminist Publication on Art and Politics* and encouraged Billops to participate in these largely white feminist spaces.[21]

Browne remembered her first two meetings at the Tombs, noting that the inmates "wanted to learn drawing and they didn't want to just draw and present a marvelous picture," but rather that "they wanted to begin at the beginning and build up." Accordingly, she opened her second session by teaching geometric forms and shading,

> and then we translated it into making the head—because they're very much interested in drawing people—so from there they could find out the structure of the head and the structure of the face and they did that . . . When I went back the next week apparently they practiced all week so then we were able to go beyond that and make the head turn and go up and down and do a really good job of shading and things like that.[22]

Browne made expressive paintings inspired by her visits such as *The Prisoner*, 1972. The built-up energy of the work echoes her experiences: "It's a very intense time—not only do they want to draw but they also want to talk, and I can't teach and talk with them personally and make everything go, so it's a jam packed two hours and you come out shaking because it's been so tense."[23]

Not all of the BECC's work took place in prisons. Andrews's journal from 1971 also lists meetings: with MoMA's Junior Council for financial backing; with Jakobson to select artwork for an exhibition of prison works in the Deputy Mayor's office; with New York University president James Hester; and with Bill Keith of the Malcolm X Art Center, among others. At the same time throughout 1971 and 1972, Andrews and Joseph—on behalf of the BECC—were working on the *Attica Book*, in

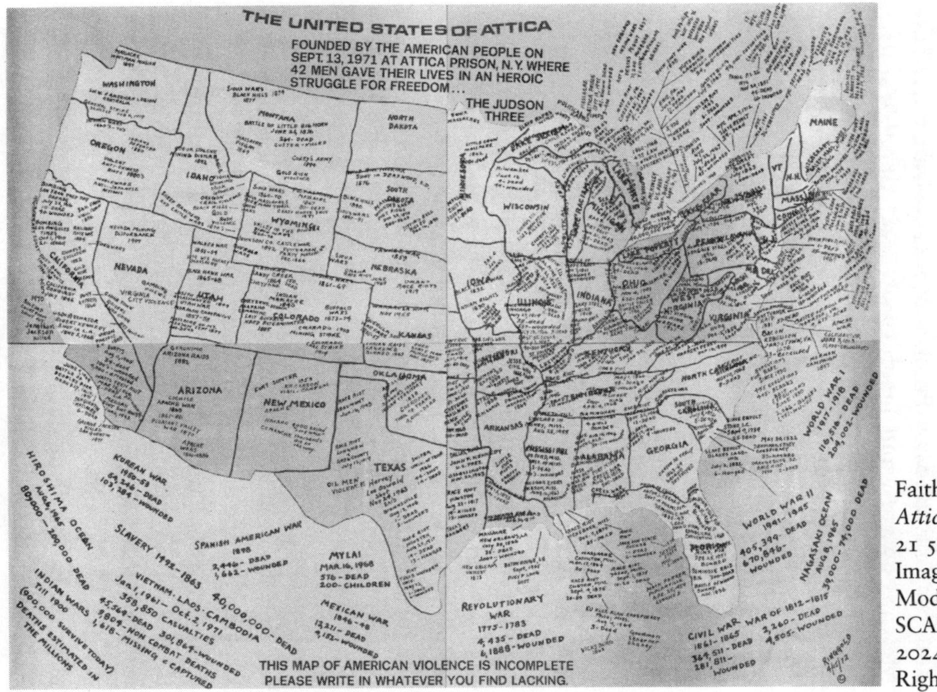

Faith Ringgold, *United States of Attica*, 1972, offset lithograph, 21 5/8" x 27 3/8" in. Digital Image © The Museum of Modern Art/Licensed by SCALA/Art Resource, NY © 2024 Faith Ringgold/Artists Rights Society (ARS), New York.

partnership with the organization Artists and Writers Protest Against the War in Vietnam.[24] Their objective was to sell this relatively low-cost artbook as a fundraiser to buy art materials for inmates, to pay teaching artists for their work, and to cover the cost of the book's production so that copies could be given freely to those incarcerated.

The publication features black-and-white reproductions of works commissioned from forty-eight artists (including Andrews, Browne, Mary Frank, Nancy Grossman, Carl Andre, Melvin Edwards, and Jacob Lawrence). Ringgold's offset poster *The United States of Attica*, 1972, is the first artwork in the book. She has written that this was her most widely distributed poster of the 1970s—"about two thousand were made and I sold them for a dollar or so each."[25] The red, green, and black piece offers a counternarrative of the nation's history, emphasizing the historical continuity of violence as a defining characteristic, by showing a US map overwhelmed with her handwritten notes of both uprisings and acts of state-sanctioned brutality in each state since 1776 against Indigenous and Black people. Ringgold also includes military imperialist violence committed by the United States abroad, for instance in Japan and Vietnam. Realizing that she would not be able to revise annually, she included a curt invitation to the viewer to add further acts of dispossession and labor and racial exploitation. E. C. Feiss has rightly proposed that the placement of Ringgold's work first was key, that the book "contextualizes its own intervention by beginning with Ringgold's poster, memorializing the dead and elucidating its own coalitional politics as part of a long and varied history of opposition."[26]

The center of the *Attica Book* features a separate collection of handwritten poems by incarcerated writers, which were produced in the BECC's prisons programs with BECC teacher Michael Salgo. Upon seeing the book and his name in print, Ronald King, a prisoner-poet wrote to the BECC: "The only time previously I saw my name in print was on

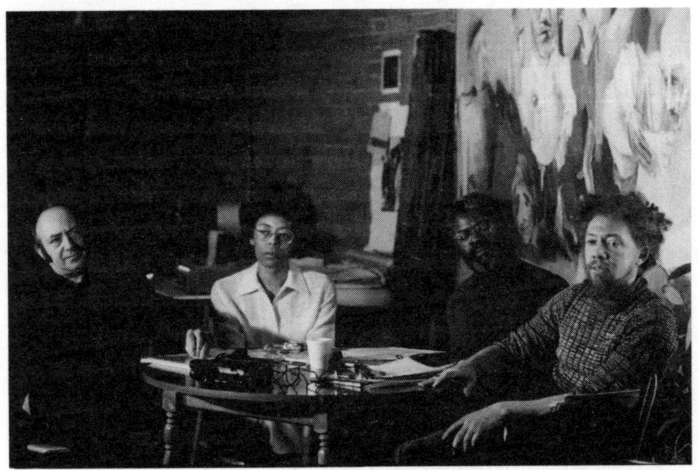

Rudolf Baranik, Vivian Browne, Cliff Joseph, and Benny Andrews working on the *Attica Book*, 1972. May Stevens and Rudolf Baranik Foundation, Courtesy of Ryan/Lee Gallery, New York.

a court calendar."[27] The BECC included this compelling line in a 1973 letter to *Artforum* cowritten by the coalition and Artists and Writers Protest in response to MoMA refusing to sell the *Attica Book* in its bookstore. The missive, which called for a protest on Easter Sunday, argues that the book is a crucial statement on art of the time—an "*art event* as well as a statement of conscience"—and one that they felt fell in line with the Art Workers' Coalition *And babies* poster discussed in in the previous chapter.[28] Much of the artwork in the book makes a powerful case to link the Vietnam War with Attica and other atrocities of the day, including the expansion of the prison system in the United States.

With the rise of prison populations beginning in the 1970s through the 1980s and the solidification of a law-and-order response to criminality, arts programs created among educators, activists, and prisoners grew too, though, as Nicole Fleetwood notes, "there have been periods in this time frame when programs have been cut or underfunded due to state and federal budget priorities."[29] The coalition was always careful to balance prisoners' needs for their programs with the prison's needs to manage the swelling numbers of the incarcerated.

The BECC also likely knew that for some prison staff, including Green, such programming was a way to mollify the prisoners, akin to the yoga and meditation classes that began to be implemented around the same time. The coalition tried to maintain some control. Andrews adds in the radio interview:

> One thing we made very clear is that we did not want the correction officials to apply any kind of standards, as far as being artistic or not, because we felt it would limit it too much. For example, we are able to handle about sixty students in a class

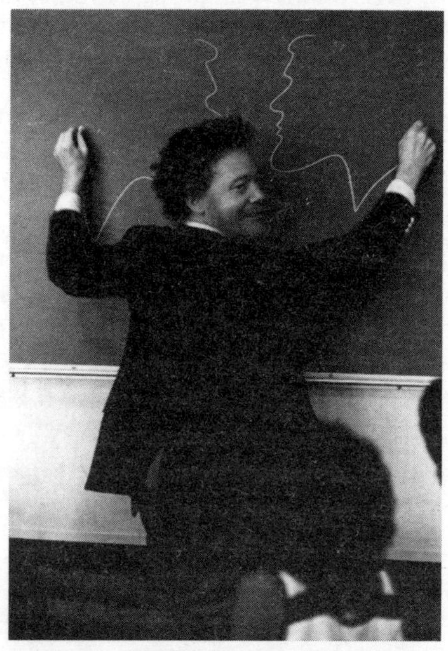

Benny Andrews giving a drawing demonstration to students at Alabama State University in Montgomery on October 10, 1975. Courtesy the Andrews-Humphrey Family Foundation.

at the Tombs—and the Tombs consists of 1,300 inmates, so you can imagine that's just a drop in the bucket—but to eliminate the ones that don't show talent on first coming would just be atrocious.[30]

By 1973, Andrews would take students to accompany him to his prison-based classes as teaching assistants. (In addition, the BECC was simultaneously advocating for an art center for ex-inmates at Queens College, though this wasn't achieved.) Typically, in a session there were at least four teachers—two permanent teachers and a few volunteers or students. The class was broken up into four groups, ranging from advanced to experimental.[31] Of the teachers, the primarily Black "permanent" staff were professional artists, and though some also taught in colleges, in the prisons they offered a different pedagogical approach. Andrews also noted in the radio interview that this appealed more to the incarcerated, who may have had strong feelings about the disciplinary and traditional aspects of their previous schooling. He added that the program had already served about 4,500 inmates—with classes every week of between forty and sixty people—and a roster of ninety artists working permanently and another roster of about 100 volunteer artists. These teachers always had to negotiate a fine line between not coming off as a threat to prison staff and not appearing as state agents to the incarcerated.

In 1976, teachers were paid $25 per session.[32] While there was a curriculum, teachers were encouraged to find their own way with the students. This meant that different styles—abstraction, figuration—were accepted, and that the mediums were based upon the supplies available and funds for buying them. It seems most classes were focused on drawing and painting exercises. Joseph, who was an accomplished art therapist, brought his training into the mix:

My approach was strictly an art therapy approach because when I went in, I tried to help the fellows deal with the problems that

> got them into prison in the first place. And much of this found its way into their art. That might have been done anyway, but I think it was beneficial to them to sit down in a group and think through some of the things that they were trying to deal with and not to use this just as an expression of anger—to see it as a therapeutic exercise, something that could help them to flush out and really get into what it was that got them on the wrong track in the first place, to deal with working that through.[33]

Andrews was known for his unique techniques to create group comradeship, such as drawing with both hands on the blackboard, sometimes backwards, and invoking elaborate narratives of a particular scene (such as a couple going out on a date) outside the prison that he would then ask the inmates to reproduce.

The BECC's rich, reciprocal creative endeavors and speedy beginnings in prisons seems virtually impossible today. But at the time, they were not so astounding. Lee Bernstein writes that the Black Arts Movement and the simultaneously changing prison culture "demonstrated widespread hopes for collective liberation brought about by a revolutionary movement with incarcerated people among its vanguard." He adds: "It was not simply that culture could sustain inmates and connect them to one another; during the 1970s cultural expression became the vehicle for incarcerated people to participate in political and social movements seeking to transform and improve society as a whole."[34] A slew of articles about the BECC's efforts in 1973 confirms this. From January to February that year, the Community Church Art Gallery at 28 East Thirty-Fifth Street in New York held an "Art of the Prisons" exhibition. In February, the Tombs hosted its first-ever public art show, titled *An Inside View of An Outside Expression*, which featured more than 100 works in its eleventh-floor library. The *New York Times* covered the show and reported that some of the pictures were to be sold and that funds would be put into the artists' commissary accounts, while others were to be exhibited at the Metropolitan Museum of Art that June.[35] Mimi Poser from the Guggenheim's radio show attended the opening and interviewed William vanden Heuvel, the New York State chair of the board of corrections, who claimed that "if we could expand this to every prison in this city and state, I think that would be of great benefit to all of us."[36] In 1976, Andrews curated *Echoes: Prisons, USA* at the Studio Museum in Harlem, which featured work by seventeen men who had taken BECC workshops while incarcerated.

Art by the incarcerated was also being exhibited on-site. In a report titled *BECC Prison Cultural Exchange Report*, likely written for MoMA's Junior Council and presented in January 1972, the BECC reported that "the art produced by the inmates of the Manhattan, Bronx, and Queens Houses of detention is being effectively used to enhance the appearance of the recreation rooms, kitchen, dining halls, libraries, hallways, and other areas used by the prisoners." The brief continues, "This extensive use of the productions of those involved in the art program being conducted by the BECC is to the benefit of the entire prison community and is a salient factor in the maintenance of the highest morale possible under prison circumstances."[37]

The BECC's plan, from the beginning, was to grow the project across the United States: "The Black Emergency Cultural Coalition is a national organization; we have artists all over the country who have membership in our organization, and we have a number of people designated in different parts of the country as regional directors in their areas to carry on similar programs."[38] The BECC archives reveal several letters from artists around the country wanting to help, as well as from the incarcerated asking the organization to create more programs and best practices. After the BECC's Prison Arts Program was funded by the New York State Council on the Arts and the National Endowment for the Arts, it had an annual budget in 1974 of $35,000 that helped the organization achieve its national goal.

A BECC statement written by Benny Andrews in 1975 claims that "the visiting artist program is now at Rhode Island Children's Facility; Boston, Mass City Jail; Washington, DC (artists recruited through Howard University); Tallahassee State Prison, Florida; Auburn, Alabama; Atlanta, Georgia; Chicago, Ill.; Columbus, Ohio and Cleveland, Ohio; Berkeley and Los Angeles, California; Detroit, Michigan."[39] By that year the program was offering a wide range of workshops in art, writing, theater, and performance at federal and state prisons, and city, juvenile, and women's detention centers.

The BECC began to publish a newsletter with images of work being made in the program and reports from teaching artists and workshop participants. The 1980 bulletin features a Prison Arts Program Directory that lists thirty-seven programs in fourteen states, including in very old and large prisons such as San Quentin, in California. By 1989, Andrews reported there were about "forty programs in twenty states."[40]

Andrews encouraged the inmates to go back to school and to teach in the BECC after they were released. As he indicated, "A number of ex-inmates now teach in BECC programs. Ronald King, a published poet, teaches creative writing at Wards Island and in Bedford-Stuyvesant. Sinbad Lockwood, a painter and a sculptor, is helping develop a program for juveniles in Brooklyn and teaches at Bedford-Stuyvesant Restoration. And Akili-Nali studied at the School of Visual Arts and now teaches at Wards Island."[41]

"Art and the Ex-Con," a persuasive essay in the 1980 newsletter written by King, whose work was also featured in the *Attica Book*, describes his journey from being a former prisoner at New York's Auburn Correctional Facility and taking BECC classes there to becoming a teacher in its program.[42] Additionally, an "Honor Roll of Teachers" in the 1980 newsletter lists King as "the Field Director of teaching for the BECC," for which "he orients and oversees new teachers coming into the program."[43] The artist Nene Humphrey, Andrews's widow, recalled training with King and teaching drawing classes on Wards Island with him in 1981–82. "He was an inspiration—he was highly influenced by the BECC and went on to teach with them and get a few masters' degrees. He was devoted to giving back," she said. She further remembered witnessing the inmates' creative impulses: "They had all this creativity and they needed somewhere to put it. We did simple exercises—we were given pencils, you couldn't bring anything in—so it was a modest situation with the supplies, usually. But even so, you could see the inmates having so much to say on the page. I found it really rewarding."[44]

In 1981, after ten years of hard work, the BECC was given notice by the New York Department of Labor, Unemployment Insurance Division, regarding their liability for contributions that should have been made since January 1, 1978. This note from their archive seems to mark the beginning of the end of their prison programs. The new Reagan administration also stopped the NEA from funding prison arts programs and in 1982, the NEA lost 14 percent of its $151.3 million budget.

A letter to Andrews from A. B. Spellman, director of the NEA's Expansion Arts Program, dated March 25, 1982, states, "I am in receipt of your letter of March 11 requesting a reinstatement of the grant for the Black Emergency Cultural Coalition (BECC). I am well aware of the good that the BECC has accomplished in recent years and I regret that the current policies of the Expansion Arts Program mitigate against support of prison arts projects and therefore against awards to BECC."[45]

The records of the official work of the BECC cease after 1982, the year they were denied funding by the National Endowment for the Arts. There is evidence that some instructors continued their programs in various institutions, but it is unclear whether they ever received compensation for their work or for how long they continued to offer classes. However, what's perfectly clear is that the BECC in part collapsed when it lost its most significant funding source, after a political shift in the 1980s under the Reagan administration toward more retributive prisons and the corresponding lack of government funding for education and cultural enrichment programs.

What the BECC offered went beyond education and enrichment. And that's what makes its downfall so unfortunate. In a 1973 article in *Art in America*, Andrews maintained, "The communication that takes place between us (the artists) and the inmates really transcends teaching art: it becomes a human exchange experience, and our being artists quickly becomes secondary."[46] Luckily, although the BECC fell apart right when it seemed to be doing its most vital work, Andrews carried its spirit into the NEA. He became the director of the Visual Arts Program for the NEA, and frequently worked in Washington, DC, from 1982 to 1984. By then, the personalities in the coalition "were going in different directions, taking on new roles," as Humphrey shared.[47] A combination of factors ultimately led to the BECC's demise—yet its legacy lives on.

Today, prison arts programs are highly administered affairs. There have also been many changes in funding streams—the government offers less—but seeds of the radical practices forged by the BECC continue in different ways and are carried out by contemporary prison arts educators and collaborators. Yet, the history of the BECC's efforts is mostly unknown to these groups. The same could be said for the contemporary art world's lack of study of artists such as Andrews, Billops, Browne, and Joseph, which is due to structural issues in museums and the obliviousness of art historians and curators.

The BECC's antagonizing of museums also engendered a strong legacy. To cite just one example: on May 13, 1991, Godzilla: Asian American Art Network wrote a powerful letter to David Ross, then the director of the Whitney Museum, condemning the lack of Asian American artists in the 1991

Whitney Biennial, of diversity in previous Whitney Biennials, and of Asian American representation in the museum, exhibitions, collections, and the executive boards. Godzilla strategically sent the letter to key museum directors and curators, Whitney board members, government funders, and the art press, which was a tactic employed slightly earlier by the activist collective AIDS Coalition to Unleash Power (ACT UP). Perhaps taking a cue from the BECC, Godzilla also reprinted the letter in its newsletter that winter alongside an article about the meeting written by the art historian Margo Machida.

Ross agreed to meet with the group on September 20, 1991; Godzilla member Tomie Arai remembered that he only wanted a few people from Godzilla to attend and that the collective insisted that he meet with the group. "There were at least twelve of us who showed up and we were all totally intimidated," she recalled, adding:

> I remember thinking, "wow, we got this far!" It was really something that had an enormous impact on me, even though I wasn't a principal player in that meeting. All along the way, in terms of Godzilla's advocacy and all the things that we managed to do collectively, there was this feeling that we were in it together. We were building a kind of cultural power together that would live with us for the rest of our lives. It totally impacted me.[48]

After the conversation, Godzilla issued a follow-up letter. "As discussed, the regrettable absence of Asian American visual artists in the last Whitney Biennial remains symptomatic of a larger issue—the lack of awareness, or often even interest, among curators in many major institutions, of the numerous artists emerging from Asian American communities and their significant and growing contributions to the public discourse," they wrote. "To remedy this problem, mechanisms must be established by which staff at the Whitney can become familiar, on an ongoing basis, with the rich range of work produced by Asian American artists."[49]

Godzilla next prepared resources on a dozen Asian American artists and sent them to the Whitney's curatorial staff, suggesting that all the artists were available for studio visits. Additionally, Godzilla recommended consulting with an advisory board of diverse artists and hosting education programs. This concerted effort to reform the institution is in line with the BECC's corrective tactics. It was crucial for both groups to point out institutional gaps in knowledge and their effect: the way artists are valued. While we've come a long way since 1991, this kind of action is still relevant today for activist groups putting pressure on museums. Yet, any effort would likely be fruitless without learning from the past.

4

Top Value Television, 1972–79

The Top Value Television (TVTV) collective was a bunch of "blue-jeaned video freaks," who did what other news outlets didn't.[1] By producing iconoclastic documentaries on politics and culture in the 1970s, TVTV spearheaded the global development of independent video, broadcasting the first tapes from the guerilla media movement across US networks. The collective emerged out of earlier groups—Videofreex, the Raindance Corporation, Ant Farm—who championed an emerging, cutting-edge consumer tech: the cigar box–sized Sony Portapak, which was groundbreaking in those years for its "lightweight" twenty-five-pound batteries and its seven-pound hand-held camera. The recorder was also a mainstay of early video art, even though it was expensive, and cost around $1,500 in 1970. Though some of its members identified as artists, and their works have been recently shown at the Museum of Modern Art in New York and other intuitions, TVTV did not operate within the art world.[2] And while TVTV didn't initially set out to marry art and activism, ultimately, they did.

Most of the members, like other video guerrillas, came out of 1960s-era counterculture, journalism, documentary filmmaking, and other backgrounds. These collectives were determined to use video to invent new forms of art—to document protests and local grassroots organizing, and to capture textures of everyday life. To begin, TVTV focused on revolutionizing the news and going after major political players through verité techniques, such as unfolding conversations and atmospherics instead of traditional terse sound bites and studio backdrops—which one sees throughout their first two grainy, black-and-white videos, *The World's Largest TV Studio* and *Four More Years*. Each about an hour long, in these works we are taken behind the scenes of the 1972 Democratic and Republican conventions, respectively. The tapes capture a volatile American moment and a sobering view of the '70s. They transform from documentary to activism in two ways: TVTV turned the mic over to Vietnam War veterans protesting the Republican convention and to Black feminists at the Democratic convention, who unpack intersectional values before that term was even coined. What's more, TVTV ensured that these urgent voices were broadcast across the United States shortly after, thus challenging the politics of the news, which did not cover these groups.

Though the technology TVTV wielded has long been surpassed, its breakthrough tactics and early DIY ethos remains admirable, albeit too little known. Many members hoped that in the future everyone might have access to a portable video camera and that the resultant proliferation of visuals would quickly change hearts and minds, producing a more democratic society through an early form of citizen journalism (or what Marshall McLuhan called the "global village"). TVTV essentially paved the way for today's deluge of verité footage on social media. They could never have imagined the outcome.

TVTV was formed by three principal members: the married couple Michael Shamberg and Megan Williams, and Shamberg's college roommate and cofounder of the Portola Media Access Center in Menlo Park, California, Allen Rucker. (After TVTV broke up, Shamberg gave up on independent media and became a Hollywood film producer—his credits include *Pulp Fiction* and *The Big Chill*—the latter may have been influenced by the group of friends in TVTV—while Williams continued to work as a documentary filmmaker and Rucker taught and wrote several books.) Together they invited Chip Lord, Hudson Marquez, Curtis Schreier, and Doug Michels from Ant Farm,

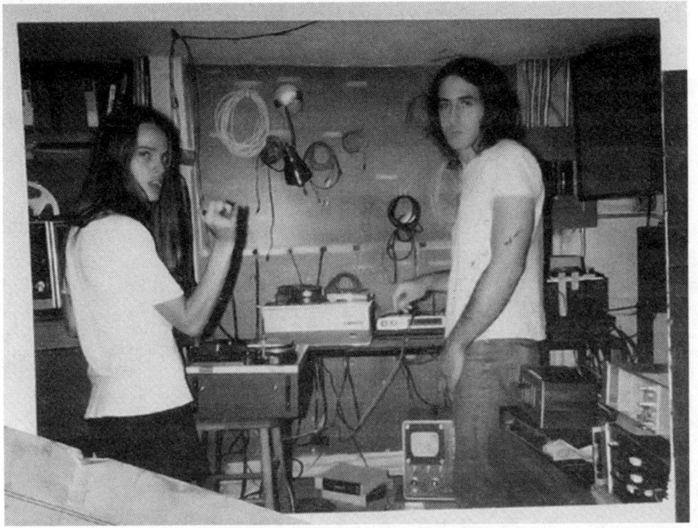

Megan Williams and Michael Shamberg surveying video gear in the lead-up to the 1972 Democratic National Convention.

and Skip Blumberg and Nancy Cain from Videofreex to join. Emerging video makers Jody Sibert, Anda Korsts, and Tom Weinberg got involved early as well. Producer Wendy Appel, journalist Maureen Orth (later a special correspondent for *Vanity Fair*), and Paul Goldsmith (who directed a documentary about TVTV in 2018) also joined and provided essential technical skills.[3]

Shamberg had written previously about video and had been to the chaotic 1968 Democratic convention in Chicago, where he worked as a freelance journalist for *Time* and *Life*. In 1970, he took a Sony Portapak to the National Citizen Committee on Broadcasting, a conference assembled by Metropolitan Museum of Art director Thomas Hoving, and created *Media Primer for Raindance* with his filmed interviews and event coverage. (In 1971, with members of Raindance, Shamberg wrote *Guerrilla Television*, a book-cum-manual influenced by the do-it-yourself ethics of the *Whole Earth Catalog*, Stewart

Brand's countercultural magazine and product catalog published several times between 1968 and 1972.) By February 1972, Shamberg wanted to take this guerilla approach to documenting US politics a step further with a collective at that year's conventions. TVTV was formally established in April as a media collective when it set up a live/workspace in San Francisco six weeks before the July Democratic National Convention in Miami.

They needed money for the project and so went to cable companies (which were then called CATV) for funding—including Teleprompter, the nation's largest cable system, Sterling Cable in Manhattan, Continental in Ohio, and Cypress Communications of Los Angeles—which could air the tapes. Maureen Orth reported in *Rolling Stone* that at the time those three systems reached "more than one million cable subscribers—about twenty percent of the current US CATV market—potentially the largest audience ever to view a program produced by alternative TV."[4] While TVTV waited for funding, they put all their expenses on their credit cards.

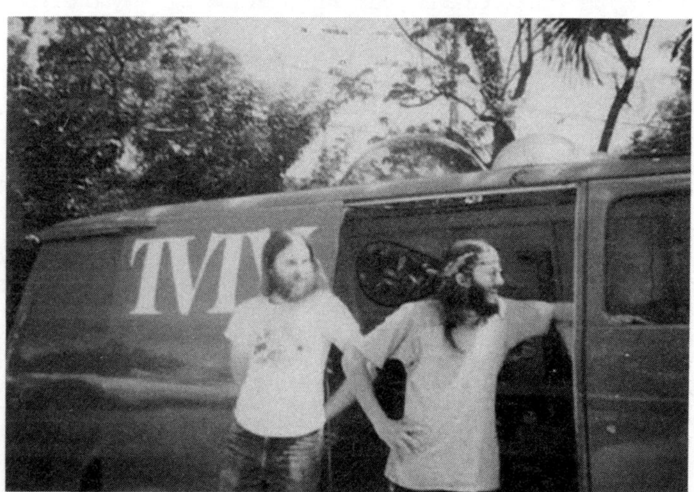

Hudson Marquez and Chip Lord pose in front of the TVTV Media Van.

When the time came, members piled into Ant Farm's "media van" and drove from San Francisco to Miami with portable video gear—including twelve Portapaks. They rented a two-story white stucco house with a pool in a pricey neighborhood, and the group of about twenty-eight filled every single room, "like members of a commune or a rock band," as the art historian David Joselit has quipped.[5] Some were directly involved with TVTV while a handful of others with various expertise came to help.[6]

Media scholar Deirdre Boyle notes:

> Once the Democratic Convention began, activity sprawled from upstairs bedrooms where crews logged tapes, down into the living room—an informal screening room and mission control center cluttered with Sony Portapaks, tapes, wires, cables, newspapers, and large hand lettered signs and assignment sheets—and out around the azalea-bordered pool.[7]

TVTV did not have its press credentials in place before arriving in Miami, but they obtained them with no problem, as one of a hundred officially accredited non-network, international TV groups given access to the conventions. The Democratic National Convention was swarming with reporters meeting in hotel lobbies—often the journalists were more interested in the other writers on the ground than the delegates and politicians themselves.

TVTV wasn't interested in competing with the major networks—ABC, CBS, and NBC. At the conventions, their well-coiffed reporters were usually stuck in a booth or a specific spot next to large, million-dollar cameras shooting on two-inch "Quad" tape, ready to read whatever was given to them. Meanwhile, TVTV roamed around the Convention Center, capturing the texture of the events through on-the-ground interviews, stray audio and visuals, and behind-the-scenes meetings. Skip Blumberg recalled that "by just keeping the camera rolling, you could get the most amazing footage, even when people thought it was off. They didn't even know we had sound; they would talk thinking it was Super 8 movies. The innocence on the world's part for underestimating what this equipment could do was important."[8]

TVTV provided concise briefing instructions to their crews.[9] "Things to Tape" included: *Delegates*: "Specifically, we should try to be with delegates at dinner, in caucus rooms, in their hotel rooms, at parties, etc. We already have pledges of access . . . The continuing saga of a delegate may make a good continuity device in the final edit." *The Media*: "You should also make friends with newsmen as they'll give you tips about events and processes. Chances are they won't feel threatened by us but will be amused and want to help." *Pseudo-Events*: "Better to have spontaneous behavior which happens in process (as in hanging out with delegates)." *Confrontations*: "Our feeling is that confrontation tape is a cliche of Porta-Pak video and we're tired of it . . . We're not into declarative, explicit typed action or statements done wholly for the media. At best, we want to cover the media covering those actions and cover the people planning for or reflecting on them. The actions themselves are of negligible importance to us."

These directives play out turbulently inside the convention hall (which is, of course, the world's largest TV studio) and outside too. In interviews with TVTV, Dan Rather confided that having so many politicians around made him feel like "a kid turned loose in a candy store." Walter Cronkite proclaimed, "I enjoy an open-ended broadcast. It gives you a chance to say a few things." NBC's Cassie Mackin, the first woman "floor reporter" for the networks, told Maureen Orth, "It's a piece of cake. There's nothing a woman couldn't have done a long time ago."

While the '68 Democratic convention was the most violent, the '72 Democratic convention was likely the most confusing in its history, as delegations challenged convention rules and new constituencies fought for inclusion and diversity. The establishment included Senators Hubert Humphrey and Edmund Muskie, Governor George Wallace, and nominee-apparent Senator George McGovern. The new factions included California Assemblyman Willie Brown, Congressman Ron Dellums, and the Reverend Jesse Jackson. Onetime presidential candidate Shirley Chisholm—the first Black woman ever elected to Congress—was deceived by Dellums at the convention and dropped out of the race while Congresswoman Bella Abzug focused on women's rights with feminists Gloria Steinem and Betty Friedan. McGovern had persuaded many feminists to support him over Chisholm. But he would later betray them, by telling his delegates not to support a plank that would legalize abortion and by also violating a promise to the women by permitting an anti-abortion activist to speak from the floor.

One spontaneous conversation showed the type of remarkable things TVTV captured that few others did. The National

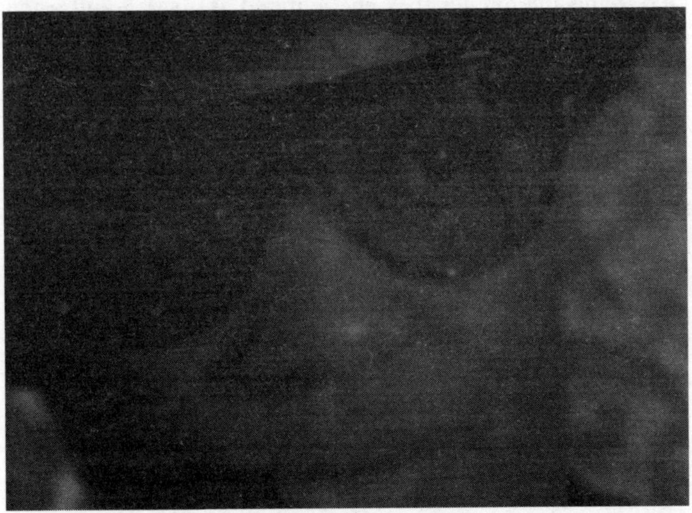

Still from TVTV, *The World's Largest TV Studio*, 1972, black-and-white, sound, 59 minutes. Margaret Sloan-Hunter.

Women's Political Caucus, which had been founded the previous year, held a press conference regarding their proposals for the party's platform featuring Abzug, Sissy Farenthold, Friedan, and Steinem. It received almost no television coverage. However, TVTV was there. A reporter spoke with Margaret Sloan-Hunter, who pointed to the exclusion of Black and lesbian women from second-wave feminism: "My involvement in the women's movement follows out of my involvement in the Black movement, except now I'm addressing myself to the needs of the majority of the Black nation, which are Black women," she explains in a lesson on intersectional feminism. Flo Kennedy and Margaret Sloan-Hunter went on to become founding members of the National Black Feminist Organization the next year.

The tapes are full of these kinds of revealing discussions about class, gender, race, and politics, but in addition to these kinds of candid conversations, TVTV also turned the camera on themselves. The collective took great care to reveal their tactics and the hitches they encountered as a small and often suspect crew trying to enter the convention. "At the first convention we were just long-haired, scruffy people with these 'Mickey Mouse' cameras, as the engineers called them. They treated us with disdain because we were so bush league, but we didn't care—we were making television," Skip Blumberg shared.[10] Several scenes show Secret Service staff on the convention floor asking TVTV members for press credentials.

Richard Reeves, a reporter for *New York* magazine, told readers that the video is "the best electronic coverage of the Democratic Convention that I've seen. And I've seen too much."[11] John J. O'Connor devoted an entire column in the *New York Times* to *The World's Largest TV Studio* the day it was cablecast in New York. "Occasionally, the documentary verges on that peculiar brand of smugness that infects many underground visions of on-the-ground society," he commented. "It verges, but fortunately doesn't succumb. On the contrary, the most devastating moments are devoted to an ego-tripping Jerry Rubin and some assorted members of his tribe."[12] In the segment "Whatever Happened to Jerry Rubin?," TVTV shows the countercultural activist Rubin gaining one delegate vote, after much cajoling on his part.

Boyle, in her book *Subject to Change*, says:

> The mere fact of a full-length *New York Times* review gave the tape and TVTV the kind of credibility the group desperately needed. The day before the review appeared, Sterling Cable (later Manhattan Cable) had reneged on its promise of $1,000 to produce the Republican Convention tape, but after the review, the cable company agreed to make good on its offer. TVTV considered O'Connor's review responsible in large measure for their ability to raise funding for the second show.[13]

Ultimately, TVTV lost money on the endeavor. It spent roughly $16,000 to create *The World's Largest TV Studio*, including buying tape, equipment, a trip to New York for editing, transportation, and living expenses for some of the collective's members. They put most of this on credit cards and ended up in debt—but awash in accolades. "We knowingly took the risk and it paid off," Megan Williams said, referring to the high praise in the *New York Times*, which enabled TVTV to secure funding for their second production.[14]

One month later, the crew went into action again, taking a cue from Joe McGinniss's *The Selling of the President 1968*, a penetrating account from inside of the second presidential campaign of Richard Nixon. *Four More Years* shows TVTV's continued prowess in gaining access. Nixon's Republican convention in August 1972 was a highly organized outfit. Yet the party's monopoly on control backfired: "The media inadvertently had been handed the Republicans' minute-by-minute script of the Convention, including all the 'spontaneous demonstrations' held by the Young Republicans," Boyle writes.[15] This meant that TVTV needed to search elsewhere for off-the-cuff material, and since Nixon's nomination was inevitable, the collective turned its cameras to events mostly occurring outside the convention hall.

The best segment of the tape occurs when protesters outside were given access inside—by TVTV. Hundreds of members of Vietnam Veterans Against the War (VVAW) arrived to march up Collins Avenue to try to delay proceedings. While much of the press was either in the convention hall or at the Miami International Airport waiting for Nixon to arrive, TVTV captured a large-scale protest led by the Last Patrol—three men in wheelchairs, including the paraplegic ex-Marine sergeant Ron Kovic. The procession of about 1,200 men in army uniforms confronted 500 heavily armed police stationed at the Fontainebleau Hotel and demanded to go inside. On tape, TVTV shows Republican congressman Pete McCloskey negotiating his way through the police line to speak with the vets and convince them that an assault would not work. The VVAW

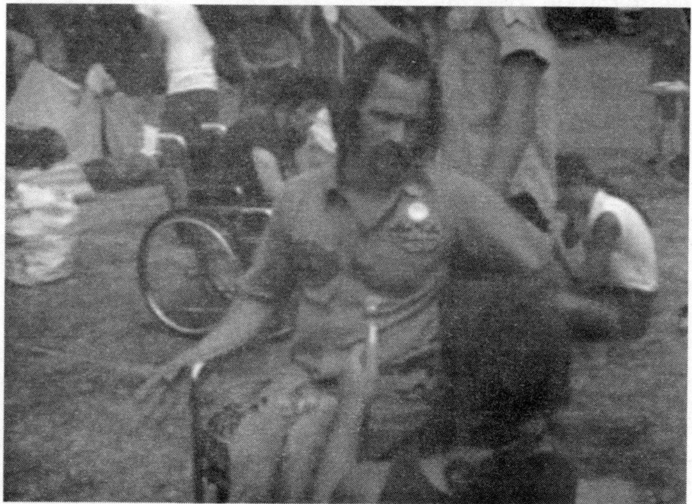

Still from TVTV, *Four More Years*, 1972, black-and-white, sound, 61 minutes. Ron Kovic.

settled for a series of bullhorn speeches including one by Kovic. As Hunter S. Thompson noted, "His words lashed the crowd like a wire whip . . . If Kovic had been allowed to speak from the convention hall podium, in front of network TV cameras, Nixon wouldn't have had the balls to show up and accept the nomination."[16]

TVTV continued to follow Kovic around Miami. According to Boyle, "On the last night, Hudson Marquez gave Kovic his TVTV press pass so that Kovic could get onto the convention floor."[17] The footage TVTV captured here is the most moving part of *Four More Years*: amid the crowd of cheering Nixon supporters, Kovic's voice is nearly drowned out, but a vignette of him shouting, "Stop the bombing . . . Stop the war. Stop killing human beings!" is powerfully chilling. Director Oliver Stone was clearly influenced by this footage: his 1989 film *Born on the Fourth of July* shows Tom Cruise as Kovic bellowing the same words.

TVTV also focused more intensely on interviews with the media this round: Dan Rather talks about being bored on the floor while Walter Cronkite explains why he didn't stand during the *Star-Spangled Banner* (he was working). Regarding the controversy and scrutiny that ensued over that incident, he told Megan Williams and Skip Blumberg in his office that the introspection it prompted in him was "not good for a journalist." Meanwhile, Cassie Mackin notes it's "been very dull . . . It looks to me like it's a very packaged plastic kind of thing, with very little spontaneity."

In an almost five-minute outtake shot outside the convention hall, Maureen Orth asks the late congressman John Lewis and the activist Tom Houck for their thoughts on "the young people here tonight," after what was clearly a long day of working on their separate voter registration initiatives. Houck compares the group to the "voices that stayed silent and particularly calm when Hitler was taking over"; the association is reinforced by a clip where Young Republicans chant "four more years" while

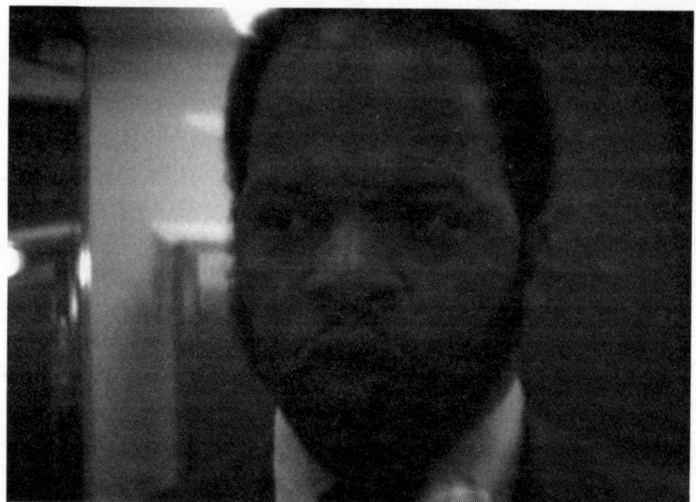

Still from TVTV, *Four More Years*, 1972, black-and-white, sound, 61 minutes. John Lewis.

doing something of a Sieg Heil salute. Lewis, who was there to register African American voters as Democrats, speaks about his civil rights activism and nonpartisan ethics: "There comes a time in the life of a country and the life of a people when you stand for something—and you don't stand for it because of a party or a particular man but because it's *right*."

Scholars and critics have noted that *Four More Years* is a surprisingly objective, nonpartisan, and evenhanded tape. Viewers are left to draw their own conclusions through the lack of voice-over narration and any overt editorializing. Certainly, the work speaks to TVTV's journalistic integrity, but in this exhaustive chronicle, TVTV also allows the various players to speak for themselves—and in many ways to hang themselves on their own words. In one standout scene, Orth speaks with National Security Advisor and Secretary of State Henry Kissinger, who offhandedly remarks, "We don't care what effect the peace process is having on domestic politics." Kissinger also appears right after the scene showing Kovic gravely shouting on the convention floor. TVTV boldly cut from that to a frenzy of screaming Nixonites around Kissinger, who applauds the renomination of Nixon while a deluge of balloons pours down on the assembled devotees, including a young man who shrieks until he can only croak: "Four more years! Four more years!"

After *Four More Years* was cablecast, TVTV was approached by Westinghouse Broadcasting, which offered to pay the collective $4,000 for a ninety-minute version of *The World's Largest TV Studio* and *Four More Years*. The tapes were edited and transferred onto two-inch quad tape, which was then standard gauge for broadcast transmissions. It may have been the first moment that half-inch portable video tape was bumped up to broadcast.

After TVTV re-edited the convention tapes for broadcast on Westinghouse television stations in October 1972, the group began to be more interested in that format instead of cable, which meant making a different—much less activist and more commercial—work. In March 1973, they received $2,200 from public television station WNET in New York to produce a tape about *Rolling Stone* for its "Behind the Lines" series. The result is a fawning, seventeen-minute tape mostly centered on the magazine's young and brazen cofounder Jann Wenner. "A far cry from the rough but complex storytelling of the convention tapes," as Boyle says, "*TVTV Meets Rolling Stone* has the look and feel of bad boys getting off on being young, hip, smart, and successful."[18]

Some of TVTV's subsequent films, such as 1973's *Lord of the Universe* and 1974's *Adland*, show some activist potential, but by 1974 the collective had markedly changed its goals. "We believe now that building an enclave within the existing system is a viable strategy for change," TVTV declared in its book *The Prime Time Survey*.[19] Revolutionizing broadcast nonfiction television from within became TVTV's new objective. Not long after its final work, the NBC comedy pilot *The TVTV Show*

(1977), was rejected by the network, TVTV ceased operating. This infiltration into the mainstream was unsuccessful, though perhaps TVTV was doomed to fail from the beginning—even when its goals were loftier and more concerned with democratizing video.

Of all TVTV's output, *Four More Years* serves as an ideal example of guerrilla television's activist tactics. The work relies on timing and on the specific equipment they used. As Williams said, "No one was familiar with the Sony Portapak. Unlike 16mm film, our equipment was silent. We also included ourselves in our coverage, which in some way often endeared us to our subjects, who couldn't envision that we were really making TV!"[20]

Wielding their Portapaks, TVTV knew how to be in the right place at the right time. Lucy Lippard has written that "activist art is all about time—the intensity of that moment that needs elucidating; the time away from the studio, friends, family, and wage earning; the time it takes to launch a major activist project; and the time past, the time ahead, into which the action must fit."[21]

Relatedly, the artist Tania Bruguera has developed her idea of "Political Timing Specificity," when an artist or collective intervenes in a political situation. As she argues, "Political-timing-specific art not only confronts power with its own tools but creates a temporary juncture where those in power do not know how to respond to others' defining what is political . . . Political-timing-specific art exists within the time it takes for those in power to react."[22]

TVTV's intervention into the tumultuous 1972 Democratic convention was a case in point. To put it plainly, the networks were trying to control the narrative and TVTV found a way to break it. TVTV entered with precision, during the right moment for political action; an *occasione* as the Italian Renaissance philosopher Machiavelli might say.[23] Or, per Boyle:

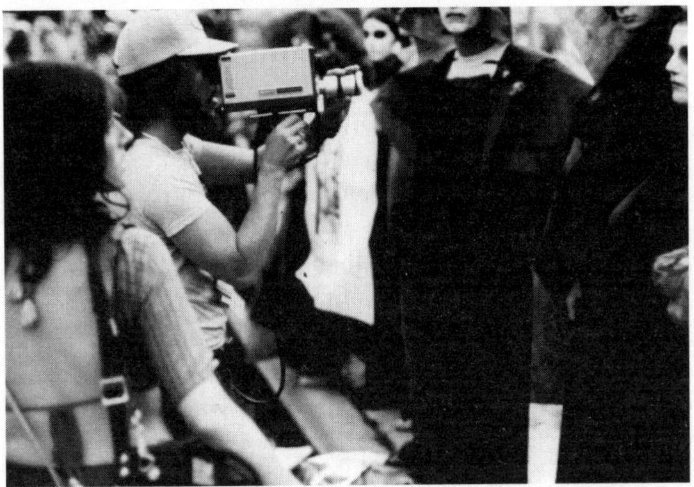

Bart Friedman and Wendy Appel filming a protest during the 1972 Republican National Convention.

"TVTV succeeded where their establishment 'betters' failed. Machiavelli with a Portapak."[24]

Writing about Bruguera, the art historian Claire Bishop has traced the *occasione* to the later concept of the conjuncture, which can be found across leftist political theory—from Antonio Gramsci to Louis Althusser, and from Stuart Hall to Ernesto Laclau and Chantal Mouffe.[25] Hall articulates it most clearly: "A conjuncture is a period during which the different social, political, economic, and ideological contradictions that are at work in society come together to give it a specific and distinctive shape."[26] For him, conjunctural analysis "forces you to look at many different aspects, in order to see what the balance of social forces is and how you might intervene, or have a better idea of how to intervene effectively."[27]

Bishop contends that "works of art that are political timing specific often appear too closely tied to the particularities of their moment" and "now require considerable explanation to be understood."[28] Such is the case with TVTV's political tapes.

The 1972 Democratic National Convention was a complicated affair; "byzantine," according to Hunter S. Thompson. It was particularly significant as the first implementation of the reforms set by the Commission on Party Structure and Delegate Selection, which McGovern had chaired before deciding to run for president. This commission led to eight "procedural rules and safeguards." Among the most significant of the changes were new quotas mandating that certain percentages of delegates be women or members of minority groups.

While TVTV's coverage was immediately legible at the time, it now requires *considerable explanation to be understood.* Journalist Renata Adler, for instance, remarked that the winner-take-all California primary "was explained [by the networks] as though it were Gödel's theorem to be communicated with sympathetic expressions of puzzlement, to subnormal grade-school children." "Top Value Television," she continued, "did much better . . . in simply eavesdropping."[29] Though it wasn't exactly that, Adler's point is that TVTV could often infiltrate closed-door conversations—whether because of their unobtrusive Portapak or because they simply looked so different from the rest of the press. And while the times and technology have changed dramatically, it's important for young media activists who wield new tools to remember how TVTV pushed video into a new activist art form. In doing so, the collective offered novel tactics, creating the widest possible audience they could, almost thinking like politicians to do so.

5

Agnes Denes, 1931–

Artist, activist, and writer Agnes Denes has long fought independently and collectively for social and ecological justice. She was a member of Women Artists in Revolution (WAR) in the late 1960s and early '70s—a splinter group of the Art Workers' Coalition that, as the reader will remember, fought for greater representation of women in museums. In January 1971, she pushed administrators and curators at the Whitney Museum of American Art to meet with representatives from WAR, the Ad Hoc Committee of Women Artists, and Women Students and Artists for Black Art Liberation, though the meeting does not seem to have transpired. She realized early on that activism can work in less predictable ways than a letter, a meeting, or a protest.

Still, her penchant for working communally carried into her art, most of which pre-dates "social practice" or community-based engagements that largely began in the early 2000s and mostly tended to occur outside of museums and galleries. Her work is activist for the ways it is grounded in getting things done—by actively addressing issues such as food insecurity and climate change rather than representing or simply describing them.

Today, she is most known for her ecological artworks, which she began in the late 1960s. Over the ensuing decades she has been called a visionary, a polymath, and a sage. "She has basically carved out an independent, label-free niche for herself and has been occupying and expanding it for over fifty years," as critic Holland Cotter notes.[1] This is why it is hard to place Denes in the early lineage of the Land art movement;

unlike most major Land artists—such as Walter De Maria, Andy Goldsworthy, Nancy Holt, Richard Long, and Robert Smithson—she has been more interested in restoration than intervention. Alongside Denes, artists ranging from Betsy Damon, Helen and Newton Harrison, Aviva Rahmani, Bonnie Sherk, and Alan Sonfist made artworks in the 1970s and '80s with a focus on ecological repair and sustainable food systems. In their wake, Carolina Caycedo, Allison Janae Hamilton, and Mary Mattingly are just a few of the artists now addressing harms to the environment, often through an ecofeminist lens.

Denes was born in Budapest, Hungary, in 1931. Her family survived World War II and fled to Stockholm in the late 1940s, moving in 1954 to the US, where they encountered the toxic combination of Cold War paranoia, the nuclear arms race, and a consumerism that stood to destroy the planet. Moving around, coupled with the challenges posed by constantly learning new languages, caused Denes to seek consolation in visual art. She studied painting at the New School and Columbia University in New York but abandoned the medium, due to the constraints of the canvas, and turned to poetry, which she later called visual philosophy. She is a prolific writer. For example, before the wave of treatises on our planet's impending demise, there was her *Book of Dust: The Beginning and the End of Time and Thereafter* (1989). A heavily researched investigation of the death of all matter, written between 1972 and 1987, the book is full of passages that ring clear as a bell today:

> The paradoxes of our existence: alienation in togetherness, uniformity in specialization, illusions of freedom in group mentality, ignorance in the midst of information overload, greed in the face of neglect, self-aggrandizement in response to ineffectuality. It is comparable to going into the ice age and the heat wave of the greenhouse effect simultaneously.[2]

Typically, each of her art projects begins with a basic equation or a question, which blossoms into a diagram, drawing, or installation that often suggests an obscure code for some mysterious process of transformation. Her work is driven by an understanding that technological advances, no matter how utopian, are always in danger of becoming tools of oppression. It's as if she wanted to grasp the roots of intricate abusive systems so that she could understand how to break them apart—and this is perhaps her greatest contribution as an activist.

Denes was one of three women included in *Software—Information Technology: Its New Meaning for Art*, the groundbreaking 1970 group show at New York's Jewish Museum, where she exhibited *Trigonal Ballet*, 1970, a foray into the nascent field of digital animation, with sound. (One of the first artists to work with computers, Denes began building digital models from a basic geometric unit—the triangle—in the late 1960s.) She had planned to also show several programs she'd written.

In a letter published in the December 1970 issue of *Artforum*, she claimed the Jewish Museum had not delivered on its promises, making it impossible for her to present her works as she'd intended. Even the computer displaying the animation eventually broke down and was not replaced. "My work and I were treated as a joke . . . I blame no one person," Denes wrote, "I was caught in the gears of a system within which shows of this type are financed and publicized with complete cynicism, and the end always justifies the means. The waves close over it and nobody gives a damn."[3]

Denes didn't mention sexism in her letter, but its role in the shabby treatment she received is implicit in her statement. Lucy Lippard spearheaded a group letter to *Artforum* in support of Denes's "protest against the mistreatment of her work and of herself as an artist." The missive, published alongside Denes's letter, claims:

> The issue here is not merely the mistreatment of one person and one person's art. It involves the lack of respect shown all artists and their work by art institutions in general, and it involves the reluctance of most artists to make their grievances public. The reasons are understandable—distaste for publicity, fear of retribution from other institutions, the time that must be spent in any sustained protest . . . This, combined with the absurd fact that the show, in its almost totally inoperative state, is going to travel to the Smithsonian, makes it all the more necessary to make public *now* the inequities and iniquities suffered by Miss Denes.[4]

The dispatch was undersigned by other artists (all men) in the exhibition, including Vito Acconci, John Baldessari, Robert Barry, John Giorno, Hans Haacke, Douglas Huebler, Joseph Kosuth, Les Levine, and Lawrence Weiner.

Two years after the *Software* fiasco, Denes became a cofounder of A.I.R. Gallery in New York City, a space dedicated to supporting women. Although self-identified as feminist, Denes didn't set out to make explicitly feminist art. From the late 1960s into the '70s, she was focused on the critical shift from Land to Ecological art. The debacle at the Jewish Museum perhaps prompted her to work outdoors more, but not necessarily to abandon her studio all together: It was essential to Denes to keep producing her drawings and prints, such as the series *Isometric Systems in Isotropic Space—Map Projections*, 1973–79, wherein the Earth is warped and twisted into trigonometric shapes: a snail, an egg, a hot dog. Similarly, the drawings in her series *Restless Pyramids*, 1983–, slough off any rigidity associated with the form, taking the shape of a flying fish, a bird, an egg, and a teardrop. While they are an allegory for environmental collapse, Denes in her most portentous mode has imagined them as blueprints for post-Earth dwellings: easy to repair, self-contained, and self-supporting.

From the start, Denes's large-scale projects have required a living, generative format, which she often found in agriculture, as in her *Wheatfield: A Confrontation*, 1982, which was commissioned by the Public Art Fund. Beginning on May 1, with a small team of unpaid volunteers, Denes planted a shimmering field of red spring wheat over two acres of rubble in Lower Manhattan's Battery Park Landfill: $158 worth of grain on a piece of land then valued at $4.5 billion. (The history of the ersatz "beach" here and other art projects is a fascinating topic for another time.) Considering the truly haunting mediagenic photographs of those amber waves of grain rippling in the shadow of the Twin Towers—images that register as elegies—it's tempting to read something clairvoyant in this project, some supernatural attunement to violence yet to come. In truth, of course, Denes didn't need to see into the future to imbue her work with such foreboding. She needed only to comprehend, as so few people did, the trajectory of Anthropocene devastation. This began at an early age: Denes had witnessed needless mass destruction while living underground as a young teenager during the 1944–45 bombing of Budapest, her birthplace, at the end of World War II.

Wheatfield was also teeming with allusions, from its proximity to the historic immigration station at Ellis Island to Denes's particular choice of grain. Critics have compared a famous photograph of Denes walking through her field with flowing tresses and a staff as a modern-day Demeter, the goddess of the sheaf. As the artist has said, "The work had to have a meaning, a strong message, and, of course, the paradox . . . a large golden field of grain on land meant for the rich, on expensive real estate."[5] The enigma, in other words, was that Denes was planting her relatively small field of wheat in a country that was building a new infrastructure for a globalized debt-based economy, which was already generating recurrent food crisis.

Her choice of wheat was also symbolic. Wheat is one of the most commonly grown grains in the United States—which

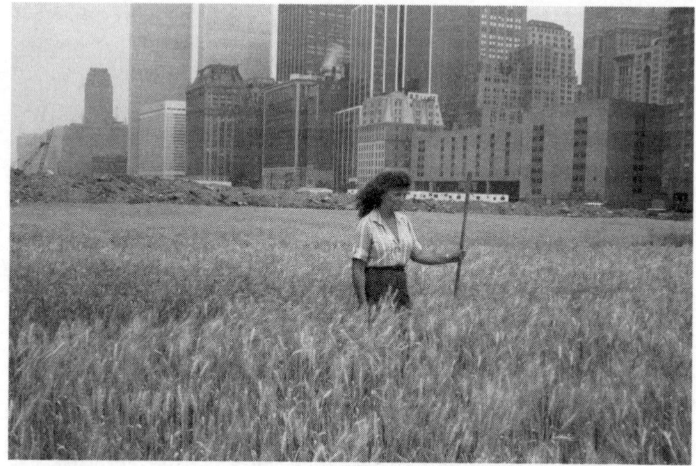

Agnes Denes, *Wheatfield: A Confrontation*, 1982. Courtesy of the Public Art Fund, New York. Photo by John McGrail.

exports nearly 50 percent of its wheat production. Yet, despite being produced in nearly every state, it is not a native grass to the country and was likely first planted during the colonial period (1492–1783). It's important to acknowledge that the work originally transpired on the ancestral homelands of the Munsee Lenape and that Land and Ecological art does not have a good track record of recognizing such facts. As Indigenous artists Marina Hupfield and Jason Lujan have argued, these genres are "explicitly connected to an ongoing narrative of conquest and ownership over Native people's land, governance, and bodies."[6] It's also interesting that Denes chose to plant a monocrop, which again speaks to how her project was meant to be symbolic, short-lived, and aesthetically pleasing.

"Did it hurt a little bit to cut it down?" asked Jane Pauley, during a televised interview with Denes about *Wheatfield* on NBC's *Today* in August 1982. Denes confirmed: "Oh, yes. I lived out there for about four months." After over 1,000 pounds of wheat was harvested from the site, Denes gave the hay to the mounted police of New York for their horses, and made packets of the seeds, which were distributed across at least eighteen cities in a large traveling group exhibition called *The International Art Show for the End of World Hunger*.

The landmark show was co-organized by Ana Cristina Bozzo and Marcia Godosky and traveled to cities including Philadelphia, New Orleans, Minnesota, Høvikodden, Göteborg, Cologne, Paris, London, Milan, Rome, Buenos Aires, São Paulo, Caracas, and Mexico City.[7] In addition to Denes, the exhibition featured works by many notable artists, including Joseph Beuys, Louise Bourgeois, Nam June Paik, Robert Rauschenberg, and Andy Warhol. The project lasted approximately a decade, from its inception in the early 1980s and debut at the International Monetary Fund (IMF) in Washington, DC, in 1986, through its final stop at El Museo del Barrio, New York, in 1991.[8] In the show, the curators installed images of *Wheatfield*, complemented by Denes's seed packets. The packets were free to take, and the seeds were planted in solidarity and hope.

Forty years later, Denes offered wheat seeds again. Tinworks, an experimental nonprofit art space in Bozeman, Montana, was the site of the first US commission of *Wheatfield*. When I arrived there in June 2024, on the heels of an unusual summer snowfall, the acre of wheat had grown several feet already and was beginning to sprout spikes of seeds at the top. It was well on its way to becoming a highly sensorial piece, at half the size of the original work.

The organization had partnered with a local farmer, Kenny Van Dyke of Hyline Farms—a commercial wheat operation in Belgrade, Montana—who helped to plant the Bobcat winter wheat seeds in fall 2023 and would be back to help process it in October 2024. A popular nearby bakery, Wild Crumb, had plans to use the wheat flour for a special bread that winter, which would be made available to local food banks. I could easily see that it was no easy feat to maintain the plot, which required constant weeding and surveillance (ground squirrels were common interlopers).

KAMUT brand wheat grains—an ancient, more nutritional variety—were distributed for free that spring for locals to plant in solidarity and were already sprouting too—there was one small patch at the local public library and a larger one in a yard in nearby Ennis. In addition, a host of educational and community programs were underway, including seed swaps and a robust talk series at the Rialto Theater on Main Street. (I was there to speak about Denes in the context of food, activism, and farming.) These informal, conversational events were a success, which brought the local community together to discuss issues related to food insecurity, Indigenous farming, and the complexities of balancing the needs of environmental sustainability and affordable food, topics frequently avoided in most public discourse.

Van Dyke, for example, is a fourth-generation Montanan and a first-generation grain farmer who struggles with investing in soil health on land he can only afford to rent, and that will likely be developed in this rapidly gentrifying and sprawling city. It wasn't hard to see why the area has caught the attention of the wealthy who have been moving there since the mid-2000s—it's beautiful, nestled in the Gallatin Valley, between snow-capped mountains. (A Whole Foods that was recently built near the Bozeman/Yellowstone airport is apparently a one-stop shop for staff who hop off private jets on their way down the highway to private clubs in the mountains.)

But that wealth has nothing on Denes's cultural capital, which she has accrued (too) slowly. The world was finally waking up to her that summer: she was having numerous solo and group shows around the world at the time. But to see her new *Wheatfield* in Bozeman recalled her concerns in the 1980s regarding greed, exploitation of land, poverty, and climate change. As director Jenny Moore explained to me, even Tinworks was slated to become a high-end development.

But the art took hold during 2020–21 (prime outdoor Covid times), and in 2022 the board of directors realized that the site is great for art, and that art should stay there. Still, as Bozeman is one of the fastest growing cities in the United States, Moore estimated that in two to five years every other lot surrounding Tinworks would be developed into condos and mixed-use buildings.

In Bozeman, Denes essentially reclaimed a field that was used for trash and parking while the block just across the street from Tinworks was developed into a mixed-use building with luxury housing. It was reminiscent of her building the first *Wheatfield* on the site where debris from the construction of the World Trade Center had been. It was exciting to see the community acting as stewards of the new *Wheatfield*, and to realize that this was just what Denes intended when she set out to make living, generative artworks. Her point, in a way, was to bring people together and in conversation and community through a largely symbolic and radically resilient artwork.

Two earlier projects by artists also advanced the food activism introduced in *Wheatfield* and *The International Art Show for the End of World Hunger*, by successfully effecting change in actual food systems. These undertakings also speak to food justice, which according to Rasheed Hislop includes "the struggle against racism, exploitation, and oppression taking place within the food system that addresses inequality's root causes both within and beyond the food chain."[9]

Los Angeles–based artist Lauren Halsey's organization Summaeverythang distributed fresh produce to residents of the South-Central Los Angeles and Watts neighborhoods and was particularly important in 2020 during the height of Covid-19 pandemic. And filmmaker, curator, and artist Linda Goode Bryant's nonprofit Project EATS, which was founded in 2009, also distributes fresh produce, grown from its own urban farms in New York City. Project EATS continues to serve communities experiencing food insecurity through its small-plot, high yield farms. Its goal is to increase access and consumption of locally grown, healthy, affordable food in food-insecure communities in New York City and beyond. It has grown from artist-led activism into a large and robust nonprofit, akin to Houston's Project Row Houses, as discussed in chapter 9.

It comes as no surprise that after *Wheatfield*'s debut, Denes turned to more durable land reclamations, including *Tree Mountain–A Living Time Capsule–11,000 Trees, 11,000 People, 400 Years*, 1992–96, the first planned "manmade virgin forest" in the world, which was commissioned by the Finnish government and announced on World Environment Day in 1992. To produce the work, Denes invited 11,000 volunteers to plant the equivalent number of a variety of pine trees in the village of Pinsiö, Finland, forming an upward spiral that tapers toward its peak, a summit of nearly 100 feet. The site (about a two-hour drive north of Helsinki) is lawfully protected against deforestation for the next four hundred years.

Tree Mountain was intended to restore the land: it was built upon a former gravel pit along with another work not too far away—Nancy Holt's *Up and Under*, 1987–98, a sinuous tunnel-and-berm construction made in a sand quarry. In Finland, the law mandates that mining companies must repair a completed working site so that it is safe and not a blot on the landscape. As gravel pits are often in remote places, they are prone to trash dumping and other illegal acts. To avoid fines, mining companies sometimes suspend operations indefinitely before they deplete the quarry and have also used art to meet reclamation requirements, which can be less expensive—and less regulated—than restoring a quarry according to reforestation specifications.

In the late 1980s, a local arts collective named Strata began advocating for artworks in southwestern Finland and produced an environmental art group show in 1992 at the Tampere Art Museum in Finland. Here, Denes presented her forty-five-foot sculpture *Hot/Cold Earthship with Heartbeat*, 1992, an old barge filled with earth—freezing one side and warm on the other, which also emanated a heartbeat—as well as drawings of *Tree Mountain*. Her reforestation plan had been brewing for ten years, and it gained the attention of the Lohja Rudus mining company, which had mined gravel pits in Pinsiö. The company decided to implement the piece.

The initiative soon found additional support from Finland's Ministry of the Environment, which announced plans for its creation. The United Nations Environment Program then supported the project with a $50,000 endowment. Somewhat romantically, the planned 11,000 trees were to each have a human "caretaker." During the inauguration ceremony, the president of Finland, Martti Ahtisaari, planted his tree, and many more trees were assigned other wardens that day while the Tampere Art Museum handled future applications. For example, tree 8838 is assigned to Muammar Gaddafi; tree 7894 to John Major; and tree 8815 to Hosni Mubarak. The mountain thus became a portrait of the political era.

After all of this, *Tree Mountain* settled in for a period of growth, yet unfortunately, due to poor soil quality and the monoculture of planted conifers, many of the trees have not survived. "What this work now communicates about monocultural agronomy, and the effects of soil degradation exceeds its original intentions and planned design," the art historian James Nisbet has argued.[10] Moreover, the site was not properly maintained. To begin, the preservation was divided between the gardening departments of the larger towns of Nokia and Ylöjärvi. Groundskeeping was later outsourced to the Pinsiö village association and men's choir. Invasive and pioneering plants sprouted all around, and trash was often left at the site.

The Finnish artist Eero Yli-Vakkuri, who was hired in 2013 as part of a small team to restore *Tree Mountain*, has written that the gardeners that initially worked on the site were critical of the plans from the beginning, as the design made exceptional

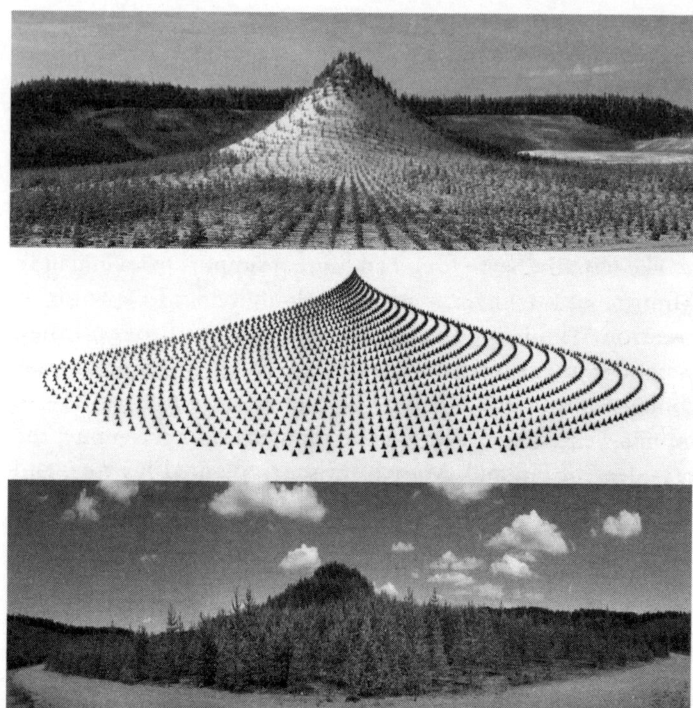

Agnes Denes, *Tree Mountain—A Living Time Capsule—11,000 Trees, 11,000 People—400 Years* (triptych), 1992–96. Courtesy of the artist and Leslie Tonkonow Artworks + Projects.

demands on the plants. The geometric spatial conditions, he notes, also made "superhuman demands on the people designated to maintain them."[11] And while the site was difficult to execute and later maintain in many ways, it turned out the local public, who neglected to tread lightly here and often left trash, also took issue with the work. "The presence of our conservation team was met with hostility," Yli-Vakkuri says. "People stole equipment stored on site, broke structures that we built to guide visitors, and continued to vandalize the artworks."[12]

Though the future of *Tree Mountain* seems uncertain, perhaps the only way forward is to rethink certain aspects of the work, such as its rigid geometric design and its lack of biodiversity, and to respond to the lack of community investment. Yli-Vakkuri discovered that "restoration causes more problems when done properly because more details which call for work are revealed." "Our assignment was to solve problems, which, with the resources we had, served the overall protection of the artwork," he said.[13]

Tree Mountain predates the many recent high-profile programs aimed at planting billions of trees worldwide, such as the World Economic Forum's tree program, 1t.org, which aims to grow and conserve one trillion trees. China is also on track to plant 87 million acres (35 million hectares) of trees in its northern arid areas by 2050 to make a "Great Green Wall" the size of Germany. However, an increasing number of scientists have claimed that these massive new projects have wrecked natural ecosystems, dried up water supplies, damaged agriculture, and pushed people off their land. They have also stressed that planting new trees and even restoring global forests cannot

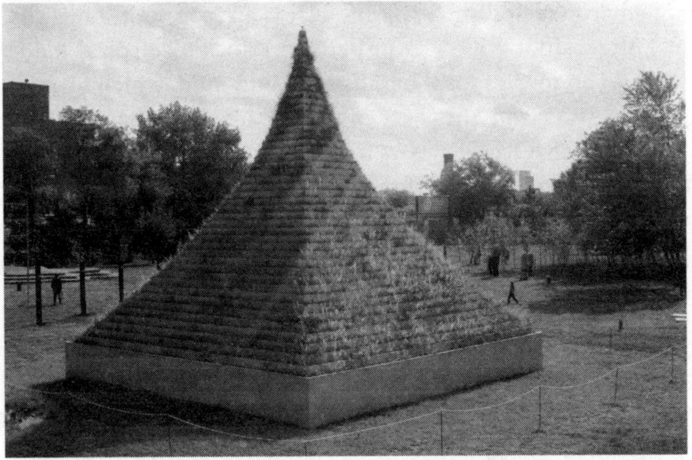

Agnes Denes, *The Living Pyramid*, 2015, grasses, flowers, vegetables, earth, wood. Installation view, Socrates Sculpture Park, Queens, New York, 2015.

take the place of cutting greenhouse gas emissions. Trees are not a silver bullet for climate catastrophe. But termination of fossil fuels and carbon emissions could be.

While the mound on which *Tree Mountain* tries to grow is Denes's largest pyramid to date, her second New York public commission, *The Living Pyramid*, 2015, at Socrates Sculpture Park, took a different approach. The several tons of grasses and wildflowers planted in this thirty-foot-tall triangle were eventually recycled back into the site's grounds as the temperature cooled and fall set in. The regenerative work struck me at the time as antagonizing the adjacent East River panorama of phallic luxury high-rises, erections that would eventually fall.[14]

Denes has long been compared to the American artist Robert Smithson (1938–73). Some have even said she is the "true heir" to his legacy. But that's not quite right—let's not forget that Smithson believed in entropy and inevitability, not environmentalism. Smithson's best-known work, *Spiral Jetty*, 1970, is a prime example of how, as Denes remarks, "manipulation is not environmentalism."[15] *Spiral Jetty* is a 1,500-foot-long (460 m), fifteen-foot-wide (4.6 m) counterclockwise spiral made with 6,500 tons of local basalt rocks and mud, which forms a jetty that juts from the shore of the Great Salt Lake near Rozel Point in Utah. Over the years it has accumulated a patina of salt crystals when the level of the lake is low. (At the time of this writing, the lake is dwindling to its lowest levels in recorded history and raising anxieties about toxic dust and economic consequences.) Smithson wrote that he deliberately chose the site due to its proximity to a derelict oil jetty and its dryness, which meant it could not become a conservationist site; he was interested in sites like the former gravel pit where *Tree Mountain* sits, which have been degraded by humanity, but he was not focused on land restoration. Smithson saw "the idealistic ecologist" as "hopelessly going over the same waterfall" as the "profit-desiring miner."[16]

I've wondered if Smithson meant something more terrifying when speaking about the cataclysm of capitalism, something closer to Leonardo da Vinci's late-career black-chalk drawings of torrential flooding. Leonardo had a longstanding fascination with destruction and wrote at length about watching meteorological or geological phenomena overpowering a landscape. For him, and for Smithson, there was no stopping the chaotic processes of either nature or its ostensible other—civilization. But Denes holds out hope that entropy can be slowed. When she accepts a commission, she often uses legal contracts to make individuals and governments abide by her conditions (such as the proviso that *Tree Mountain* will be protected for four centuries), implicitly endorsing the idea that our species does have agency in saving itself and the planet. I think that's implied in the way that she made 11,000 individual people responsible, in a way, for this artwork—to care for it and steward it into the future.

In Denes's 2019–20 retrospective at The Shed in New York, she seized the opportunity to channel and exert that agency again. The institution commissioned three works from Denes's repository of unrealized pieces. Most vital was an architectural model based on *A Forest for New York*, 2014–ongoing, Denes's optimistic plan to turn the nearly 255-acre Edgemere Landfill on the Rockaway peninsula in Queens, New York, into a forest of 100,000 trees suited to the brackish environment. Denes writes that this endeavor, once realized, will address Far Rockaway's "public health problems, such as the current epidemic of widespread asthma . . . through the positive effects of a forest to remove carbon dioxide from the air, purifying it, to clean groundwater, and to create a healthy ecosystem."[17] The Rockaway Waterfront Alliance has sponsored the project, though progress toward its realization has been stagnant at best. At the site, Denes proposes to have a visitors' center, café, restrooms, and a place for celebrations, exhibitions, and concerts, with parking facilities along its perimeters. "It will create many jobs and millions in tourism," she writes.[18] While planting trees will not stop climate change, as noted, this is an admirable project to improve current living conditions in Rockaway.

At the time of this writing, at age ninety-three, Denes is still pursuing the project. As she told me, "I'm going to keep doing this work until people understand."[19] While there have been successes and failures in Denes's various restoration efforts, she has been one of the most daring artists to challenge us to fully repair our broken relationship to the land—to understand that as it cares for us, we must care for it.

6

fierce pussy, 1991–

This chapter is dedicated to Nancy Brooks Brody (1962–2023), a core member of fierce pussy who passed as this essay was being written.

In 1991, artists Joy Episalla and Carrie Yamaoka, two cofounders of the New York–based collective fierce pussy, were respectively working freelance graphic design jobs at *GQ* and *Traveler* magazines. During quieter moments around the office, they ran off hundreds of fierce pussy posters on the copy machines. No one seemed to mind. Perhaps that was because Episalla and Yamaoka weren't alone. In *Adjusted Margin: Xerography, Art, and Activism in the Late Twentieth Century* (2016), Kate Eichhorn offers an account of some of the most vital urban activism of the '90s: Employees using their corporate gigs at NBC, Microsoft, and so on, staying late to "churn out all this political stuff," as Marion Banzhaf, a former member of ACT UP put it.[1] It turns out these corporations played a large part in disseminating incendiary thoughts and words: capital goods for the common good.

Episalla and Yamaoka, a couple, worked various day jobs that allowed them to keep their studios. Episalla was born in Bronxville, New York, in 1957, and grew up in Hartsdale, New York. After receiving a BFA from the California College of the Arts, she moved to the East Village in 1979. She became involved by 1990 in an ACT UP affinity group of about twelve activists called The Marys, and was crucially involved in their disruption of the "MacNeil/Lehrer NewsHour" on January 22, 1991, wherein several Marys walked onto the set chanting

"Fight AIDS!" and chained themselves to the news anchor desk and other places in the studio. Episalla had ingeniously made the fake IDs that allowed The Marys to enter the building. Yamaoka was born in 1957 in Glen Cove, Long Island, and grew up in nearby Manhasset and spent five years in Tokyo. After college at Wesleyan University, she also moved to New York in 1979, landing in an apartment on Lafayette and Spring Streets.

At a Monday night ACT UP meeting, Nancy Brooks Brody met Episalla and Yamaoka, who had caught wind of a potential gathering of women involved in ACT UP during a demonstration at the police station in Hell's Kitchen. Brody, who was born in 1962 in Manhattan and attended the School of Visual Arts in the 1980s, was already friends with the person organizing that meeting—Zoe Leonard.

Leonard was born in 1961 in Liberty, New York, and grew up in Harlem. As a teenager, she moved to the Lower East Side and attended the City-As-School High School in Manhattan, but dropped out at age sixteen and began taking photographs. By the late 1980s, Leonard was part of an ACT UP splinter group that communally wrote the *Women, AIDS, and Activism* handbook, published by South End Press in 1990—and began talking to other members about forming a women's group, out of a desire to say something "about lesbian visibility, desire and pleasure—something that wasn't only about illness."[2] Word spread and the announcement for fierce pussy's first meeting happened during an ACT UP assembly at Cooper Union's Great Hall, through an open call on the floor that there would be a meeting for women at Leonard's apartment on a certain night, come one, come all.

At the time, women were mostly left out of media coverage of the epidemic, due to the misconception that they were immune to HIV infection. Of course, that wasn't the case—in 1991, about 40 percent of HIV-positive individuals and 12 percent of AIDS patients were women. The definition of AIDS used by the Centers for Disease Control and Prevention (CDC) was skewed toward men's experience with the disease, failing to recognize opportunistic infections that commonly affected women with AIDS, such as pelvic inflammatory disease and cervical cancer. As a result, 65 percent of HIV-positive women died without ever being diagnosed with AIDS. These women were ineligible for vital health care provided by the Division of AIDS services, including at-home nursing attendants. The CDC's exclusionary definition led to severe medical misogyny: clinical trials for developing HIV/AIDS treatments excluded "pregnant and non-pregnant" women.[3]

This moment of fierce pussy's emergence *always* bears repeating because the trauma they experienced in the 1990s endures—and in many ways seems to be replicating itself. To paint an inevitably incomplete picture of that damage: It was the institutionalized homophobia that so greatly intensified the AIDS crisis. It was the ravages of years of conservative rule in the United States. It was increasing violence against gay people. It was Anita Hill being interrogated after having been sexually harassed by Clarence Thomas, and Thomas being confirmed anyway. It was a nationwide housing crisis during which New York Mayor David Dinkins controversially evicted the homeless from Tompkins Square Park.

But it was also a time in the city when many abandoned buildings and ubiquitous construction projects were covered in graffiti, announcements, and fliers, and when artists such as Jenny Holzer and the Guerrilla Girls seized the opportunity to add their own responses to the decaying mix. Enter fierce pussy. During their first meeting, at Leonard's East Village apartment, they produced three no-frills posters on the spot using whatever was near at hand and cheap, if not outright free. "I AM A lezzie, butch, pervert, girlfriend, bulldagger, sister, dyke, AND PROUD." This was the first of the "List Posters," 1991 to the present, each of which sandwiches a jagged litany of pejoratives between the phrases "I AM A" and "AND PROUD." The group decided that at every other meeting a work would be made then and there, fast, and dirty. Imperfections and visual noise were embraced from start to finish. They also decided to speak as one, as *her*, with intimacy, humor, and rage. They didn't see their work as direct action–oriented, per se:

> Not everyone who came to the fp meetings was from ACT UP and not everyone was an artist. We put the word out in a lot of different ways. But because we were putting so much energy into our activism, our art practices were kind of getting pushed to the sideline. Part of the call was to create an art collective. We didn't pitch it as doing direct action—it was more cultural action. And we wanted to make art in this really fast and dirty way, in an activist spirit.[4]

At various points the membership roster has included Pam Brandt, Jean Carlomusto, Donna Evans, Alison Froling, and Suzanne Wright, to name a few, but the group continued to employ that single, strong voice, that direct first-person address, always looking inwards to project outwards. Three decades later, they sometimes say that they feel like the Rolling Stones of queer activism. (Though, of course, the Stones have done nothing to destabilize heteronormativity through political speech . . .) They also tend to talk about fierce pussy in the singular: "She's her own artist." "She's got a lot of opinions." Akin to most millennials, she's pissed at abuses of power and ready for a better tomorrow.

Running parallel to their collaboration, fierce pussy's members have maintained individual practices. Dealing with the same exhaustion that many AIDS activists felt by the mid-1990s, fierce pussy went on a hiatus in 1994, though some members continued to collaborate on projects, primarily campaigns against the Iraq War. The group officially reunited in 2008 when they were invited to participate in a "semi-retrospective" hosted by Printed Matter:

> We sent out a call to everyone who had been in the group that we could remember, something like forty people. We emailed everyone saying, "We're going to do this show, come join us." And somehow, we were the only four people that showed up. So, we figured we're the four that still want to be doing this.[5]

The four thought: "What if we just continue on? We all really like each other and still have things to say, together." And so, they did.

A redeployment of language plays a crucial role in nearly all of fierce pussy's projects. The group understands that language is being made and remade constantly, they liken it to a living, breathing entity. Their work reminds us that it was originally in feminist consciousness-raising groups, and not in legal scholarship, that many of the most important feminist redescriptions were generated: *sexism*, *sexual harassment*, *marital rape*, and so on. Their speech is always excitable, their politics always performative and ahead of the curve—or, as they joked in our interview: "Judith Butler was reading us." They likely were.

In the wee hours of the night, walking around the city with buckets of water—no one had cars—the group wheatpasted posters in strategic locations, more *sight* specific than site-specific. They "bombed" entire walls with prints, combining different works to make a composition. Even though this was illegal, and they were rushing with buckets of wheatpaste, they were still making a composition. And they knew their art could be used as evidence against them, having learned from David Wojnarowicz's lawsuit against Reverend Donald Wildmon and the American Family Association in 1990—but they were never deterred. Their initial campaigns focused on raising lesbian visibility (before capitalism found a solid market for that) and speaking directly to their community (before social media found a market for that).

fierce pussy's identity remains relational and unfixed yet situated—"fierce pussy crafts 'queer identity' as a continuum experienced in historical time," notes Tara Burk.[6] Their mission, too, has evolved in a dynamic yet coherent way. One of their earliest objectives was to claim territory. They wanted to leave a noticeable trace, but not by using money, power, prestige, or any of the other forms of capital that art accrues as it moves through its normative contexts and markets. And they wanted to do it *fiercely*, with desire and pleasure, as in that word's Latin roots, *ferus*, feral. Maybe the point was not to overthink it. This wasn't about making or having an art career. This was life or death.

As time plodded on, as overt homophobia became increasingly stigmatized and words like *dyke* became mainstream, fierce pussy tested whether seemingly positive changes constituted substantive progress. Retooling older posters became a habit—the reunited group's meetings were often, as they say, "writing sessions that became editing sessions, refining sessions, expanding sessions."[7] In 2008, on the occasion of their "semi-retrospective" at New York's Printed Matter, they updated the "List" posters, replacing "AND PROUD" with the teasing provocation, "AND SO ARE YOU." The new posters covered the storefront window of the venerable nonprofit. Moments after they went up, police arrived to relay concerns expressed by neighbors and passersby—which demonstrated that the processes of language reclamation and of redescription are far from passé.

For another early poster project, in 1991, fierce pussy took on the homophobic Christian right and its allies by pairing family and childhood photos with text; a prominent example shows a beaming baby with the word DYKE in large typeset at the hem of her striped apron. Twenty-seven years later and not far from where the work debuted on the streets of SoHo, it was one of several fierce pussy pieces that engulfed the windows of the Leslie-Lohman Museum of Art in 2019. It's

I AM A
lezzie
butch
pervert
feminist
amazon
bulldagger
dyke

AND SO ARE YOU

fierce pussy's *List remix* postcard, 2008–, ink on card stock, 6" × 4".

also fierce pussy's most unnerving campaign—where vulnerability meets the insidious ways language can cut to the bone and scar, sometimes for life. "Oh, this is hilarious," I overheard someone saying about the project as they entered the museum. I'm not so sure.

In 1992, fierce pussy used stencil lettering and spray paint on cardboard to rename streets along a gay pride parade route in Manhattan, replacing Christopher Street with Tomboy Turnpike, Hudson Street with Audre Lorde Lane, and Sheridan Square with fierce pussy Plaza. (In 2022, Hunter College followed suit with the naming of Audre Lorde Way on its campus.) In 1993, they paired an image of a suffragette held by two cops with the text: "1906: This woman was arrested for wanting the right to vote. 1993: How many women will lose their jobs, homes, or kids for being lesbian?"

In October 2018, before the midterm elections, they updated that second line to: "2018: Do not take democracy for granted. VOTE!" The new version, as grainy and unkempt as the original, made the rounds on social media with emojis to embellish and exclamatory comments. It was a sight for sore eyes. Since then, fierce pussy has steadily made more posters, free to download from their website. In 2020, the collective memorably paired an image of the Freedom Riders' mugshots alongside the reminder: "People have the power. We have the power. VOTE."

From their initial phase of by-any-means-necessary mimeography and wheatpasting, fierce pussy went on to produce stickers, billboards, mail art campaigns, and a permanent installation in the bathroom of the New York LGBT Center.

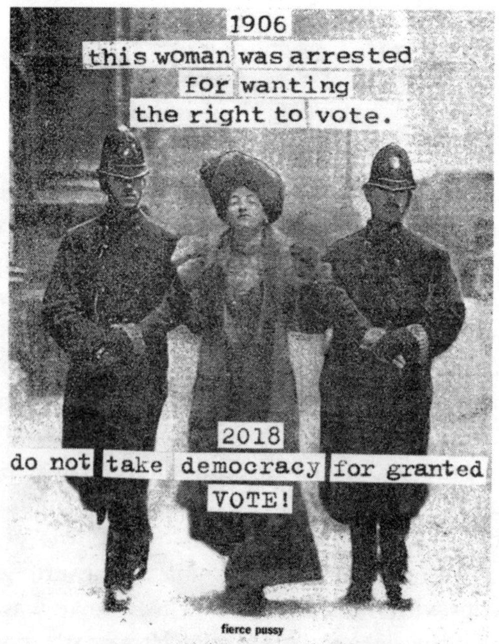

fierce pussy, *Vote*, 2018, poster, 17" × 11".

These have been pragmatic projects on freedom, and not just because they deal so deeply with language. The group has always conformed their art's format to the most efficient mode of distribution, in order to make the biggest splash, even though they're well aware that they are trading impact for durability. The typical ephemerality of their primary material—paper—stood out when I visited their archive at the New York Public Library. Their Xeroxed projects from the 1990s, still in decent shape, filled just one box. The only item I found there that wasn't a photocopy was a picture of the group with the activist Barbara Gittings from 1994. An accompanying letter to her read: "You are a heroine to us all," and then: "Enjoy the posters."

A fierce pussy billboard on the side of a van driven through Manhattan and into a West Village pride march that same year read:

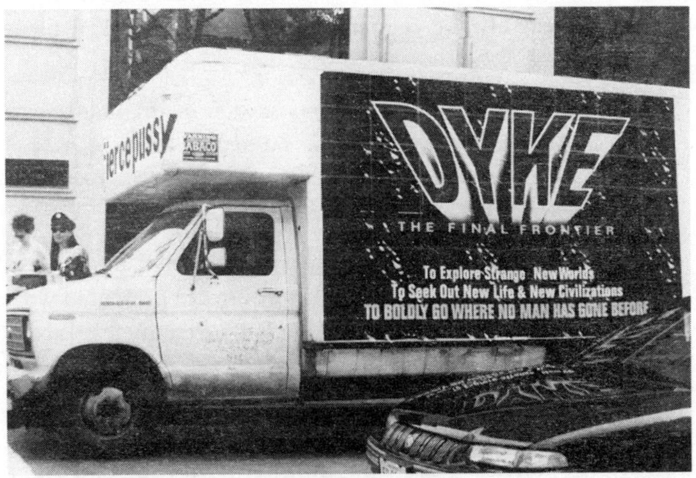

fierce pussy, *fierce pussy truck*, 1994, three color-Xerox posters, wheatpasted on truck.

DYKE
The final frontier
To Explore Strange New Worlds
To Seek Out New Life and New Civilizations
To Boldly Go Where No Man Has Gone Before

With the letters in "DYKE" rendered in dramatic one-point perspective, the sign played with the tropes of commercial advertisement and campy sci-fi; there's an inevitable association not only with *Star Trek* but also with the famous *Star Wars* opening crawl.

The billboard seems like a precursor to *Transmission*, an ongoing series of comically inflected visions of an alternative future. Written as open letters from a century yet to come, and employing the squared-off font that in the '80s was used to suggest advanced technology, the *Transmission* texts ingenuously question the barbarism of the present: "What is 'police'? . . . What is this word 'rape'?" The letter is revised and updated between each iteration; most recently it was produced as a poster, free for the taking. One version of the communiqué from our unearthly "descendants in the free state of transplendency" begins:

> *Dearest beings of 2018, we are re-transsending our transmission wave across time. Our transscholars, translators, and transcribers continue to transmonitor your data. There is still much we wish to understand—please reply all.*

As with the collective's previous projects, the wish to understand and the desire for individual freedom are presented with caustic wit. But despite the satirical edge, a genuine liberatory impulse finds expression in these missives, which do, after all, optimistically envision a new society and a higher mode of consciousness. "Do you need sustainable farming transniques and energy harnessing?" they inquire. "We can send right away! Of course telepathic communication is easiest or do you prefer Dropbox?"

Richard Rorty, an indispensable bad object for feminism, tried, and failed, to pragmatize theorizations of gender parity in the early '90s, when he was arguably the most famous living American philosopher. In 1993, he contributed an essay to *Hypatia* in which he claimed that pragmatists such as himself, and deconstructionists, can only offer feminists "bits of ad hoc advice—advice about how to reply when masculinists attempt to make present practices seem inevitable." Three years earlier, Rorty and Nancy Fraser had engaged in a heated dispute about feminism, and his light touch in the *Hypatia* piece—"advice"—may have stemmed from a desire to avoid being seen as overbearing, since he had not won the earlier debate. He continues:

> The most effective way to criticize current descriptions of a given instance of the oppression of the weak as "a necessary evil" (the political equivalent of "a negligible anomaly") is to explain just why it is *not* in fact necessary, by explaining how a specific institutional change would eliminate it. That means sketching an alternative future and a scenario of political action that might take us from the present to that future.[8]

If you dare to envision a future, you might as well do so with panache. And if you're going to imagine radical, structural change, you should—like the young Simone Weil—also acknowledge that such change can never be known in advance. You might also acknowledge that such ideals are still a dream: We don't know what equality, equity, or even dignity is, because it hasn't happened for all humans, yet.

> *In your earlier transmissions you described a civil rights movement. We noticed an increased breakdown in social relations. We know you call yourselves human—is there an 'e' on the end of that?*

The poster version of the queer futurism and "time travel tactics" (per scholar Jill Casid) proposed by *Transmission* was created for fierce pussy's five-month-long exhibition at the Beeler Gallery at Columbus College of Art and Design (October 2018–March 2019), curated by Jo-ey Tang. Its blessedly slow programming, in four "chapters" that changed every five weeks or so, allowed for leisurely presentations of individual work from each of the four pragmatic prophetesses in addition to presenting their collective output. Surprisingly, it was the first time their individual practices had been put into conversation in public.

The show's title, "arms ache avid aeon," references a quietly political work by Yamaoka titled *A is for Angel* (1991), for which she plucked four words beginning with the letter *a* from correction ribbons she had sourced from friends' typewriters. When asked about the show's title, Tang said: "From intimacy, resistance (arms), through grief and desire (ache), light and activism (avid), and time (aeon). The missing *a* word—AIDS—which brought them together in the first place, hovers."[9]

At the Beeler Gallery, Brody, Episalla, Leonard, and Yamaoka each had a room to themselves. A final gallery was reserved for fierce pussy herself and offered ephemera and archival materials from the collective's projects. In the fall of 2019, a fifth chapter was realized at the Institute of Contemporary Art in Philadelphia. Chapter 6 will take the form of a book.

Chapter 7 took place at the Palais de Tokyo in Paris from February to May 2023, as part of the "Exposé·es" exhibition inspired by Elisabeth Lebovici's book *Ce que le sida m'a fait. Art et activisme à la fin du XXe siècle* (What AIDS Has Done to Me. Art and Activism at the End of the 20th Century) (2017). For an installation that spanned the museum's large front windows, fierce pussy printed text on newsprint so light would filter through the paper. Up close, the wheatpasted paper on the windows looked like skin, with small wrinkles and tears.

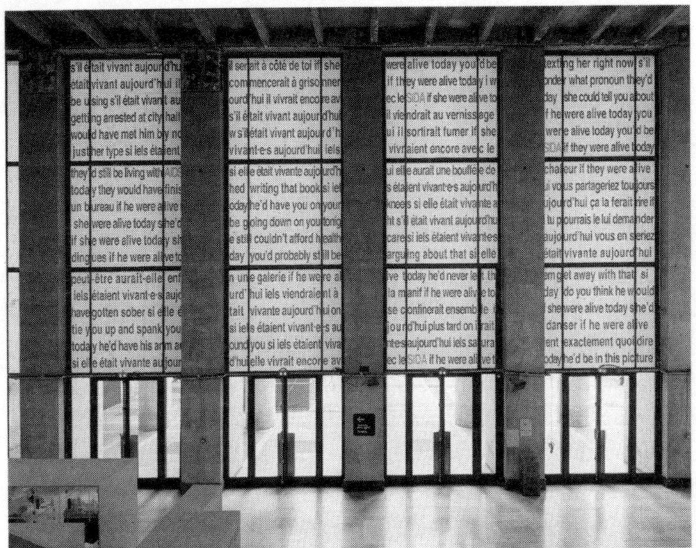

fierce pussy, *For the Record*, 2013–23. Newsprint wheatpasted to windows at Palais de Tokyo, Paris, 2023. Photo: Aurélien Mole. Courtesy the artists.

The collective has also used the mail as another form of distribution. After an invitation by the Ford Foundation to produce a work for *Indisposable: Structures of Support After the ADA*, fierce pussy made *Transmission VI*, 2022, featuring work printed in braille over type, which they disseminated through a large-scale mailing as well as showing it in the gallery.

Since 2018, as fierce pussy has been increasingly invited to show in museums and galleries, the group has always figured out a way to participate that feels in line with its ideas and politics. They will often make a stack of giveaway posters, or engage with windows, doorways, or available outside space where their art can be visible to any passerby. The group generally doesn't sell any work; fierce pussy is cash poor. Rather, their focus is on getting an institution to fund the work and then pay for free distribution of it.

> All of our history comes along with us when we show our work in museums and institutions. We approach the institution as another platform through which we can deconstruct different institutional hierarchies and disrupt the way that the museum normally functions. This brings up questions about who museums are for, who feels comfortable in them, and who is going to feel welcomed by our work.[10]

For fierce pussy, tone is a tactic. As they think about language and different forms of address, they are also thinking about how affect can be a method, or a political vehicle, to connect. Viewers in a museum aren't used to being addressed directly or being able to take a work of art back home with them. While fierce pussy often takes an incendiary approach—from their name to the content of their output—they're also actively attempting to transmit affect, by giving their work away for free and by sharing their rage and grief. "We're saying: this is for you."[11]

These institutional celebrations of these artists' impact and of their robust and sustaining mode of direct-action documents how far we've come, but also how far we need to go. At the moment, simply resisting atrocity seems challenging enough, let alone making progress. Yet effective activism requires that we think in terms of forward motion. "The mind-set of 'the resistance' is slippery and dangerous," as Michelle Alexander put it.[12] "There's a reason marchers in the Black freedom struggle sang 'We Shall Overcome' rather than chanting 'We Shall Resist.' Their goal was to overcome a racial caste system—to end it."

Effective activism also requires knowing when to memorialize and when not to. In 2008, after participating in the landmark traveling exhibition *ACT UP: New York: Activism, Art, and the AIDS Crisis, 1987–1993*, the founders of fierce pussy felt that a large part of their lives had been historicized even though in reality the art, and the mourning, went on. The loss is ongoing. They realized they wanted to make a new work that could be a conduit between the past and present. But they wondered: How do you speak to people about something that's almost impossible to describe?

> There was a symposium associated with the show and it was this very strange, out of body experience that we all shared with each other afterward, of listening and watching your own life and experiences become historicized in front of your eyes and having people speak with authority and describe how it was. We were so moved and undone by this—realizing how upset we all got and how much unprocessed grief we still had, because our grief had never really been acknowledged by larger society. To this day, there has never been an actual acknowledgement by the US government or mainstream media of what we all went through in that epidemic. How many of our brothers and sisters we lost and took care of and how many we buried and mourned and are mourning still. We carried on in our lives and shoved those feelings aside, like this dirty secret amongst survivors, but the magnitude of the loss wasn't acknowledged by our larger society and still hasn't been reckoned with or addressed.[13]

They wanted to produce something that foregrounded the kind of desire that makes the past present, the longing that will not consign the past to history. The result was *Get Up Everybody and Sing*, 2010, which later became the poster *For the Record*, 2013. The latter was originally made as a project for Visual AIDS and the annual Day With(out) Art, and was also featured in "Greater New York" at MoMA PS1 in 2015–16. "If they were alive today they could tell you about getting arrested at City Hall / If they were alive today they'd be outside smoking / If she were alive today she'd never let you get away with that / If he were alive today he'd still be living with AIDS."

It goes on, each "if" followed by a statement in the present conditional, conjuring up the glancing specificities of human lives that were so enragingly contingent. The text gives voice to a group of people trying to survive against all odds, against their deeply homophobic and prejudiced government, by saying to readers—to us: You didn't get to know them, but you might have really liked them. You might have loved them, even.

"Sometimes there's just this chasm where either someone has no idea, or they have a very romanticized idea of what it was to be an activist during the AIDS crisis. They've seen some footage, but they don't understand why we were that angry or that desperate," they've said. *For the Record* is an attempt to educate, but not pedantically. The work bridges a gap by using the present tense and again, a particular tone: a means of address. "We've always felt a responsibility to go forward and do the things that everyone we lost couldn't do. So, some of that present voice is an echo of that energy. It's about wanting things to change, wanting a future. It's about both trying to survive and showing a possibility of a way to survive."[14]

The piece tethers a responsibility to witness to a refusal to forget. Personal grief becomes a public proclamation. "We're the witnesses to what happened, and we carry our lost friends with us. We're trying to share as much information with the world as possible. We're frank about the loss and the pain, but also recognize and honor the voices—living and dead—that give us strength, hope, and encourage pleasure."[15] These liberatory actions and values have shaped and continue to shape fierce pussy's ethos and ethics.

At the time of this writing, fierce pussy has just opened Chapter 8 of their ongoing "arms ache avid aeon" project at PARTICIPANT INC in New York City's Chinatown. Curated by Jo-ey Tang, and dedicated to Brody, the show puts the artists' individual and collective practices in dialogue and differs from past chapters because it is a homecoming. What does it mean to see this *fierce pussy: amplified* exhibition in New York, thirty-four years after they first convened? A new poster, *I got all my sisters with me* (2025), which accompanies the show, provides one response. It is a declaration of inclusive, non-biological forms of kinship on all streets, and anywhere else. Citing a line from Sister Sledge's 1979 disco anthem "We Are Family," which was written by Bernard Edwards and Nile Rodgers, the eponymous poster, like others before it, will appear as a stack on a milk crate—free for the taking—at various art organizations and nonprofits across the city. It is an act of love, within an oeuvre that has always been a labor of love, and yet another way of saying, "this is for you."

Underwriting the art of fierce pussy are continual wishes for overcoming, anchored by decades-long radical camaraderie. The group has likewise created a longstanding sense of solidarity, not only within AIDS and lesbian activism, but across time. Just as ACT UP drew from the civil rights movement and the feminist movement—and therefore from artist-led activist groups such as the Black Emergency Cultural Coalition and Women Artists in Revolution—so too does fierce pussy sit on the shoulders of their chosen ancestors, of the "many people who have sacrificed their light, their lives, and their brilliance."[16]

7

Dyke Action Machine!, 1991–2008

Capital goods for the common good—remember that corporations perversely played a large part in some of the most vital urban activism of the 1990s. Artists slyly used their day jobs as designers and production assistants to make activist posters and leaflets in the off hours, where hundreds if not thousands of pieces of paper were produced for direct-action campaigns. "These were the same people who designed your shampoo bottle and the ad for your Verizon account," the artist Carrie Moyer has said of those workers who helped her "realize how important graphics were to successful activism."[1] If graphics were the means, wheatpasting custom posters on temporary wooden walls and boarded-up windows was the main mode of address.

Moyer was born in 1960 in Redford Township, Michigan. In 1985 she graduated from Brooklyn's Pratt Institute with a BFA in painting, after interning during her senior year at the influential and collectively run New York feminist magazine *Heresies* (1977–93). In 1990, Moyer earned an MA in computer graphic design from the New York Institute of Technology and began working in the "bull pen" of a large advertising company, using some of the earliest design software (well before there was InDesign, Illustrator, and Photoshop) on standalone, Unix-based computers.

In the evenings she painted in her Williamsburg studio, but was growing disillusioned with the medium, which had a thriving market at the time for male artists practicing Neo-Expressionism and no room, it seemed, for women. She wasn't quite sure what painting meant anymore and struggled with its context, too often divorced from social and political struggles.

Moyer wasn't alone in feeling fed up with idealist conceptions of art, or the notion that the social function of art is merely to transcend the current moment and inspire. In 1987, the art historian, critic, and AIDS activist Douglas Crimp had warned against this, arguing for a merging of social justice and art: "We don't need a cultural renaissance," he claimed, "We need cultural practices actively participating in the struggle against AIDS."[2] For Moyer, painting just could not mirror the urgent queer and feminist activism she had been observing since the late 1980s, which saw a return to Conceptualist approaches, including alternative means of production and distribution, such as creating political works of agitprop inspired by public signage and mainstream advertisements. (For at least a century, *agitprop* has referred to a combination of agitation and propaganda. It is sometimes used in direct-action campaigns, including protests.) Using this style, artists found new opportunities to create a direct address to their audiences, and a distinctive array of tactics to draw upon.

There are many important examples of this kind of work, but two iconic pieces were crucial for Moyer: Barbara Kruger's 1988 billboards emblazoned with the message, "We don't need another hero," her feminist riff on advertising sponsored by the Public Art Fund in New York, and the iconic *Silence=Death* (1987) poster by Avram Finkelstein, Brian Howard, Oliver Johnston, Charles Kreloff, Chris Lione, and Jorge Soccarás, aka the Silence=Death collective. This type of public-facing, often communally made work, which was intended to exist outside of the gallery and the art world, was indicative of "something of a loss of confidence in the power of the aesthetic image itself, or a need to separate from dependence on the image as manipulated by art critics, dealers, and curators," as Lucy Lippard has aptly noted.[3] During this era of oppression, disinformation, and outright silence—stained by Reagan-era politics and economics, the ongoing threat of nuclear war, and the AIDS crisis—artists knew that to condemn, dissent, and to say *no more* was one way to mobilize.[4]

In 1990 Moyer joined Queer Nation, a group founded by four ACT UP members, which is often credited with reclaiming the word *queer* from those who would use it as a pejorative. Moyer designed their first press kit and stickers. A chant used by the collective during demonstrations, "We're here! We're Queer! Get used to it!" became a popular rallying cry. In addition to street protests, Queer Nation organized several direct actions. For instance, on April 20, 1990, the group appeared at the Macy's Herald Square department store, where Olympic gold medalist Greg Louganis was promoting a new swimsuit line. Queer Nation members arrived holding Wheaties cereal boxes with the swimmer's picture pasted on the front, to remind onlookers that the company had rejected Louganis as a spokesperson, even though he hadn't come out yet. (Wheaties eventually featured him in 2016). Several more campaigns followed, often with a focus on injustices faced by gay men. Queer Nation was largely male focused—and Moyer remembered being turned off by that.

Like Moyer, the artist Sue Schaffner admired seeing Queer Nation's *Absolutely Queer* poster campaign plastered around Manhattan in 1990. Created by a working group of Queer Nation, sassily named Dyke Action Machine! (aka DAM!), the project outed celebrities such as Jodie Foster by riffing off Absolut Vodka ads. (Six years later, Absolut ran their first Absolut Pride campaign.)

Schaffner was born in New York City in 1964 and moved to suburbia a year later. She attended Syracuse University in the 1980s and arrived in the West Village in 1990 to start a freelance commercial photography studio under the moniker Girl Ray. She began working with advertising companies and soon joined Moyer in the DAM! working group. There were roughly twenty to thirty people in the initial collective, though numbers dwindled as time went on.

With DAM!, Moyer attended the first National Lesbian Conference in Atlanta in April 1991. Not long after, she was given a flyer during a June Pride March for a new group, the Lesbian Avengers, which she also joined—and soon became its de facto minister of propaganda. When the slightly larger DAM! collective disbanded after the conference, Moyer and Schaffner continued their work together, extending the anonymous spirit of the cadre. They "liked the idea of fronting as a 'machine' with untold anonymous members working on the frontlines of the culture wars," as Moyer has said.[5]

The group's anonymity nodded not only to the laborers who tend to capitalism, but also to the advent of digital publishing, which, at the time, was frustrating and glitchy. Moyer and Schaffner could see that, not too far in the future, a single person would be able to do nearly all the tasks in the "bull pen"—from typesetting and layout to retouching to pre-production. But at the time, DAM!'s sleek and polished work appeared as though it required many different workers to produce. And so, the idea of a big advertising agency named "Dyke Action Machine!" took hold.

The first posters that they plastered around the city were 1991's *Gap Campaign*, which mocked Gap clothing ads by substituting lesbian activists for celebrities. These served as a pre–social media noticeboard, essentially saying to other lesbians, *we see you*. Akin to fierce pussy's work, DAM's output foreshadowed the development of the meme. But riffing off advertising could be divisive: for some, the images looked a bit too much like the Gap's own insipid and slick ads, while for others they elegantly exposed the lack of lesbian representation in American pop culture.

It wasn't until 1998 that Moyer and Schaffner came out of the "activist art closet" through their direct-mail campaign *Meet the Muffiosi* with 2,000 postcards mailed to individuals

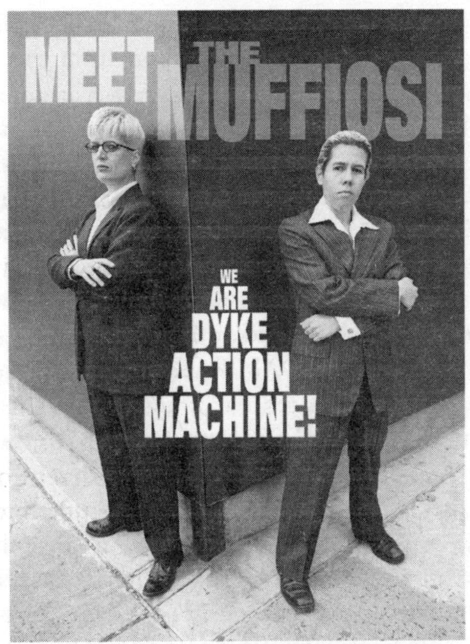

Dyke Action Machine!, *Meet the Muffiosi*, 1998, paper, 4 ¼" x 6".

and the press. By that year, DAM! had received public recognition through grants and exhibitions, though they were still producing agitprop at their day jobs, after hours. "By then our work had gained traction in the art and gay press," Moyer has said, adding, "Plus there were other activist groups putting out agitprop and design, some who preceded DAM!, some who followed. We wanted to plant our flag on a kind of messaging that seemed very new and particular to the moment."[6]

For DAM!, high production values were important, which is an ethos carried over from their professions. It would take months to set up a photoshoot, borrow makeup and props to be able to execute it, and schedule volunteers to help and model. A project typically took four to five months to produce. Because DAM! was such a small team, Moyer and Schaffner held each other accountable and built up an internal momentum while also receiving critical support from peers, friends, and art institutions.

Their 1993 poster campaign *Do You Love the Dyke in Your Life?* served as a rejoinder to Calvin Klein underwear ads from 1992 featuring the actor Mark Wahlberg, not long after the Gay and Lesbian Alliance Against Defamation condemned him for his homophobic remarks. In the work, five queer-identifying women pose with their arms crossed while wearing their Calvins, a popular brand at the time among lesbian and gay consumers. In 1992, DAM!'s second poster project riffed on advertisements produced by *Family Circle* magazine and again affirmed that visual representation is powerful: "Dykes were family by golly, before families became trendy," proclaims one image accompanied by a picture of a pregnant lesbian family. DAM! also fruitfully excavated the aesthetics of bridal magazines, public service announcements, educational websites, and movie posters. Between 1991 and 2004, DAM!'s public art campaigns culminated in an annual installation of nearly 5,000 posters wheatpasted around the streets of New York City. This mode of reclaiming public space was focused on speaking directly to the citizen *and* the consumer, as both always have the capacity to act.

While sometimes the posters had an intrinsic evanescence built in—as it would only take a few hours for someone to come along and wheatpaste another sign over the top—DAM! created other tongue-in-cheek campaigns, including websites, matchbooks, pins, stickers, an interactive phone line, stretch vinyl murals, advertisements in lightbox kiosks, and postcards. Throughout, DAM! was learning how to work with new technology—their production timeline extends from the emergence of desktop computers in ad agencies to the invention of the iPhone. "It was dinosaur times in terms of technology," when they began, as Schaffner noted, but, as the tools of the trade changed, DAM! noticed dominant culture shifting too.[7] Seen today, DAM! nearly predicted how financialized capitalism would absorb queer lifestyles into new markets.

In 1994, an IKEA ad famously featured a gay couple; it was one of the first advertisements to do so. The American Family Association mounted boycotts against it, and a bomb threat was called in on an IKEA store. Also that year President Bill Clinton's "Don't Ask, Don't Tell" policy, which stated that gay people could serve in the military so long as they didn't reveal their sexual orientation, went into effect. And, finally, in 1994 DAM received its first grant, from the foundation Art Matters, which resulted in a poster titled *Straight to Hell* that riffs on 1970s-era B-movie ads. The work exposed one of the targets of Clinton's program—the first catastrophe of his presidency—namely racial and ethnic minorities whose

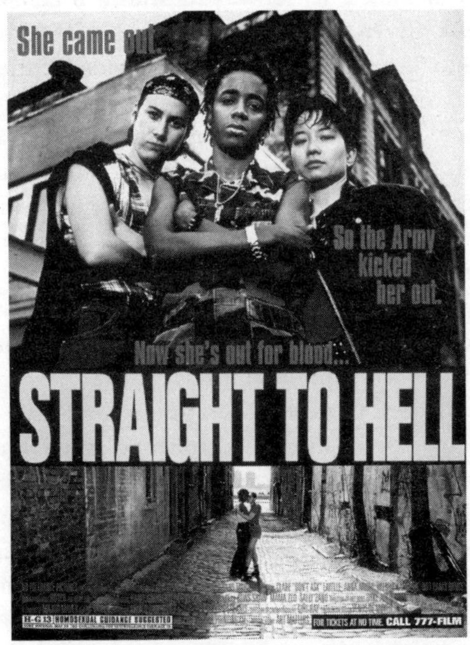

Dyke Action Machine!, *Straight to Hell*, 1994, four-color offset poster, 19" x 25".

discharges increased over time. According to the Williams Institute, "In the late 1990s, approximately a quarter of discharges were women and similar proportions were racial/ethnic minorities. In recent years, those proportions have increased to more than a third of the DADT discharges."[8] The text for the fake revenge film—rated "HG-13," as in "homosexual guidance suggested"—reads: "She came out. So the army kicked her out. Now she's out for blood." A trio of vengeful butches stares back at the viewer.

Thanks to the grant, DAM! was able to pay for snipers (or workers who wheatpaste posters on billboards for a living) to put up 5,000 of these posters around Lower Manhattan in June. With the funds, DAM! could occupy the same spaces and use the same snipers that corporations used to promote their wares. Yet, it took a seasoned pedestrian to pick up on the differences between regular advertising and DAM!'s agitprop.

DAM!'s tactics are key examples of 1990s culture jamming or "subvertising," which often entails using mass media to produce ironic or satiric commentary. The work was ultimately more about gaining visibility and representation than placing specific demands on a museum or infiltrating a political convention, as noted in previous chapters. In this way, DAM! appears as an inheritor to the brilliant agitprop accomplished by their stated influences, especially the Guerilla Girls, a New York–based group that formed in 1985 to expose gender discrimination and corruption in the art world.

In 1994, the artist Collier Schorr pointed out that for DAM!, "there is no sense of dire emergency, no meeting points, or targeted officials. Their efforts are effectual reminders that k. d. lang is not the only lesbian in the world." For Schorr, the *Straight to Hell* campaign was DAM!'s most successful, because it "underscores the existence of a ticket-buying lesbian audience, while also offering up an array of agendas within its slick comic-butch construct."[9]

But this "ticket-buying," overly commercial, lesbian audience began to trouble DAM!, and within a few years the duo took an anti-consumerist stance, which is evident in the red, white, and blue 1998 poster *Lesbian Americans: Don't Sell Out!* The work uses a direct address to urge lesbian consumers to see through the consumerist efforts of "gay friendly" companies. Recalling the aesthetics of US 1940s-era, war-time posters (and even earlier Soviet agitprop of the 1920s), this piece positions the butch lesbian as the ultimate American patriot—the real, anti-capitalist revolutionary. Once more, DAM! hired snipers to wheatpaste 5,000 of these posters in Lower Manhattan in June 1998.

"Are you even 'present' in American society if you can't be pictured as a consumer group?" Moyer once asked.[10] By 1997, Ellen DeGeneres had come out on her sitcom show, and though many companies pulled their ads, it was obvious that a market

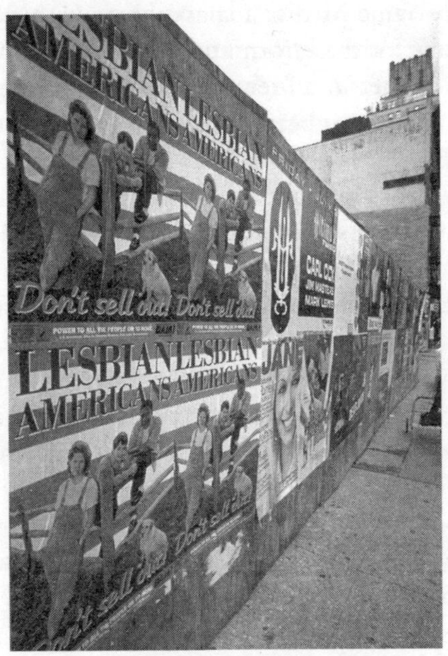

Dyke Action Machine!, *Lesbian Americans: Don't Sell Out!*, 1998, four-color offset poster, 24" x 36". Street view.

had opened for lesbians. Realizing the voracious nature of capitalism, DAM! shifted from wanting to perform "the role of advertiser and truth teller" to resisting co-optation: "Was a depiction of a lesbian couple in a Subaru ad the ultimate goal after all?," Moyer wondered, referring to the brand's playful coding in the 1990s.[11]

Standing strong among DAM!'s anti-consumerist projects is *Gynadome*, 2001, a website that marked the group's tenth anniversary. Embedding 1970s lesbian, separatist, and back-to-the-land culture into science fiction, the site announced the running tagline: "No Electricity. No Computers. No Men." It featured the tales of three neo-Luddite women: Marsha (code name Ditto, born deaf and left for dead on the Microsoft campus), Renee (code name Womewaccka, the subject of a nefarious scheme to produce originals for cloning), and Crystal (code name Media, a shapeshifter with overly peaceful inclinations for the information-war era), who live on the only lesbian planet in a "remote biosphere" where "women are Women, men have been put out to pasture, and computers are just Big Paperweights." In addition to the site—which showcased videos and interviews—the project was advertised on twenty-five large-scale lightboxes around San Francisco in summer 2001.

Notably, this wasn't DAM!'s first website or critique of the concurrent internet boom. In 1995 they created *The Girlie Network*, a witty glimpse at an all-lesbian television network. The "prime-time line-up featured such Sapphic classics" as *Leave Us the Beaver* and *The Snip Squad*. With the debuts of Logo and Here, two American cable channels devoted exclusively to gay content, as well as Showtime series such as *Queer as Folk* (2000–5) and *The L Word* (2004–9), DAM!'s tongue-in-cheek concept of an all-lesbian television network is now seen as prophetic. What's more, when the former media conglomerate Viacom was developing Logo—a channel originally dedicated to lifestyle and entertainment programming targeting

LGBT audiences—they tapped into the "pink tank" of 1990s queer activist artists, including DAM! "Were we delighted that the media had finally acknowledged our contribution to making lesbians and their concerns visible? Hell yes. We always knew Dyke Action Machine! would make a great ad agency," Moyer has remarked.[12]

In 2001, when asked about the difference between wheat-pasting in the streets and the relatively new frontier for virtual campaigns, Schaffner noted:

> Although our online output does allow us to reach a far wider audience than our street campaigns, there is something incredibly satisfying about actually seeing (and greeting) the end user of our art. A virtual world does not allow you to walk down Fifth Avenue with a bunch of dykes that have plastered *Gynadome* tattoos all over their very real bodies. Ephemera's qualities of collectability and nostalgia aren't relevant yet to digital works. I don't think we will ever give up the object work.[13]

That was true. For their final project, in 2008, DAM! produced a darkly satirizing pamphlet-cum-stewardship report titled *Dyke Action Machine INCORPORATED,* an "industry leader in lesbian messaging." With pages featuring the headlines "Abundance: The Courage to Be Rich" and "Outreach: Embracing Ambiguity," the thin, glossy, zine-like publication was produced for the *Artists & Activists* series commissioned by the New York nonprofit bookstore Printed Matter. "At last, Dyke Action Machine has figured out how to convert lesbianism into a viable commodity that can be bought, sold, and traded," proclaims DAM!'s website: "DAM Incorporated (DAM Inc.) is our indispensable guide to selling out."[14]

Moyer and Schaffner used stock photography for the images, which are mostly pictures of empowered-looking women. To write the text, they looked at a then-current Raytheon stewardship report and banking promotional material for the sale of mutual funds and credit cards. "Usually, mutual funds just tell you about all the wonderful places they invest and how dollars will make the world a better place, which, of course, is in most cases not true," as Schaffner told me, adding: "But God bless the language they come up with . . . They're just absolute maestros. Why shouldn't we take advantage of that illustrious language?"[15]

DAM!'s swan song points to the absurdity of capitalistic conditions—to the creation of a lesbian consumer group and the restriction of the same people to equal political and legal rights. With this project, DAM! recognized their "responsibility to restructure and work from within the system," as they write in a letter that opens the pamphlet:

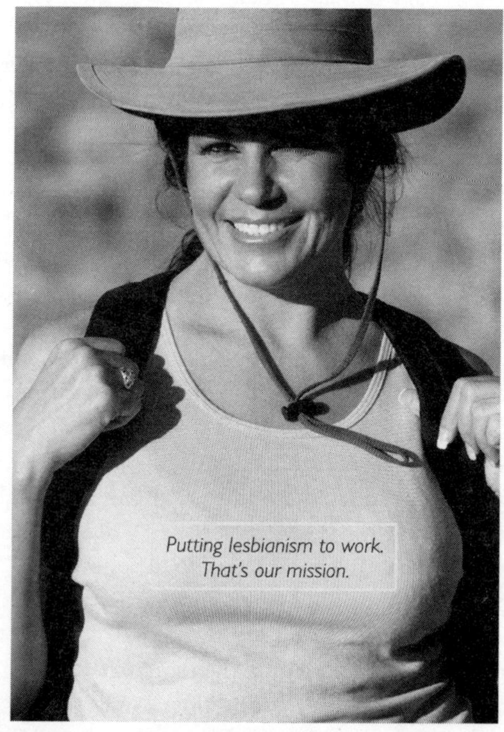

From *Dyke Action Machine INCORPORATED*, 2008.

Dear DAM Inc. Stakeholders:

We live in extraordinary times. From widespread financial insecurity to escalating climate change, each day society is faced with new and often daunting challenges. Together communities and corporations are learning to become responsible global citizens as we face an uncertain future together.

Since 1991 you've known Dyke Action Machine! as a team of media watchdogs who operated from the margins of mainstream culture. Today, instead of testing the status quo, we now recognize that it's our responsibility to restructure and work from within the system. Turning Dyke Action Machine! into DAM Inc. is the first in a series of exciting changes you'll begin to notice in the days and weeks ahead.

Our new identity presents us with ground-breaking opportunities to work with lesbianism as a commodity that can be bought, sold and traded. DAM Inc. also embraces the responsibilities posed by doing business in the 21st century, investing old-school lesbian values such as worker advocacy and good stewardship in every project we undertake. While American big business practically invented the term "supersize," our corporate ethos goes one better—by always putting large, assertive lesbians front and center.

We care for precious resources by focusing on universal quality-of-life issues, encouraging our employees to become change agents at work and in the bedroom. Employees may elect to enroll with Partners for LifeTM to obtain Population Offset Credits, volunteer their time at intake centers for young, fundamentalist women or invest their pensions in Third-World ecotourism.

As you get to know some of our programs, we hope you come away with a sense of DAM Inc.'s commitment to something greater than itself. We were founded more than 15 years ago when "dyke" was not even a household word. Now that we are in the forefront of Lesbian Branding and Messaging Systems, we are committed more than ever to building a company of immediate, ongoing, and lasting value. We will do everything in our power to continue to earn your trust.

Sue and Carrie
Chairwomen and CEOs
DAM Inc.

By the 2010s, and in part due to its own efforts, DAM! had become ineffective as a political venture within commercial, media-savvy urban centers, such as New York City. It seems that DAM! had grasped the limits of what representation could accomplish through culture jamming. “Maybe the work wasn’t done, but the strategy was done,” Moyer posits.[16]

In the years since DAM! concluded, there have been a few contemporary art groups that have explored what it means to make effective agitprop. The collective New Red Order (NRO), to take one example, created a carnivalesque theme park in an empty lot near the aboveground 7 train in Long Island City, New York, in September 2023, and aptly titled the installation *The World’s UnFair*. Among the works on view were posters

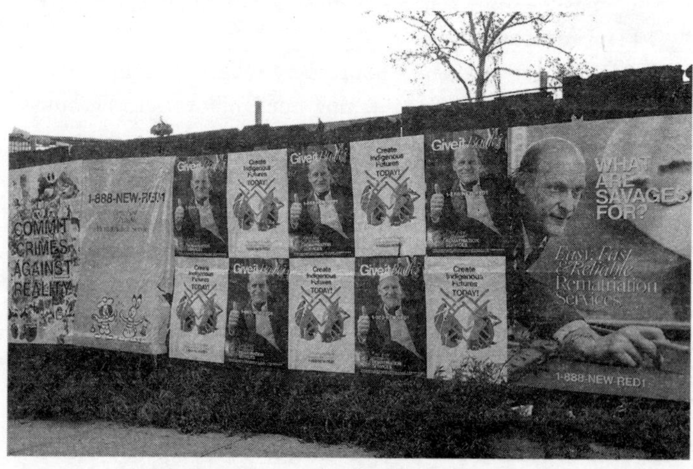

New Red Order, *The World’s UnFair*, 2023.

wheatpasted on the seafoam construction fences around the site. One read: *What Are Savages For? Easy, Fast, and Reliable Rematriation Services*, while another asked, *Sick and Tired of Living on Stolen Land? Give Back Your Dreamhome*. Working with the tropes of publicity and advertorial frameworks, akin to DAM!, NRO aimed to move beyond symbolic gestures by creating a call to action.

New Red Order is a "public secret society" facilitated by three "core contributors": the Tlingit artist and filmmaker Jackson Polys and the Ojibway filmmakers and brothers Adam Khalil and Zack Khalil. (The name of the group riffs off an extant American secret society based in Waco, Texas, "The Improved Order of the Red Men," which is the country's oldest whites-only fraternity. In this case, anonymity provides a cloak for the powerful.) For many of NRO's works, the collective engages with networks of "informants" and "accomplices," often to draw attention to both the destructive past and Indigenous futurity. (Past informants include Ashley Byler, Tali Keren, Kite, Erica Lord, Noelle Mason, Del Montgomery, Laura Ortman, Tony Oursler, Jeremy Pheiffer, and Kate Valk.) In *The World's UnFair*, the collective presented a range of work—from videos to talking animatronic sculptures—that sprawled across a site expected to become a new condominium tower.

The show, which was organized by the New York nonprofit Creative Time, echoed NRO's boisterous installation resembling a tech showroom/marketplace/conference center complete with merch in *Indian Theater: Native Performance, Art, and Self-Determination since 1969* at Bard College's Hessel Museum of Art in Annandale-on-Hudson, New York, which I had caught earlier that summer. In both, NRO's message was straightforward: land back. (Also referred to as #LandBack, this is a global campaign that emerged in the late 2010s among Indigenous people and their allies who seek to reestablish Indigenous sovereignty, including political and economic control of their ancestral lands.) Appearing across advertisements and videos in both outings was the actor Jim Fletcher, who joined the NRO Informant Pilot Program after acting as an "Indian" in 2015 for the Wooster Group's *Cry, Trojans!*, a play that casts the *Iliad* as a colonial fable. In NRO's video *Never Settle: Calling In* (2018), Fletcher performs as a spokesperson, as if in a New Age ad campaign. "Be a part of the solution, leave behind a better world, never *settle*," he declares, presenting NRO as an organization enabling sanguine decolonial action.

Because they tackle different issues, it's futile to try to draw a neat line from DAM! to NRO, but it was exciting to see such well-done agitprop fusing satire and sincerity in 2023—and furthermore to see it outside of the museum setting, which often promotes quiet, passive, and regulated viewing. During my visits, I noticed groups of visitors talking with one another, speaking to staff about the themes of the show, and leisurely hanging out. The location was key: many passersby in this busy area stopped in to see what was happening on their way to the subway. By leveraging some of the resources of contemporary art—funds, publicity, visibility—NRO created a larger audience for itself, beyond museums and galleries. Selecting the installation as the finest of the year, the artist Josh Kline wrote, "*The World's UnFair* is proof of what's possible when visionary artists with a message and a desire to communicate with people outside the art industry are given public space and a budget."[17] I only hope they'll be able to take it on the road.

8

Hock E Aye Vi Edgar Heap of Birds, 1954–

In the early morning hours of November 20, 1969, when the Cheyenne-Arapaho artist Hock E Aye Vi Edgar Heap of Birds was fifteen years old, eighty-nine Indigenous Americans landed on Alcatraz Island in the San Francisco Bay and did not leave until nineteen months later. Occupying the landmass by "right of discovery" and citing the terms of the 1868 Treaty of Fort Laramie, which granted abandoned federal property back to its ancestral owners, these self-described "Indians of All Tribes" reclaimed the rock "in the name of all American Indians." Adam Fortunate Eagle has recalled of the event: "Our protest involved people from many Indian nations. Tlingit, Iroquois, Blackfeet, Chippewa, Navajo, and virtually every other Native American tribe were represented among the thousands of Indians in the Bay Area."[1]

Since the closing of the island's infamous prison in 1963, Alcatraz had been abandoned by the federal government and California was slow with new plans for it. The activists offered to buy it in glass beads and red cloth, in reference to the sale of Manhattan over three hundred years earlier. Their list of demands included the return of Alcatraz and sufficient funding to build, maintain, and operate a museum and a center for Native studies. There had been a few slightly earlier and very brief occupations on the island by Sioux groups, yet the nineteen-month takeover was the first time that Indigenous activists clashed with the government and did not step back. A headline on the front page of the influential Indigenous broadsheet *Akwesasne Notes* read: "Silent too damn long: ALCATRAZ TAKEN BACK."

The event was a catalyst, initiating "a nine-year period of Red Power protest that culminated in the transformation of national consciousness about American Indians and engendered a more open and confident sense of identity among people of Indian descent," as scholars Troy Johnson, Duane Champagne, and Joane Nagel have written.[2] Between November 1969 and July 1978, there were more than seventy property takeovers by Indigenous activists, as documented in *Akwesasne Notes*. To cite a few examples: In August 1970, members of United Native Americans, with support from the American Indian Movement (AIM), ascended 3,000 feet to the top of Mount Rushmore to reclaim the land that had been promised in perpetuity to the Oceti Sakowin (The Great Sioux Nation) in the 1868 Treaty of Fort Laramie. On November 3, 1972, protesters from the Trail of Broken Treaties Caravan occupied the Bureau of Indian Affairs (BIA) offices in Washington, DC, for six days. On February 27, 1973, about 250 Sioux Indians, led by members of AIM, converged on South Dakota's Pine Ridge Reservation, launching the seventy-one-day occupation of Wounded Knee (the location of the 1890 eponymous massacre). On August 15, 1975, nearly 100 Native American protesters took over the Bonneville Power Administration (BPA), a federal agency that markets power produced by federal dams in the Pacific Northwest, in Portland, Oregon. And, on July 15, 1978, "The Longest Walk"—a five-month, 2,800 mile trek for Native American justice, which began with more than 300 people on Alcatraz Island—ended in Washington, DC, with over 2,000 marchers and eight days of demonstrations, protests, religious ceremonies, and educational workshops.

Fast forward to April 1, 2016, to the beginning of one of the greatest organizing efforts to protect land and human rights ever known: the Dakota Access Pipeline (DAPL) protests, also known as the Standing Rock protests, which commenced with a large encampment near Cannon Ball, North Dakota. The effects of this protest were immense. Zack Kahlil of New Red Order (NRO), the collective discussed in the previous chapter, has perhaps said it best, "Post–Standing Rock exploded the level of visibility for Native American people here in a way that seems totally unprecedented."[3]

The protesters were there to stop the construction of a fossil fuel pipeline by the Texas-based company Energy Transfer Partners. The 1,172-mile underground channel runs from the Bakken and Three Forks oil fields in western North Dakota to southern Illinois, crossing beneath the Missouri and Mississippi Rivers, and under part of Lake Oahe near the Standing Rock Reservation. Members of Standing Rock, which is home to the Dakota and Lakota nations, and surrounding communities consider the pipeline to be a serious threat to the region's water—a resource that is both medicine and gift, requiring nurture in return. "For just as water was given certain responsibilities for sustaining the world, so were the people," as Potawatomi botanist and author Robin Wall Kimmerer reminds us.[4]

In addition to posing a threat to the environment and ancestral homelands, the pipeline's construction also directly threatened ancient burial grounds and sites of historical importance. Critics contend it's a matter of when, not *if*, the pipeline will leak, and they point to Energy Transfer Partners' poor track record on other pipelines. The protests near Cannon Ball, which drew nearly 10,000 people at their peak and included many violent clashes with police, dismally ended in February 2017, when law enforcement cleared the site.[5]

"I wish they had kept going—there was a wonderful momentum," Heap of Birds said in our interview that April. "And I hope it channels into more activism and engages more non-Native communities. Because it was inclusive, and we appreciate help. So, it was wonderful in many ways, but the violent way it ended and how pushy it became was simply awful. Though I saw it coming when Obama left office."[6] To date, the protests—the momentum—continue, however, on a smaller scale.

For decades, Heap of Birds has made art about land rights and the protection of Native people. He often creates text-based works on paper, which can look like protest signs—or a "kind of symbolic or semiotic warfare," as the scholar Bill Anthes has noted.[7] Through this practice, it's as if Heap of Birds is continually protesting, without attending marches, or even leaving his home in Oklahoma. "I was proud of how the tribes came together for the Dakota Access Pipeline protest, but I didn't get too involved . . . We have a joke: 'We're Indian every day.' So that's how I look at it, from the tribal standpoint. We did this activism before, we do it now, and we'll do it later."[8]

The joke is a wry one, and it recalls an essay titled "Indian Humor" by the Standing Rock Sioux writer Vine Deloria Jr., which appeared in his first book *Custer Died for Your Sins* (1969)—which, coincidentally, was reviewed in the Alcatraz-headlined issue of *Akwesasne Notes*. "Humor, all Indians will agree," he writes, "is the cement by which the coming Indian movement is held together."[9] Often this humor is dark, and as Deloria notes, shaped by centuries of violence. Comedy sometimes keeps a lid on the unspeakable.

Here is New Red Order on Native jokes:

> Our humor is a way to unpack (stay a while—yet never settle) things without feeling overwhelmed, to cope with the absurdity of our history and find a way to live together in this public secret. The immensity of this seeming incommensurability expands and percolates, grows so much as to become a joke.[10]

As mentioned previously, NRO is a "public secret society"—a long-repressed rejoinder to the genocidal campaign aimed at Indigenous extinction and forced assimilation in the United States.

Heap of Birds's work, like NROs', is a form of scrutinizing and prompting a dialogue about this subjugated history and how it produced knowledge. At the same time, he constantly questions history's biases, creating works that are activist for the ways they refuse to forget or cover up. For, as the Laguna Pueblo activist Paula Gunn Allen says, "the root of oppression is loss of memory."

The subject of our 2017 interview was a monoprint series Heap of Birds had been making since the 2016 US election titled *Genocide and Democracy*. As he told me, the works, "illuminate the profound lack of electoral standing Indigenous communities hold in democratic systems because of depleted population numbers and broadly dispersed demographics that span across many states and provinces, often from forced removal."[11] Today, many Native Americans living on reservations continue to be excluded from the democratic process, often the result of voter suppression efforts.

In 2017, Heap of Birds had been making monoprints for over ten years, mostly in Santa Fe, New Mexico, with the late Michael Duane McCabe, a master Diné (Navajo) printer who had showed the artist a process of painting backward on clear glass with a clear liquid. "The result feels a little elusive," Heap of Birds said, "but I like it, because it's different than my public art, which is more in your face with bold text. With these new monoprints, I never know what's going to happen because of the liquid. Recently with *Genocide and Democracy* I started using solvents too, dissolving the letters even more."[12]

To create the texts, he took excerpts from American patriotic songs and combined them with his own writings to produce statements such as "Red Skin Bounty Tis of Thee" and "Suffer Dance Run Sweet Land Liberty." Typically, Heap of Birds will first write a note, sometimes in his phone or on index cards in his studio, with the words. Before going to the print studio, he puts his three-word phrases together into two, for a total of six words, stringing texts together in a way that recalls concrete poetry. They have a rhythm, like a drumbeat or a heartbeat, but

Edgar Heap of Birds, *Genocide and Democracy*, 2016, ink on paper, 15" x 22" each.

Edgar Heap of Birds, *Standing Rock Awakens the World* (detail), 2019, twenty-four primary mono prints and twenty-four ghost prints on paper, 90" x 176".

they are also devastatingly abrupt. As he remarked, "In some ways the prints in *Genocide and Democracy* look like they're coming out of some bloody, violent event—blood is pooling on them, and there's a violence implied by the words. I write texts, but I also edit other documents, like the Declaration of Independence, which, if you just cut it down in a particular way, gives you the truth of a nation."

"It's a racist document," he added, "with its talk of the savage Indians and so forth. I also found lines in songs like 'God Bless America' and 'The Star-Spangled Banner' that show the hypocrisy of justice, health care, sovereignty, and education in America and just put them together."[13]

In 2020, Heap of Birds made a monoprint series inspired by the Standing Rock protests and exhibited it in his solo show at Fort Gansevoort in New York City. *Standing Rock Awakens the World*, 2019, another mural-like piece made of forty-eight monoprints, echoes *Genocide and Democracy*. The words in the newer work are similarly astute: "Stop Settler Terror" and "Water Is Our First Medicine" appear in stark white across a blood-red ground. For this piece, Heap of Birds began to use a "ghost print," which is the second print made after the first, bright primary print. For Heap of Birds, the ghost print is a political metaphor for the way Native people are often represented in the media—subdued, muted, gentle. Of course, as he points out, they are often much more like the vibrant print.

Heap of Birds's use of text in his art dates to his days in graduate school in the late 1970s, and to listening to the new wave band Talking Heads, who often employed short phrases, such as (and perhaps most famously) "stop making sense." "On a formal level, that phraseology and cadence fascinated me," Heap of Birds once explained, adding, "So, I used to make little notes to myself, with a few words or short phrases. I hung these notes on the wall, and later I realized I could make bigger pieces out of them in pencil and pastel."[14]

An early example of his unique hand-lettering of words can

be found in *American Policy II*, which he began in 1986 and which refers to the massacre of Cheyenne and Arapaho at Sand Creek in 1864, the deadliest day in Colorado's history, and the Washita massacre in 1868, which happened in present-day Cheyenne, Oklahoma. In a 1988 version of this work, twenty-four pastel drawings form an ensemble of hand-drawn, stream of consciousness phrases such as "Know Young Death" and "Relocate Destroy," all written in a prickly, barb-like script. If they were objects, they would strike with the force of a spear.

Heap of Birds has long likened his art practice to sharp rocks, to arrowheads; his 1986 solo show at the New Museum in New York was titled *Born from Sharp Rocks*. In the same year, he wrote, "In touching these weapons, I have found clues as to the useful current day defensive and preservation tactics that can serve living Native Americans."[15] To make novel forms of community protection, Heap of Birds needed to grasp something even more powerful than stone—something symbolic, ideological, political, and that demanded attention.

There are many reasons why Edgar Heap of Birds has made language so central to his art. In the 1960s, text became prominent in contemporary, conceptual art, and many art historians have connected this to the larger "linguistic turn" of postmodernism and critical theory of the time. Coming up as an artist in the post-conceptual generation, Heap of Birds was aware of this history, but a more obvious reason goes back even further. The settler colonial nations of Europe not only robbed land but also language from Indigenous peoples in the Americas. "Had history been different," as Robin Wall Kimmerer, writes: "I would likely speak Bodewadmimwin or Potawatomi, an Anishinaabe language. But like many of the three hundred and fifty Indigenous languages of the Americas, Potawatomi is threatened, and I speak in the language you read."[16] English was also Heap of Birds's first language and like Wall Kimmerer, his ancestors were subjected to an enforced English schooling in US government–led boarding schools.

Often Indigenous nations were identified by their rivals with sobriquets, and the colonizers adopted the same terms: "Cheyenne" is an incorrect name "as it is a mistaken form of a Lakota word meaning 'Unintelligible Speech,'" as Heap of Birds notes. "The correct word is *Tsistsistas*, which means 'ourselves.'"[17] Heap of Birds's first public artwork, *In Our Language*, premiered in October 1982 and made this clear. On a Spectacolor light board—an 800-square-foot array of 8,000 red, white, blue, and green 60-watt bulbs—in New York's Times Square, which usually featured advertisements, he melded English and Cheyenne to create nine short phrases. Every twenty minutes, the series of texts would flash in rhythmic fashion across.

IN OUR LANGUAGE
TSISTSISTAS 'CHEYENNE'
SPEAK OF VEHOE
TSISTSISTAS SAID VEHOE WRAPPED UP
TSISTSISTAS SAID VEHOE FENCED IN
TSISTSISTAS SAID VEHOE CATCH YOU

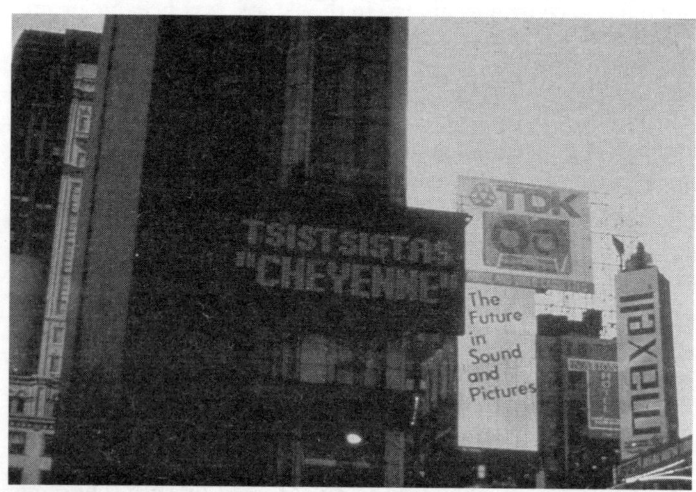

Edgar Heap of Birds, *In Our Language*, 1982. Times Square. Photo: John Marchael.

TSISTSISTAS SAID VEHOE TRAP YOU
TSISTSISTAS SAID VEHOE SPIDER
TSISTSISTAS SAID VEHOE WHITE MAN.

The messages repeated more than fifty times a day for two weeks, wedged into a twenty-minute loop of computer-animated commercials. This early work exemplifies how Heap of Birds approaches language as a discursive realm to be reclaimed against the colonizer. To do so, he inverts the colonizer's subjugation, returning the agency and privilege to name to the Cheyenne. While originally *vehoe* meant "trickster" and referred to an Algonquian hero, later the word also meant white man and is a homonym with the word for spider.[18]

However brief, these texts served, again, as an activist form of remembering. And while the overall effect of the piece may seem short-lived or hard to quantify, it paved the way for Heap of Birds to continue exploring the relationship of language and decolonialization in his public artwork. For decades now, he has emphasized through his art that language is never a neutral, clear, or transparent vehicle for communication. For Heap of Birds, using words is a way to antagonize and shatter complacency, and to involve the viewer in a direct address. His aim, in part, is to lead his audiences to question the authority of "official" discourses, histories, and the laws that shape one's identity and place in the world.

In Our Language was sponsored by the Public Art Fund as one of twelve pieces in a project titled "Messages to the Public." It was curated by artist Jane Dickson, a member of the collective Collaborative Projects (or Colab), who was working for Spectacolor, Inc., as an ad designer and computer programmer at the time. The endeavor also featured art by Keith Haring and, perhaps most famously, Jenny Holzer, who has also engaged with text throughout her long career to "offer content that people—not necessarily art people—could understand."[19]

Yet, for Heap of Birds, much more so than other artists who have employed language in their art, there is always a critique of English and the systems of representation it entails. Even though English appears in his work, he is always dissecting it and destabilizing it, and this has continued for decades. Reviewing Heap of Birds's 1987 exhibition at New York's American Indian Community House Gallery/Museum, Jean Fisher wrote, "Like many colonized peoples, Native Americans quickly learned that language was a weapon to be used against them. However, in Heap of Birds's work the blade has turned around. He cuts, dismembers, or reverses the English language."[20]

Reversing letters in colonialist and settler names became a habit, which helped the artist to reflect on the historical experience of Native diaspora and challenge "official" histories. For one important but lesser-known text-based work, he made in April 1989, Heap of Birds made five billboards in red text on a white background that reads:

SOONERS [in reversed text]
RUN OVER
INDIAN NATIONS
APARTHEID OKLAHOMA.

The Sooners were the white citizens of Oklahoma that prompted the seizure of Native reservations in 1889 and the displacement of thirty-nine Native Nations, from what was then called "Indian Territory" by the US government. The billboard was the artist's contribution to a major community effort and rebuttal against the centennial Land Run celebration in Oklahoma City, which was then marking 100 years of statehood. A local program called the Indian Youth Project secured funding to support the production of the billboards and four were placed downtown along a main road (with one near a high rise), while one was installed along the highway to Norman, Oklahoma.

On April 22, 1989, nearly 200 people marched along the street where the billboards were deployed and then gave

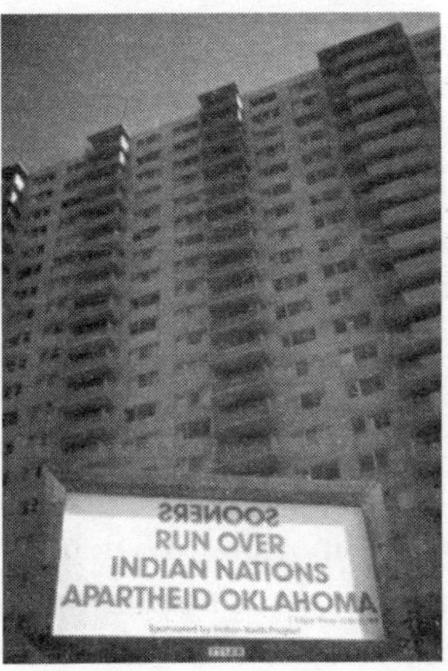

Edgar Heap of Birds, *Apartheid Oklahoma*, 1989. Five billboards, each 5' × 9'. Installed throughout Norman and Oklahoma City, Oklahoma.

speeches at the steps of the state capitol building. An important point of the billboard effort was financial independence. It was not created through funding from an art museum, gallery, or another art institution, but "only through the Native community from Southside Oklahoma City, an impoverished section," as Heap of Birds told me.

In 1989, as the minority, white apartheid regime remained powerful in South Africa, and as student groups across the United States urged their universities to divest and push back, Heap of Birds connected apartheid to the history of Oklahoma becoming a modern state. It was a timely project, but it was also one that was important for its correlation to the land where he still lives, which remains the most inspirational element in his practice to date.

Heap of Birds's text-based monoprints might be the medium for which he has received the most attention. But he has also created formidable public artworks, such as *In Our Language* and the ongoing *Native Hosts* series of site-specific signs that, like agit prop, use the visual language of institutional metal signage to reaffirm native groups' historical occupancy of land. For another ongoing body of work, his abstract *Neuf* series, which he began in the 1980s, Heap of Birds creates paintings that loosely refer to the remote canyons of his ancestral home, the Cheyenne and Arapaho reservation lands of Oklahoma.

In 1981, after finishing graduate school at Temple University in Philadelphia, Heap of Birds packed up and drove his Volkswagen bus back to Oklahoma, where he has been based ever since. It has been important to him to live near family, but also to be in his ancestral community—to be an active part of the historic Cheyenne-Arapaho nation. "It was always an activist mentality," as he has said, to stay near his community and not abandon it.[21] Heap of Birds spent part of the early '80s living in his grandmother's cabin, on a reservation in Clinton, Oklahoma. He then moved to Geary, Oklahoma, and eventually to Oklahoma City, where he taught for thirty years at the University of Oklahoma, as the first Native American faculty in its art department.

Understanding the importance of site to his work, I visited Heap of Birds in his studio, located in a single-story office complex, in February 2024. The site is near his daughter's school, and not too far from his home. Family is everything; his wife Dr. Shanna Ketchum-Heap of Birds, who is a citizen of the Diné/Navajo Nation, is a principal scholar of Native American art, theater, and performance studies.

After looking at some of his earliest drawings and paintings, which indicated his budding interests in merging text and design, I was drawn to a framed print, prominently installed in his studio, which was clearly not his art. It was a reproduction of Blackbear Bosin's famed painting *Prairie Fire*, from 1953, which was hailed as a new beginning in Plains Indian art because of the motion it signifies—animals and people fleeing burning flames—instead of a static scene. The self-taught Bosin was a mentor and remains a key antecedent, and perhaps ancestor, to Heap of Birds's art. I thought of him while we looked over a new monoprint series titled *Family*, for which Heap of Birds created a list of names derived from his ancestry that he incorporated into the six-word structure of his previous works. "Bear Shield Standing Bull Flying Coyote" reads one.

As we looked at more new work, we discussed how the monoprints have evolved. Many in his recent ongoing series, such as *Pray Protect Tribal Lives Matter*, 2021, incorporate natural elements, including brushed leaves and other elements that a traditional printmaker might see as errors, but that Heap of Birds embraces.

While we spoke about the importance of communality, Heap of Birds told me of his activism that "maybe it was always an expectation—because we're collective all the time. It goes way back."[22] Not long after moving to Oklahoma in 1980s, he wanted to foster community among local artists and so he started a collective called the Makers' Alliance, initially with Native artists Pat Russell, Shan Goshorn, and Richard Ray Whitman, which ran strong for ten years. The group had several exhibitions in local university galleries showcasing their dissimilar work in different mediums—beadwork, poetry, sculpture, and traditional baby cradleboards (by Russell). "So, the activism then was, well, you better organize a collective to do it yourself and have an exhibit and do youth workshops to get into the realm and help," as Heap of Birds recalled. "It was difficult; I didn't have a teaching job then—I was kind of a scout leader for it. But I enjoyed the grassroots nature of it."[23] Many of the artists involved in the Alliance over the years went on to develop their own art careers, but for several this was the beginning, and it was crucial.

Working collectively led Heap of Birds to continue to teach workshops and conduct community projects with local groups—with elders and youth from Cheyenne and Arapaho lands in Concho, Oklahoma—as well as all over the world.

This labor includes his visits with First Nations artists in Australia, which resulted in a large traveling group show from 1995–97 titled *16 Songs*. These projects have focused on ceremonial knowledge, such as dealing with the Medicine Wheel's meanings and directions, and the traditional tipi.

To be an activist, for Heap of Birds, is not "a one-way street with some elite idea."[24] It involves local community building but also making an array of art—including abstract paintings that deal with questions of beauty and freedom. For Heap of Birds, it's critical to offer an alternative to the protest, "a balance," as he says, with "what you love and what's productive, and generative." Here is one example of what this might mean: In 1975, Heap of Birds attended summer classes at the California College of the Arts, and while in the Bay Area he went to an AIM meeting where he first met the Native American author and AIM cofounder Dennis Banks. "He would come to our rez 30 years later on one of those treaty rights walks," Heap of Birds recalled. "Our people hosted him; he met and held our daughter when she was about four years old at our powwow."[25]

After looking at work in his studio, Heap of Birds and I head out in his 4x4 truck to meet with Randy Hawk, one of the main wranglers of the 600-head tribal buffalo herd at Concho Agency, which is about thirty minutes west of the studio. "FYI," he tells me before we leave, "the Concho Cheyenne and Arapaho Agency goes back to when Custer and his army were here after the Washita Massacre. His main captain was Captain Reno, and the town near Concho is named El Reno. There is still a Fort Reno and Custer City. Part of the treaty lands were taken from the Cheyenne and Arapaho and used to fashion a federal penitentiary at El Reno. Timothy McVeigh was imprisoned there. The Fort, Federal Pen, and Highway 81 form the eastern boundary of our reservation which once stretched west to Texas."[26]

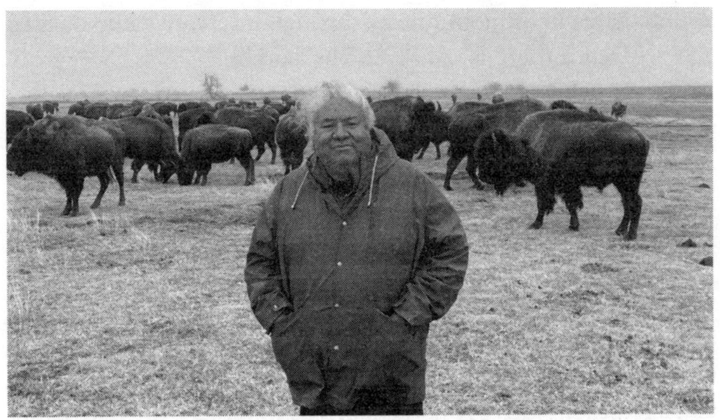

Edgar Heap of Birds in Concho, Oklahoma. Photo: Shanna Ketchum-Heap of Birds.

That warmer-than-usual February day, the buffalo were being corralled into pens and vaccinated, before being released back out onto the land. The same site holds the Earth Renewal Ceremony, which happens for several days during the summer solstice. As an elder of the Cheyenne Elk Warrior Society, Heap of Birds assists with leading this large gathering of prayer for healing. As we drive around, he shows me the remnants of the lodge from last summer and how the camp is usually set up, explaining how it looks like a small, bustling city for a week.

I learn that Cheyenne-Arapaho territory is different from other reservations in that it's a checkerboard of sorts—not just one large stretch of acreage, like the Navajo Nation in the Southwestern United States. During the time of the Sooners, Cheyenne-Arapaho domains were punctuated by land-run grabs. Heap of Birds points out when we're in Oklahoma, and when we're not; that is, when state police could interact with us, and when they cannot.

It becomes clear that sovereignty does not mean support—I'm reminded of why the artist is outspoken, why he carefully discusses the suicide rates, poverty, alcoholism, hypertension, and diabetes in his community through interviews like ours in 2017. "Death there is constant," he said:

> Some of it is self-inflicted, but a lot of it is just based on problems on the reservation. And it's not getting any better. There's so much disenchantment there now—ill health from bad food provided by the government. It's all sugar, salt, and processed foods that will kill you. They give it away for free and then you get a horrible disease like diabetes from it.[27]

Life is bucolic but not easy—there is a food bank, crisis offices, victim services. Heap of Birds's art serves as a challenge to other Native American artists to represent these truths instead of covering them up. It's also a dare to the art world, which largely chooses to be dazzled by beauty when it comes to Indigenous art. But perhaps most of all, his work inspires empathy.

On the road, Heap of Birds points out the sand plum trees, the juniper, and cottonwoods. He shows me the sweat lodges and buildings for various buildings for tribal services and administration, the powwow grounds for dances. And he points out the building where he once received an application for a scholarship to attend college at the University of Kansas (KU) in Lawrence, where he received a BFA in 1976.

In January 2021, KU announced that its campus had become home to a new art gallery dedicated to Indigenous excellence in the visual arts, thanks to a generous gift from Heap of Birds. Beginning that month, the Edgar Heap of Birds Family Gallery began to host an annual series of exhibits featuring the work of Native American artists. The inaugural exhibit, *Indigenous Space*, featured the work of Norman Akers, a KU visual art professor and enrolled member of the Osage Nation, and Heap of Birds. In a twist on the way that museums are typically funded, Heap of Birds decided to donate funds from his own pocket to give back to the schools that educated him. In doing so, he created a mandate for the schools to uplift and increase awareness of Native peoples and art.

Heap of Birds did not have a Native professor while going to school. For him, this philanthropic activism is a way to welcome, nurture, and support young Indigenous artists while giving them a place to belong at the University of Kansas. As a student at KU, Heap of Birds led the Native student group, which would often collaborate with the nearby Haskell Indian Nations University, a public tribal land-grant school in Lawrence. For the second show in KU's Heap of Birds Family gallery, Haskell students were asked to show their artworks for the first time at the more "prestigious" university.

Heap of Birds's hope is that all Native students will feel welcome in the space. His family name on the front of the gallery is a kind of activism and intervention, which, as he pointed out to me, "everyone does with wealth—they're intervening in a major way." Yet I've never heard of another artist doing this, and when I ask him where the idea came from, he says that it was always there in a way. He recalls his grandmother Lightning Woman telling him that "if you can't go with something to give them, don't go." "And we're still hard-pressed to not give something away," he adds. "Isn't that what you do? Acknowledge people with what you have to share."[28]

In February 2023, Heap of Birds endowed another space—again titled the Edgar Heap of Birds Family Gallery—this time at the Tyler School of Art and Architecture at Temple University, where he received an MFA in 1979. His gift of $200,000 served to name an area for exhibitions within Tyler's public art gallery, Temple Contemporary, and to create an artist's residency program for Native artists. A 750-square-foot space is now used primarily as a permanent residency program, where an artist can work for an extended period and then have an exhibition if they choose to. At the time of this writing, Heap of Birds is working on developing summer programs for students at universities modeled after the Oscar Howe Summer

Art Institute at the University of South Dakota (USD), which honors Howe, the longtime USD professor and Yanktonai Dakota artist, by helping educate the next-generation Indigenous American artists.

Heap of Birds's philanthropic activism offers one way for museums to move forward. It is also a call back to the vision of those who occupied Alcatraz Island in 1969, to the activists who wanted to establish their own cultural institutions. What would US art institutions across the country look like if there were more well-funded residency programs and art centers dedicated to Indigenous artists? And what if the fruits of that labor were exhibited in permanent Indigenous art wings, or galleries, in US museums, both urban and rural?

9

Project Row Houses, 1994–

No one has written more beautifully about the shotgun house than the late theorist, educator, and social critic bell hooks. While the shotgun style and name may trace back to Haiti and Africa in the eighteenth century and earlier, it was the most popular type of house in the Southern United States from the end of the American Civil War (1861–65) through the 1920s. Of these narrow rectangular residences, hooks argued:

> The traditional shotgun house is more than a powerful marker of African American cultural landscape. It is a symbol of a diasporic mode of living represented architecturally around the world by folks moving from enslavement, indentured servitude, rebellion against colonialism, and colonial occupation into freedom. It stands as a global symbol of liberation.[1]

It was with this spirit of liberation that Project Row Houses (PRH) was born in the Third Ward, a historically and predominately Black neighborhood in Houston, Texas.

In 1837, Houston was divided into political geographic districts called "wards," hence the name Third Ward. The founding of Trinity United Methodist Church in 1848, a congregation created by enslaved people, remains one of the most important events in the history of the area, as well as the establishment of Emancipation Park—land bought by a group of African Americans in 1872. From roughly the 1890s through the 1950s, the Third Ward was a thriving region for commerce and social activities along Alameda and Emancipation Avenue (then called Dowling Street). The flourishing economic and cultural activities of the area in these years—a time of enforced racial segregation under Jim Crow laws—are often compared to the Harlem Renaissance. However, infrastructural developments, such as the construction of State Highway 288 in 1939, cleaved the physical community in two. And though the Third Ward served as the center of the civil rights movement in the city, the population and services were on the decline there. After the passing of the Civil Rights Act in 1964, which outlawed segregation, some residents began to slowly move to racially integrated neighborhoods in Southwest Houston. Many local businesses closed, while discriminatory practices such as redlining—in which financial services are withheld from neighborhoods that have significant numbers of racial and ethnic minorities—stymied new growth, and Nixon's War on Drugs consumed generations of young men. This systemic oppression continued into the 1990s as poverty became endemic in the area.

In the early 1990s, the artist Rick Lowe was working as a volunteer at the S.H.A.P.E. Community Center in the Third Ward, and was thinking alongside other African American volunteers there about how to merge political theory and practice.[2] Born in 1961 in Russell County, Alabama, as the eighth of twelve children, Lowe grew up on a rural sharecropping farm about thirty-five miles from the nearest town in the southeastern area of the state. His upbringing in the South, during the civil rights era, was a formative experience, and something that he wanted to express through art. He studied painting at Georgia's Columbus College, but dropped out during his junior year in 1982, and moved to Biloxi, Mississippi, for a yearlong residency at the Springer Art Center. Here, he began to merge painting with politics, as indicative in his *Victims* series (1983–), which he exhibited in a 1984 solo show at the Biloxi Library and Cultural Center.

According to Lowe, these early paintings were "very didactic," representing victims and victimizers of gun violence to explore issues ranging from police brutality, poverty, and war. The works, in his words, are "narrowly focused on working-class issues, to speak directly to working-class folks."[3] Using standard four-by-eight-foot sheets of plywood and inexpensive house paint, Lowe distanced himself from the easel-based painting he had studied at Columbus College and instead made large-scale, modular works at a more monumental scale, to echo the magnitude of his subjects and themes. This method allowed him to produce, hang, and deinstall paintings as large as eight-by-twelve-feet with ease.

After moving to Houston in 1985, Lowe became known in the local arts community for his commitment to direct-action campaigns and for organizing through the local chapter of Amnesty International and the Union of Independent Artists, a political advocacy group that focused on freedom of expression in public art and environmental issues. In 1986, during a peace rally, Lowe presented a guerrilla art installation of his *Victims* works on the public plaza of Houston's City Hall. In 1988, he exhibited *Victims Untitled* (1987) in the First Texas Triennial at the Contemporary Arts Museum in Houston. The mixed-media installation exemplifies the blend of styles he was utilizing at the time: a crepuscular landscape is bookended by a hooded Ku Klux Klan member and a burning cross on one side, while a noose is sculpturally affixed to the surface of the panel on the other side. Below the Klan member, Lowe added texts derived from the Declaration of Independence and a history of the KKK. The work is a response to the 1981 lynching of Michael Donald by the Ku Klux Klan in Mobile, Alabama.

In April 1990, after the 1989 deaths of Byron Gillum and Ida Lee Delaney at the hands of police officers, Lowe presented an outdoor exhibition at the S.H.A.P.E. Community Center featuring paintings from his *Victims* series. The installation featured a large-scale tableau of Lowe's life-size painted plywood figures. When a grand jury decided not to indict officer Scott Tschirhart, who had killed Gillum, the community asked Lowe if they could host a press conference with his work in the background. "It was a big moment for me and solidified my art activism at that time," Lowe has said.[4]

Not long after, a local high school group visited Lowe's studio, and, as the artist has often recalled, something happened that "just shattered" him. A student noted that that while his work was hitting on all the issues that are relevant to low-income communities, the people in the Third Ward didn't exactly need a greater awareness of them. "We don't need people to come back and tell us what the issues are," Lowe remembered the student saying. "We already know; we see it, we live it. If you're an artist and you're creative, why can't you create some kind of solutions?"[5]

Lowe began to invite members from the African American activist community to rallies being held by the Union of Independent Artists, and they came. But, when Lowe invited the Union of Independent Artists to the Black activist community to protest police brutality, racism, and corruption, he received a "rude awakening": "There were people that just did not come," he recalled. "I heard rumors that folks were saying that I was trying to use the Union of Independent Artists for my own personal agenda . . . that was when I kind of stepped away from the Union."[6] The departure opened a door for Lowe to focus mainly on activism within the African American community.

In 1992, Lowe was invited on a S.H.A.P.E.-organized tour of the Third Ward with city officials, developers, and organizers to identify dangerous buildings they thought should be torn down. When the group arrived at a block of small (600-square foot) shotgun houses at Live Oak and Holman Streets, it was identified as "the worst" block on their route. (Such houses were being demolished across the South.) It was a pivotal moment for Lowe. Beyond the homes' forlorn and derelict appearances, he saw something else—a way that the area could return as a thriving community epicenter of Black culture, creativity, and commerce with a deep sense of pride. Lowe envisioned a "temporary kind of guerilla style art project," where primarily Black artists could work in one house each and create site-specific artworks.[7]

"I was also thinking about the community brain drain," Lowe remembered. "Everybody's always leaving, and nobody's coming in. I thought of myself as a part of that brain drain. The resources that I had accumulated over time were not going back into the neighborhood. So, how do you pull those things together?"[8] The twenty-two houses Lowe saw in all that day reminded him of the artist Dr. John Biggers (1924–2001), the founding chairman of the art department at Houston's Texas Southern University, a historically Black college. Biggers was born in a shotgun house in North Carolina and became known for his vibrant, complex, and symbolic murals and paintings, which often depict the dwellings. "I see them as I walk the Third Ward of Houston—the rhythm of their shadows, the square of the porch three over four like the beat of a visual gospel," Biggers said of the houses.[9] Biggers's art underscores the richness of Black culture, specifically in the community of

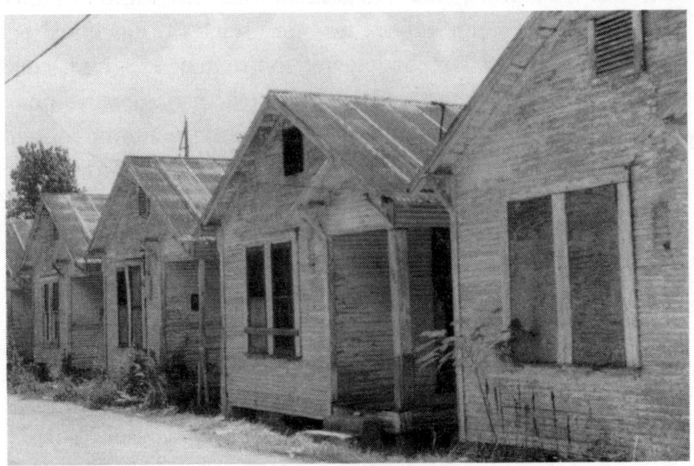

Row Houses before renovations. Photograph by Sheryl Tucker Vasquez. Courtesy of Project Row Houses.

the Third Ward, but his paintings also more generally trace the architectural style of row houses back to their roots. In these works, Biggers "conveys historical notions of home that have been crucial to African Americans," as hooks points out, adding, "Our vision of home must be mapped, charted, named."[10]

That's exactly what the founders of Project Row Houses set out to do. Lowe had been organizing with a group of intergenerational artists—James Bettison (1958–1997), Bert Long Jr. (1940–2013), Jesse Lott (1943–2023), Floyd Newsum (1950–2024), Bert Samples, and George Smith—and conveyed to them not only what was being planned for the shotgun houses in the Third Ward, but also how what he had seen that day was reminiscent of Biggers's aesthetic. At the time, the arts in Houston were taking a professionalizing turn, becoming "less wild than the 1980s," according to Lowe, when artists "felt freer to experiment and play."[11]

The Museum of Fine Arts was expanding into another building, and the Core Residency Program at the museum's Glassell School of Art was beginning to gain national attention. Yet, that didn't necessarily entail more visibility for local Black artists, even for those who had participated in the Core Program, such as Bert Samples. The group Lowe was organizing with—now called the "Magnificent Seven"—was thinking about how it would be better to create something new rather than to wait for opportunities. As erstwhile PRH curator Ryan N. Dennis has remarked, "PRH was created out of conversations, from a place that, in some ways, was responding to a lack of inclusivity from institutions and organizations throughout Houston. Black artists living and working, both collaboratively and independently, were trying to create opportunities for themselves that were not being given."[12]

Lowe began researching artists who had made art with a practical application. "I ran across a book with Joseph Beuys in it and there was a chapter called social sculpture," Lowe remembered. "He defined it as the way we shape and mold the world. It was interesting to me, and I started thinking, how do you make social sculpture?"[13] This was a moment when problem solving and questions of value began to coalesce in his mind.

Lowe began tracking down the owner of the houses, who was then living in Taiwan. He also started researching grants and recruited Deborah Grotfeldt (1950–2022), who had been working for seven years as assistant director at Houston's DiverseWorks—a multidisciplinary arts nonprofit, where Lowe was a board member. At DiverseWorks, Grotfeldt assisted with fundraising, worked directly with artists coordinating programs in all disciplines, and managed the renovation of a large, raw warehouse space into an arts facility. Grotfeldt and Lowe set up PRH as a nonprofit organization, which led to more fundraising efforts. In its first year of operation, PRH received crucial seed funding of $25,000 from the National Endowment for the Arts, which led to an additional $113,000 in contributions from corporations, private foundations (such as the Elizabeth Firestone Graham Foundation), individuals, and $136,000 in-kind construction materials over the following year.[14] The Heimbinder Family Foundation also provided a $120,000 no-interest loan for securing the properties from the present owner.

The founding artists and Grotfeldt devoted PRH's first year on-site to raising funds, developing relationships in the community, planning programs, and recruiting and managing volunteers and contractors. PRH's founders learned that to be an activist organization, they needed to speak directly to the local community: Who are the voices that aren't being heard? And what are their concerns? They also felt it was important to build PRH's board of directors from local artists, volunteers, and business owners in the Third Ward.[15]

Lowe negotiated a five-year lease/purchase agreement effective September 1993 for the entire block and a half of twenty-two houses, though he had originally only wanted to lease ten. (In hindsight, it was lucky that the owner insisted on the entire twenty-two-house package as it created an opportunity to expand PRH's public art and education initiative to later include historic preservation and more community services.) That fall, staff from arts organizations throughout Houston, including the Menil Collection and DiverseWorks, labored alongside volunteers of all ages to help the artists repair the houses. (The director of the Menil allowed Mondays to be a day off for some of the museum's employees so that they could lend a hand at PRH.) The corporate sponsor Chevron renovated the outside of the houses and organized a workday with over 300 employees. For months, volunteers numbering in the hundreds fortified porches, removed trash from lots, and hung drywall.

During the renovations, the founding artists began to think about how they could convey a visible artistic presence in the project and the neighborhood. In April 1994, with the houses' windows and doors still boarded up, PRH cofounder Jesse Lott

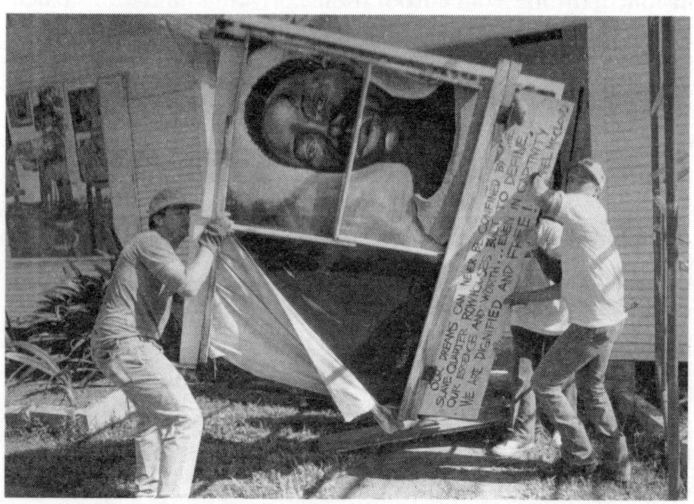

Installing *Home Free* by Israel McCloud for *The Drive By* exhibition at Project Row Houses, 1994. Courtesy of Project Row Houses.

organized *The Drive By* exhibition, and invited artists to create installations on the exterior of fifteen houses. Israel McCloud, a third-generation Houstonian artist, recalled that he wanted the mixed-media piece he created from found objects, *Home Free*, "to be a representation of one of the residents of the neighborhood looking outside with optimism and hope."[16]

McCloud, whose father was a muralist, grew up making large-scale public art by using extension ladders and scaffolds (this was before there were lift trucks). In the late 1980s, he gained attention for painting Black Power murals for businesses owned by the local Jamaican community in Houston. By the 1990s, he was one of the codirectors of the Midtown Art Center, a flourishing institution that, as McCloud suggests, was part of another Harlem Renaissance–like moment in Houston, one of "creative intensity and collective solidarity."

On June 1, 1994, renovations were finished on the first twelve of twenty-two structures. Each one was "adopted" by a corporation, a Houston-based museum, patron, or church. For instance, the Trinity United Methodist Church raised $5,000 for one house through donations, and its choir also performed on-site. After PRH's grand opening in October 1994, its art program grew to include commissioned projects, summer residencies, and fellowships. *The Drive By* show kickstarted PRH's now longstanding tradition of inviting artists to install works in and around the houses, for exhibitions referred to as the Artist Rounds, which have become a biannual event, with openings in March and October.

For the most part, the art program has remained focused on preserving the Third Ward's identity, history, and culture. Each round focuses on a theme, which often concerns politics. PRH has become a model not only for artist-led activism but also for what political art can look like and what it can do. For instance, *Round 47: The Act of Doing: Preserving, Revitalizing and Protecting Third Ward*, was curated by Ryan N. Dennis in fall 2017, and included installations such as Marc

Furi's *I Love 3W*, a house that featured a Monopoly-inspired installation about gentrification in the neighborhood. For this work, Furi also created video interviews with key local artists such as McCloud, who talks about making artwork in the neighborhood for four decades as a way of fighting for the "multifaceted collage, interdisciplinary Black Mecca" at the heart of the Third Ward's cultural identity.[17] Indeed, McCloud's murals, often painted on walls donated by business owners, have always been about "advocacy, identity, and giving face to who we are, what we are, where we are going."[18] (Seen today, they offer a strong contrast to the often blasé murals now found throughout Houston's shopping areas.)

In 1995, PRH began its arts education program and developed an after-school curriculum for local children who were seeking a creative outlet in the afternoons.[19] Many of the children were interested in Lowe's desktop computer, a then-novel technology, which he generously allowed them to explore. That year, PRH also initiated an opportunity to support and empower working single women between the ages of eighteen to twenty-six in the community with the Young Mother's Residential Program (YMRP).

The YMRP gives its residents one year of free housing, counseling, and on-site day care to allow them to finish their education. The first participants in the program moved into their homes in January 1996. The YMRP continues to be successful, with women pursing higher education and law degrees, and becoming business owners, community leaders, and even PRH board members after they leave.[20]

In just three years (1993–96), PRH created eight gallery houses for the Artist Rounds; two administrative houses; a house for afterschool and summer programs; the Sisters-in-Progress house, offering support programs; seven houses for the YMRP program; a community garden where five houses had been torn down; a house for performance programming; a woodworking shop; and a house for storage. Three years later, in 1999, PRH received the nearby and legendary Eldorado Ballroom as a gift from a trustee, Hubert Finkelstein. This historic Third Ward site of blues and jazz performances, weekly talent shows, and sock-hops remained open from 1939 until the early 1970s. Artists such as B. B. King, Sam Lightnin' Hopkins (a legendary Houston-based blues musician), and many other Black performers played at the Eldorado. After four years of renovations, the space reopened in March 2023, after a $9.6 million renovation. Notably, PRH collaborated with Houston Community College on the 2003–2005 *Eldorado Series*, presenting and recording African American jazz musicians who played at the Eldorado Ballroom from the 1940s to 1960s.

Clearly, PRH has become a unique gathering place—also known as a third place—for dialogue engaging the community in cultural, social, political, and educational debates. While PRH's art and education programs are a longstanding and valuable resource, what has really set the institution apart is its dedication to the community through enrichment programs (tutoring, financial empowerment, and food distribution) and neighborhood development (historic and cultural preservation)—and most of all, its ongoing creation of low-income housing. Though, as Lowe has pointed out, "Our interest is not *just* in affordable housing. It's also to create opportunities for artists to live here. Diversity allows people to grow."[21] Currently, PRH offers a mix of subsidized and market-rate housing, and several artists live on its "campus."

To be sure, PRH was founded as a response to the ongoing US housing crisis. At the time of this writing, there is an estimated shortage of 4 to 7 million homes in the United States, according to the Pew Charitable Trust's Housing Policy Initiative. (The mortgage finance giant Freddie Mac estimates a lower number, about four million units.) The primary culprit has been restrictive zoning that has made it hard to build homes in areas where there are jobs. Adding to this immense housing shortage is the US housing market where existing homes are bid up because high-income households are competing with low-income households for the same residences, while not enough new affordable homes are being built. Taking inflation into consideration, home prices in the United States rose to nearly 60 percent from 2014 to 2024 and about a quarter of all renters—some 12 million households—spend more than half their income on housing.

According to a March 2024 report released by the National Low Income Housing Coalition titled *The Gap: A Shortage of Affordable Homes*, no US state has an adequate supply of affordable rental housing for the lowest-income renters. Texas ranks the sixth-worst state in the United States for affordable housing for extremely low-income renters, with Houston as the fifth-worst metropolitan city in the country.[22] In the Third Ward, the housing shortage has been exceptionally severe for generations.

Beginning in the mid-2000s, as Houston's economy boomed, the Third Ward's central location made it a prime target for developers building cookie-cutter townhomes, an event aided by city government leaders committed to improving Houston's economy and residential infrastructure. (This is different from more classical gentrification wherein individuals invest capital in disinvested properties and oust longtime residents of a community.) Continual rises in property values, including an especially sharp spike in 2017 when Emancipation Park reopened after a $33.6 million renovation by the architecture and design firm Perkins&Will, created a new wave of displacement for legacy residents. Some have questioned whose needs are being met: "If the developers and municipal leaders desired to provide the residents of the Third Ward with a state-of-the-art public park," why is it that, "the renovations to Emancipation Park did not occur until real estate development flourished in the neighborhood?" ask scholars Willie Jamaal Wright and Cameron Khalfani Herman.[23]

In 1997, the Rice Building Workshop (now known as Construct), a program for architecture students at Rice University taught by architects Danny Samuels and Nonya Grenader, became a long-term partner with PRH. The earliest collaboration, Six-Square house, a two-story, 900-square foot home designed and constructed by students from 1997–99, was inspired by the architecture of the original row houses. The project became a prototype that generated a range of variations in the following years. Duplex apartments were later built by the Rice Building Workshop on Division, Francis, Anita, Napoleon, and Drew Streets from 2004 to 2013, with Department of Housing and Urban Development (HUD) funding provided through the City of Houston and in participation with many institutional supporters. The duplexes feature deep front porches and standing-seam metal roofs that are a contemporary adaptation of the typical shotgun architecture of the Third Ward. By 2013, fifty-four affordable apartment units were added to the neighborhood. These properties are overseen by the Row House Community Development Corporation (RHCDC) and a property management company it contracts with.

The RHCDC was established in 2003 as a sister nonprofit to Project Row Houses in direct response to PRH's vision to create community. PRH staff had noticed that after participants in the Young Mother's Residential Program "graduated" from it, they couldn't find any low-income housing in the neighborhood. Lowe recalled that PRH wanted "to have options and opportunities for people to maintain the connection to the community that nurtured them if they wanted to."[24] Accordingly, the Row House CDC's mission is to "develop affordable housing, public spaces, and facilities to preserve and protect the historic character of the Third Ward."[25] To accomplish the latter, the RHCDC ventures to "build low-income housing that consists of good and relevant architecture that is not only well designed, but also makes sense to preserve the community's historic character."[26] Rents range from 30 percent of median income for the area to market rate, and residents commit to engaging in twenty-two hours of community service each year.

As of 2024, the RHCDC is in the process of actively building and acquiring additional property for rental and home ownership in the Third Ward. Funding for housing is notoriously difficult to come by, and so the RHCDC develops partnerships with local organizations such as Houston's Community Land Trust. The Row House CDC ultimately envisions a variety of spaces: mixed-income housing, green areas, public facilities, artists' living/studio spaces, and historic preservation. "Our focus includes creating community through an architectural design that promotes connecting with neighbors via porches and common open space," the nonprofit asserts.[27]

A Rice University survey of more than 1,600 Third Ward residents in 2019 found that a majority were "extremely" worried about a local loss of African American culture in their neighborhood, and nearly one-third of the tenants said they were nervous about being forced to relocate within the next year. "Further, when residents were asked about the neighborhood conditions that concerned them, the construction of new townhomes was an 'extreme' concern for approximately 40% of respondents," the report also stated.[28] "The townhomes, the increasing presence of police, and the circulating white bodies of recently arrived neighbors give new meanings to a walk throughout the neighborhood," as Wright and Herman point out. "They not only show how the neighborhood has changed (and continues to do so); the presence of these structures *and* bodies-in-motion work to codify spaces as white, spaces where one's roving Blackness becomes a practice in defiance of this racial compartmentalization."[29]

PRH and other community organizations (such as the Sankofa Research Institute and the Emancipation Economic Development Council) that are resisting displacement and erasure in the Third Ward present another "practice," as a continual reminder to the city and to developers that the area is a historically Black neighborhood. And yet, only three years into its work, PRH acknowledged the role it would play in gentrification: "The really scary part of it all is that the more we do brings more attention to the Third Ward, which has got the cheapest land prices now in the city," as Grotfeldt said in 1997, adding, "Real estate speculation has already begun."[30]

Yet, it is likely that the Third Ward would have gentrified without the success of PRH—the city's lack of zoning laws and dearth of inclusionary housing requirements encouraged speculation and privatized land development beginning there in the 1990s. But, of course, the fact remains that gentrification in the Third Ward has revealed class inequality. To counteract this, Lowe felt a need to energetically "participate in the development of our neighborhood so that we're not just waiting around and watching it gentrify—we needed to be actively participating in the development."[31]

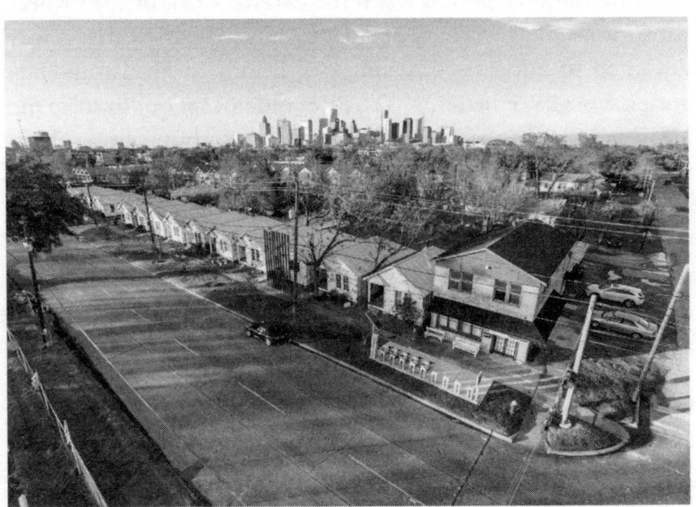

Aerial view of Project Row Houses in 2015. Photograph by Peter Molick. Courtesy of Project Row Houses.

Remarkably, the Row House CDC is careful not to demonize gentrification. Echoing Lowe's comment about diversity, it "believes that a diverse economic base is necessary for a vibrant community." "Our focus," the nonprofit suggests, "is to promote equal opportunity to live in Northern Third Ward, including low-to-moderate-income residents. This is the population that is most immediately impacted by the growing trend of gentrification that is encroaching upon the neighborhood."[32] The "growing trend" was immediately apparently to me as I roamed around the area: a new townhome was going up directly across from PRH's low-income housing, while around the corner another condemned building was being demolished, and there were numerous commercial signs adverting the sale of empty lots.

For some critics, such as the arts writer Ben Davis, the RHCDC doesn't go far enough: "The handful of properties that the Project Row Houses maintains seems like a drop in the bucket, a feel-good footnote to the real story," he says. "During the very period when the careful work of the Project Row Houses has won it worldwide praise, the issue that it was designed to address—housing conditions in Houston—has gotten worse, not better."[33] Yet, PRH did not set out to solve the housing crisis in the Third Ward, and as a nonprofit working in the face of governmental neglect it can only do so much.

But the story is also more complicated than that: across the United States, local homeowners often pack city council meetings to complain, with NIMBY zeal, about new housing developments, even affordable housing initiatives. If states could strip the cities' power to say no, more affordable housing could be built—and there is an obvious urgency to do so. Project Row Houses is just one example of artists taking the initiative to get things done, and much of this work has been recently happening in collaboration with private foundations, as public funding for the arts has dwindled.

For example, in 2018 PRH shifted its focus to conservation

through PRH Preservation, another sister nonprofit with a focus on preserving and rehabilitating older single-family housing stock. The goal of the initiative is to preserve as many row houses in the Third Ward as possible and to bring the homes into compliance with applicable codes. That year, a gift from the Houston-based Kinder Foundation underwrote PRH's acquisition and preservation of a 1.4-acre piece of property at Webster, Hadley, Nagle, and Live Oak Streets, which consists of twenty-one wood-frame structures constructed between 1930 and 1950. After the houses were renovated, the tenants who had been living there moved back in.

Lowe departed Project Row Houses around this time, and it was a "freeing moment"—the organization was doing well on its own, and he felt that his work was done there. A new executive director had been hired in 2015, and the institution was able to bring in significant funders shortly after. Effective activism needs to have an expiration date—and "that's the part to look forward to, the conclusion of the time that your work is needed," as Lowe said.[34]

Lowe continued to conduct other forms of social sculpture directly engaged with local communities (which he also pursued while at Project Row Houses, namely with the *Watts House Project* in Los Angeles from 1996–2001; *Transforma Projects* in post-Katrina New Orleans in 2005; and the Anyang Public Art Program in South Korea in 2010). His later accomplishments include 2016's *Victoria Square Project* in Athens, Greece; 2020's *Greenwood Art Project* in Tulsa, Oklahoma; and 2020–21's *Black Wall Street Journey* in Chicago. In each of these projects, Lowe conducted a dialogue with local communities and produced pragmatic solutions for the pressing issues they were facing, such as xenophobic tensions following the refugee crisis in Greece. This framework of thinking—of coming up with solutions—has become a lens to view his entire life's work. Lowe is truly a structural thinker, continually asking what it means to effect positive change in a community.

Lowe also decided to concentrate on his painting practice and participated in major exhibitions such as Documenta in 2017 and the 2022 Whitney Biennial, where he showed a painting titled *Project Row Houses: If Artists Are Creative Why Can't They Create Solutions*, 2021. His debut New York solo exhibition of paintings, *Meditations on Social Sculpture*, also opened in 2022 at Gagosian.

Today, PRH is a relatively large nonprofit, but the same questions from the early 1990s still animate its work: Who are the voices that aren't being heard? And what are their concerns? Marshella Abrams, a longtime Houstonian with generations of family in the Third Ward, told me that "although the introduction of new housing options for the community is great, the majority are financially out of range for most of the longtime residents." "Hopefully," she added, "developers and community leaders can make the historic area more equitable for many types of residents so that they can feel comfortable and still have a voice and stake in their own community."[35]

It perhaps goes without saying that another one of PRH's most pressing concerns is climate change. As I finished writing this chapter, an email arrived from the organization requesting donations to support elderly Third Ward residents who count on the nonprofit during times of crisis, including hurricanes, power outages, and soaring temperatures. "This week's hurricane has compounded the damage from the tornado in May, leaving our historic row houses with interior water damage, buckling floors, mold, and fallen trees. In addition to this, we urgently need to upgrade the generator at the Eldorado Ballroom to ensure it can serve more community members during disasters," the note states. Gentrification remains a major issue in the city and across the United States, but as more extreme weather becomes the norm, many are now wondering whether Houston will feel habitable to humans in the years to come.

10

Prescription Addiction Intervention Now, 2017–

"They were fighting for their lives. They were very well organized. They worked well together. Whatever problems they had were discussed. They knew their targets and they went after them, sometimes by creating sexy media campaigns, as we now do. The main thing is that there was a deep truth behind them."[1] That's the artist Nan Goldin in February 2020, responding to a question I'd asked her regarding the influence of the activist collective ACT UP (AIDS Coalition to Unleash Power) on PAIN (Prescription Addiction Intervention Now), an advocacy group she founded in late 2017. I was particularly curious how ACT UP New York, the "mother ship" chapter, which was founded in 1987, had guided her organizing. What were the parallels between ACT UP's direct response to the institutionalized homophobia that greatly intensified the AIDS crisis and now?

"PAIN began from my learning about the Sacklers' involvement with the opioid crisis through Patrick Radden Keefe's article in the *New Yorker*," Goldin explained first.[2] She knew of the philanthropic Sackler family through the art world, but learned through the 2017 story that they own the private company Purdue Pharma, the maker of OxyContin—a drug that has caused profound human suffering and at least $35 billion in sales. At the time, Goldin herself was in recovery, after nearly dying from an overdose related to her OxyContin addiction, which developed after she was prescribed the drug following an injury. She spent two months in treatment in rural Massachusetts and while there she realized that, once again, she was witnessing a generation being wiped out by a plague—that people were dying from governmental neglect.

She decided to react. "Becoming an activist has been more important to me than propelling my art career," she told me. And while Goldin's art practice is not the subject of this chapter, some key features of it are worth unpacking, as they foreshadow her activism.

Goldin never set out to make political art, but politics have always been in her art. Born in 1953 in Washington, DC, perhaps her most revered work is the profoundly emotional forty-five-minute slideshow and accompanying book *The Ballad of Sexual Dependency* (1986). The piece documents post-Stonewall gay subculture with a focus on Goldin's family and friends. The people in her photographs are fabulous, self-destructive, sexy, and sexual creatures. Some are outcasts while others appear nearly mythic. Several of her *Ballad* subjects had passed away by the 1990s, lost either to a drug overdose or to HIV/AIDS (including her beloved Greer Lankton and Cookie Mueller). Goldin's desire to make the work was driven by the need to remember these exemplary subjects from her "tribe," or chosen family. Taking pictures was a way for her to keep her friends constantly in mind, almost as a form of activist remembering.

So, it was "an incredible irony," as Goldin has said, to learn that her art had intertwined with Sackler funding to major institutions.[3] The Tate, which had received a total of £4 million from Sackler family trusts over several years, bought the slideshow of *The Ballad of Sexual Dependency* in 2015, when she was addicted to OxyContin. Goldin spent some of the fees she received from the sale on buying the drug from dealers, since doctors would no longer prescribe it to her.

By the time I spoke with Goldin, PAIN had already led a series of successful protests in international museums, typically on corporate-sponsored free days—including at the Arthur M.

Sackler Gallery in Washington, DC (April 2018), the Guggenheim in New York (February 2019), the Louvre in Paris (July 2019), and the Victoria and Albert Museum in London (November 2019). PAIN targeted these major institutions, in the same way that ACT UP protested in specific locations, for a reason—a *deep truth*.

Like the Tate, these museums had taken donations from the Sacklers. Goldin knew how this "artwashing" on the Sacklers' behalf came with contractual obligations, specifically naming rights to galleries. Consequently, PAIN effectively lobbied these institutions with two reasonable and attainable goals: to urge them to refuse the family's money and to remove the Sackler name from public spaces.

For each protest, PAIN took a direct cue from ACT UP's media-savvy actions, such as Seize Control of the FDA, which took place in Rockville, Maryland, on October 11, 1988, and was the first major victory for the AIDS activism movement. As discussed, this was not your usual "rally," with people marching, picketing, or listening to speakers at a symbolic location, such as the White House. Members of ACT UP, led by the artist Gregg Bordowitz and the attorney David Barr, developed a new way of thinking about protest, and a savvier way of dealing with the media. Over several months of teach-ins, regional ACT UP groups together conceived of a specific event to call out the FDA for better access to experimental drugs. More than a thousand activists attended this debut national mobilization. Affinity groups were tasked with doing small, independent actions—one crew appeared in white lab coats with bloody handprints on their chests, while another held a die-in, with cardboard gravestones. ACT UP members broke into the FDA building; 178 were arrested.

"I watched ACT UP become huge," Goldin recalled, adding:

> I wasn't really a member. I went to a few meetings and protests. But the important thing was that there was a lot of photography going on showing AIDS victims, as in Nicholas Nixon's work,

> which the community of people living with AIDS hated. They supported the work I was doing around the crisis. They told me that, and it was very important to me that I was working in parallel on some level.[4]

Goldin had attended Queer Nation die-ins in the early 1990s during Pride and other demonstrations. "I realized over the next couple of years that die-ins are a lot more effective when they're silent or have a drummer," she said. "It's much deeper and more mournful. At first, we were screaming and lying on the ground, and it seemed a little weird. But you learn as you go along."[5]

Readers will remember that in 1989, Goldin organized one of the first New York exhibitions about AIDS, *Witnesses: Against Our Vanishing* at Artists Space. While she wasn't too involved in ACT UP, she was aware of its strategies, such as pre-publicity and prepping spokespeople. ACT UP knew how to speak through the media, not to the media. Nearly thirty years later, PAIN would do this too. Like ACT UP, the group embraced an experience-based agenda—taking on issues urgent to those with opioid addiction. PAIN held Wednesday night meetings in Goldin's Brooklyn apartment, where they planned their ambitious events, and organized via encrypted phone apps outside of meetings. During gatherings, members discussed logistics for their direct actions, including email blasts to the press, securing photographers, supplies, and banners. They then had other meetings to assemble their protest props, such as putting fake OxyContin labels on orange prescription pill bottles—a prop that for many in the group was imbued with a kind of sacredness and referred to the dead. PAIN member Harry Cullen has pointed out that in these meetings Goldin consistently came back to the idea that the protests "had to be beautiful."[6]

Goldin may have had David Wojnarowicz in mind. In his work, he paralleled the body with its fragility, while always insisting on the importance and the necessity of beauty. The artist and fierce pussy member Zoe Leonard once recalled showing Wojnarowicz, at the height of the AIDS crisis, her photographs of clouds. She worried her work was too subtle, abstract, and apolitical on the surface. "I remember showing those pictures to David and talking things over with him and he said—I'm paraphrasing—*Don't give up on beauty.* We're fighting so that we can have things like this, so that we can have beauty again," Leonard said.[7]

From the start, PAIN members Alex Kwartler and Clare Carter filmed and recorded its meetings and protests. "So many of our protests were framed around the idea that the imagery—the video footage—would outlive it," Cullen noted.[8] Some of this footage is featured in Laura Poitras's documentary portrait of Nan Goldin, *All the Beauty and the Bloodshed*, which premiered on September 3, 2022, at the 79th Venice International Film Festival, where it was awarded the Golden Lion. The film has been instrumental in sparking dialogue across the world on harm reduction.

To date, PAIN has deployed key strategies such as the die-in, ACT UP's signature tactic, in which protesters feign mass death. PAIN centered on this tactic because, as Cullen said, it "communicates the gravity of the issue and brings the reality of death into the wings of the museums that were profiting from it."[9]

The die-in stems from a long history of activism in the United States that has made the body the central point of protest. Think, for example, of the February 1, 1960, Greensboro sit-in, when African American students from A&T State University convened at a segregated Woolworth's lunch counter in Greensboro, North Carolina, and refused to leave after being denied service. Think also of the lie-in as a popular protest tactic against the Vietnam War. On November 14, 1969, nearly 3,000 people with black and white balloons stretched out on sodden

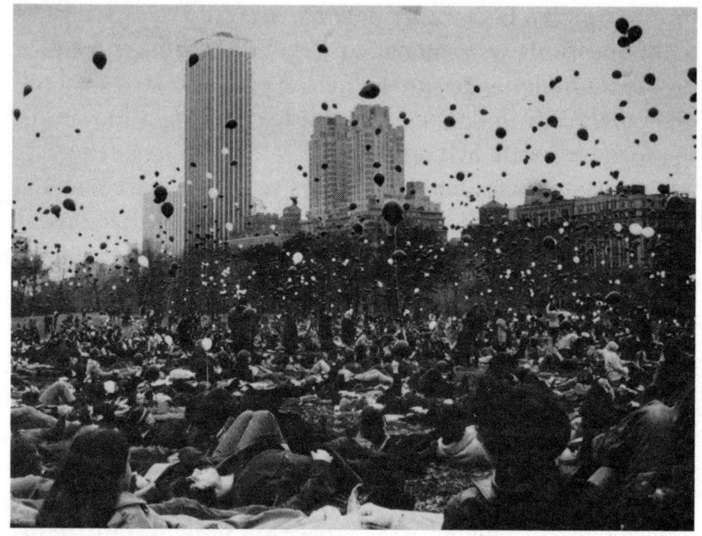

"Lie-in" protest of the Vietnam War in Central Park, November 14, 1969. Photo: J. Spencer Jones.

turf in Central Park's Sheep Meadow, while drums rolled and "Taps"—a bugle call often heard at military funerals—was played on a trumpet.

The term *die-in* began showing up in US newspapers in 1970.[10] It was perhaps first used in an article by the *Harvard Crimson* on March 6, 1970, regarding a protest being organized by Boston environmentalists to mark the first Earth Day on April 22, 1970.[11] On that day, a few dozen people, some with makeshift coffins, faked their deaths in front of ticket counters at Logan International Airport to raise awareness of pollution. According to reporter Jeremy S. Bluhm, "The coffins were placed in the middle of the lobby, and a demonstrator climbed into each one, while other students lay prone on the floor nearby. Many of the demonstrators were wearing gauze facemasks."[12] The protest was called "a festival of death."

The Black Lives Matter (BLM) movement began to stage die-ins beginning in 2014 and they quickly became an important protest strategy. Philosopher José Medina has connected these to the historical precedent initiated by ACT UP and has focused on the act of public testimony that the die-in offers: "In both cases the die-ins constitute a dramatic collective testimony of the massive losses of a community while the rest of society and its institutions remain unresponsive and unconcerned," he writes. And "in both cases the testimony is radical because it resists social and institutional silences while aiming to uproot insensitivity and to create new forms of social sensibility and responsiveness."[13]

However, unlike their precedents, BLM die-ins often commemorate the death of specific individuals: Michael Brown, Eric Garner, Breonna Taylor, George Floyd, and too many others. In 2014, the year Brown was murdered by the police, protesters across the United States remained on the ground for four and a half minutes to reference the amount of time his body lay in the street after he was killed in Ferguson, Missouri.

The die-in offers something different than a march or picket line—specifically for the camera. It often creates an image that transcends the protest, and the materials used therein, while creating a piercing emotional effect. As the historian Daniel Ross notes, "The die-in is attention-grabbing, inexpensive, and easy to organize using social media: the perfect protest for the Internet age."[14] Typically, the die-in involves the takeover of a noted public place with enough room for protesters to spread out, perhaps with props such as coffins or tombstones. These protests are sometimes silent—often to great dramatic effect, as Goldin noted—since that is where their shock value and relation to performance resides, particularly when limp protesters are carried out hastily by the police. But sometimes they are loud, with shouted slogans and singing, as the point, of course, is to educate the public and to make manifest a healthy tradition of dissent.

PAIN's debut—and most notable—die-in occurred at 4:00 p.m. in the Sackler Wing of the Metropolitan Museum of

Art on March 10, 2018. (In 1974, the Sackler family donated $3.5 million toward the new wing's construction.) That Saturday, as some demonstrators unfurled banners that read SHAME ON SACKLER and FUND REHAB, a hundred or so others laid down on the floor, positioned like corpses to reflect the death toll of OxyContin. They chanted "Sacklers Lie! Thousands Die!" and called on the family to fund rehab and education programs. Members of the press who had been tipped off to the event snapped photos and captured video. Later, the activists tossed 1,000 orange OxyContin prescription pill bottles, which they labeled "prescribed to you by the Sackler family, major donors of the Met"—into the reflecting pool that surrounds the Ancient Egyptian Temple of Dendur. After being escorted out of the museum by security, Goldin turned to face the museum and shouted, "We'll be back!"

There have been many victories (and arrests) for the group since then. As a result of the Louvre protest, the institution removed the Sackler family name from wall placards in the Oriental Antiquities gallery, formerly the Sackler Wing of

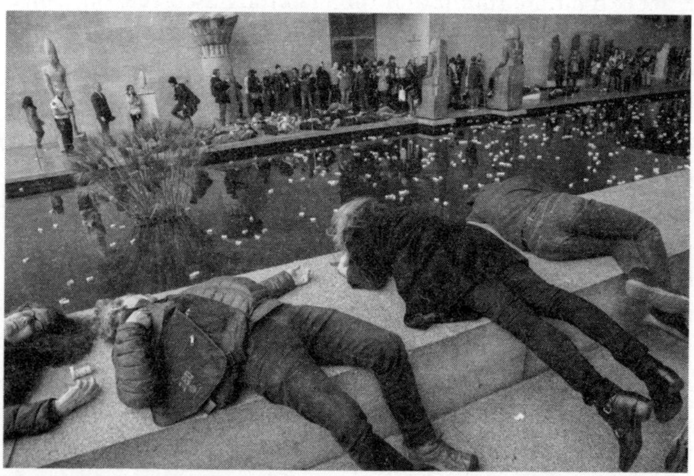

Metropolitan Museum of Art die-in, photo: J. C. Bourcart, March 10, 2018. Courtesy of PAIN.

Oriental Antiquities. Beginning in 2019, other major museums and galleries began to reject support from the Sackler Trust UK, including the National Portrait Gallery and the Tate. For another spectacular surprise protest, this time on a Saturday night at the Guggenheim—in response to the Sackler's support of the museum and its Sackler Center for Arts Education—PAIN activists released a cascading flurry of 8,000 fake OxyContin prescriptions inscribed on white pieces of paper from the upper levels of the museum's rotunda before unfurling banners and staging a die-in.

This action referenced a chilling sentiment that Richard Sackler reportedly stated upon the launch of OxyContin, that "the prescription blizzard will be so deep, dense, and white." The fake prescriptions included excerpts from communication between top Purdue executives, including members of the Sacklers, about how to increase sales of the drug and the likelihood that it would be abused. PAIN also created fake museum brochures for this protest, which were "a little bit blasphemous," as Cullen said. At the time of the protest, the famed Hilma af Klint exhibition, *Paintings for the Future*, was on view, a show that brought the museum its highest-recorded attendance. Over "one of the big circles on her pieces, I plastered a big Oxy pill," Cullen added.[15]

The Guggenheim is, of course, one of the most beautiful places to hold a protest, and there are many images to prove it. On May 1, 1971, members of the Art Workers' Coalition protested the last-minute cancellation of Hans Haacke's solo exhibition at the museum. The museum's director, Thomas Messer, had opposed showing Haacke's work *Shapolsky et al. Manhattan Real Estate Holdings, A Real-Time Social System, as of May 1, 1971* (1971)—a piece that went on to become a paradigm of a politically engaged art. Demonstrators gathered in picket lines outside the museum, while inside other protesters threw papers from the rotunda reading "Messer Makes a Mess."

Forty-three years later, the artist-led collective Global Ultra Luxury Faction (G.U.L.F.) staged a protest at the museum to draw attention to ongoing human rights violations in Abu Dhabi. Thousands of migrant laborers from South Asia were building a massive complex of condos and cultural centers—including a new branch of the Guggenheim, slated to open in 2025—on an artificial landmass there called Saadiyat (Happiness) Island while working under objectionable labor conditions, or "modern-day slavery," as one report put it.

On March 29, 2014, during a busy "pay-what-you-will" night at the institution, the group released 9,000 "1% bills" of fake currency that fluttered down the spiral rotunda from the fifth floor. Each note, meticulously designed by Noah Fisher, was illustrated with a drawing of the Guggenheim's planned new branch. "As bemused visitors puzzled over the bills, and as activists distributed agitational pamphlets, embedded journalists fanned throughout the crowd scribbling notes, taking pictures, and sending tweets," Yates McKee has written, adding, "Museum guards, aided by a phalanx of police officers, emptied the museum of visitors and shut the building down."[16] The action was well planned and well documented. G.U.L.F. member Nitasha Dhillon noted that it was inspired by Abbie Hoffman's 1967 intervention at the New York Stock Exchange, where he orchestrated the dumping of dollar bills in the middle of the trading floor.

PAIN's protests have not always occurred in suave and beautiful sites, but they have been effective and often involve other groups. On August 9, 2021, PAIN organized a die-in while protesting the ongoing and frustrating summer 2021 Sackler settlement hearings. (These began in 2019, when the Sacklers proposed to settle all litigation for $3 billion using a bankruptcy maneuver to protect them from civil claims related to the opioid epidemic, an offer rejected by attorneys general in twenty-six states.) Along with members from the nonprofit harm reduction organization Truth Pharm, a coalition of survivors and advocacy groups working in response to the overdose crisis, PAIN activists demonstrated outside of the United States Bankruptcy Court in White Plains, New York. In 2019, the Sacklers transferred Purdue's headquarters from Connecticut to White Plains so that they could file for bankruptcy in the district of corporate-friendly Judge Robert Drain, one of the only judges in the country known to grant liability releases to private owners—which he did for the Sacklers on September 1, 2021, by yielding them immunity from getting sued in civil lawsuits related to opioid deaths in exchange for contributing payments amounting to $4.5 billion of their personal wealth. After a year of feeling constrained by the Covid pandemic, this was a major blow to the movement.

By the end of 2021, however, it became clear that the bankruptcy proceedings would not be the final chapter in the Sackler's saga. Through coalition building—with groups such as Vocal New York, Housing Works, ACT UP NY, the Center for Popular Democracy, and the North Carolina Survivors Union—the activists began to win. Three nearly back-to-back events made for a thrilling and hopeful end to another miserable pandemic year. On November 22, the state of New York officially shut down the corrupt practice of judge-shopping (filing numerous lawsuits for the same claim to increase the likelihood of a favorable outcome) for mega corporations. "While we're frustrated this didn't take effect during the Purdue bankruptcy," PAIN noted on Instagram, "we're glad that we took to the streets to demand this important structural change."

Then, on December 9, 2021, the Metropolitan Museum of Art and the Sackler family announced in a joint PR announcement that the Sackler's name would be removed from seven exhibition spaces, including the Sackler Wing. The Met had already severed financial ties with the Sacklers in May 2019, but this moment of removing their name was a real victory.

Patrick Radden Keefe—author of the *New Yorker* story about the Sacklers and the book *Empire of Pain* (2021), which extensively chronicles the family—reported the day after the Met's news broke that a group of more than seventy artists had pressured the museum's board of trustees to end its association with the Sacklers. In a letter dated November 3, 2021, the artists wrote that the museum "is a public institution dedicated to art, learning and knowledge . . . Honoring the Sackler name on the walls of the Met erodes the Met's relationship with artists and the public." They pointed out that "last year, Purdue Pharma, the makers of OxyContin, pled guilty in federal court to three criminal conspiracy charges," adding:

> They admitted that they defrauded the United States government, lied to the Drug Enforcement Agency, and violated federal anti-kickback laws—paying providers to prescribe more of Purdue's products. The company also pled guilty to federal criminal charges in 2007, as did the company's President, Chief Legal Officer and former Chief Medical Officer.

Clearly it was hard to argue with that.

Finally, on December 16, 2021, Judge Colleen McMahon overturned the Purdue settlement from September, declaring that it should not move forward because it releases the Sacklers from liability in civil opioid-related cases. The ruling was yet another major blow to the family, and a triumph for PAIN's calculated warpath.

There are two galleries at the Met that to date still bear the Sackler names—those of the "good" Sacklers such as Elizabeth A. Sackler, for example, who claims she has not made any money from sales of OxyContin and has come out in support of protests (including PAIN's) against her uncles' company. However, as it's made clear in *Empire of Pain*, her father, Arthur M. Sackler, was the mastermind behind the marketing model used to sell the drug. One captivating aspect of the book is the false divide the family seems to assume between the "Valium Sacklers" and the "Oxy Sacklers": Arthur M. Sackler developed the tranquilizer Valium and the advertising for it, but he died before OxyContin was introduced by Purdue.

For some people, including Goldin, the entire Sackler-Purdue clan is evil, while for others, exceptions can and should be made. I tend to agree with Goldin—they're a dynasty of billionaires who have ultimately profited from mass death: Almost half a million people died from opioid overdoses, including prescription and illicit opioids, from 1999 to 2019, according to the Centers for Disease Control and Prevention. This public health emergency became much worse during the Covid-19 pandemic—the result of lost access to treatment, rising mental health problems, and wider availability of dangerously potent street drugs.

To finally see the Sackler name removed from the entrance of one of the Met's most iconic spaces was astounding. As Radden Keefe notes, the boards of many organizations who still list the Sackler name in their buildings "have been watching the Met to see how the museum would react. As long as the Met did nothing, inertia might have seemed like a viable option."[17] In May 2022, the Guggenheim Museum and the National Gallery in London removed the Sackler's name from their walls. Protests continued at institutions that had not followed suit: In April 2023, approximately 100 Harvard students and PAIN activists participated in a surprise die-in at the school's Arthur M. Sackler Museum, one day after a screening of *All the Beauty and the Bloodshed* on campus. Nearly five years earlier, PAIN had protested in the same place, as footage in the film shows. "It takes very little time for Harvard to name a building after a corrupt billionaire, but a long time to take it down," Anna Correll, one of the students at the protest, told *Hyperallergic*.[18]

A similarly slow process elongated the Sackler's settlement case. In May 2023, a federal appeals court overturned Judge Colleen McMahon's December 2021 ruling. The case was then

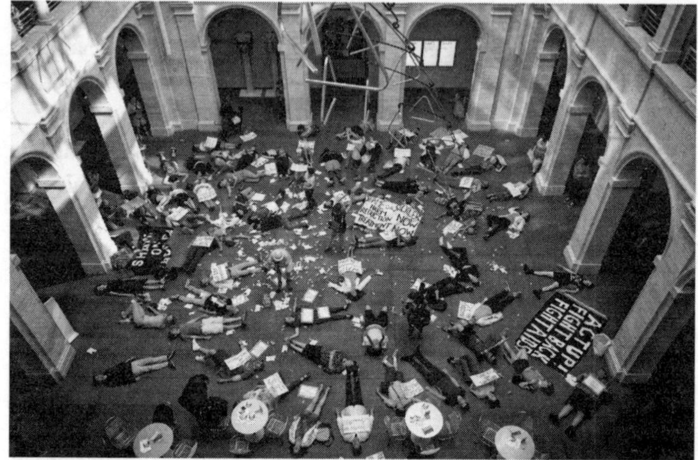

Harvard Art Museum die-in, photo: Tamara Rodriguez, July 24, 2018. Courtesy of PAIN.

taken up by the US Supreme Court. With Truth Pharm and the Center for Popular Democracy, PAIN protested outside of the court as oral arguments were heard in December 2023, and passionately demanded accountability for the Sackler's crimes. Demonstrators pointed out that the Sacklers are, of course, not bankrupt—that they have moved money to off-shore accounts—and that their proposed abuse of bankruptcy code is an escape hatch for the ultra-rich, the precedent of which could invite a flood of corporate malpractice.

On June 27, 2024, the court ruled that members of the Sackler family cannot be shielded from liability for civil claims related to the opioid epidemic. Almost echoing PAIN, Justice Neil M. Gorsuch wrote in the 5–4 decision, "The Sacklers have not filed for bankruptcy and have not placed virtually all their assets on the table for distribution to creditors, yet they seek what essentially amounts to a discharge."[19] This was another major win for PAIN, as it stopped the possibility of releasing the Sacklers from further accountability over the opioid crisis, even though it also ensured that urgently sought money would not be going toward victims, states, and tribes, among others, anytime soon. This moment in the political world was something of a crescendo in PAIN's history, akin, in the media world, to *All the Beauty and the Bloodshed*'s nomination for Best Documentary Feature at the Academy Awards (though it did not win). It will be interesting to see where the group goes from those heights.

Through all their efforts, PAIN has become a ground zero for addiction-related activism and direct-action campaigns, in ways adjacent to ACT UP—chiefly because they identified specific goals and didn't give up until change happened. The group might not have been able to meet their objectives without the star power of a major artist; most, though certainly not all, political collectives need a fierce leader with integrity who can withstand a tidal wave of institutional power. The public-facing testimony interwoven throughout Goldin's art and activism cannot be underscored enough, and it also comes through clearly in the collective's voice. As PAIN has written: "Our victories are cumulative, no matter how disparate. If we continue naming names, we continue building power. Whoever we struggle against, we must use our position as artists to tear open the void and show others the way out."[20]

To quote the firebrand Wojnarowicz one last time: "Isn't that great? It means the control of information has a crack in its wall."[21] PAIN has not only opened that crack, but, more importantly, allowed others to walk through it.

Notes

Introduction

1 Richard F. Shepard, "Drawing Class at Tombs Eases Pent-Up Emotions," *New York Times*, November 16, 1971.
2 Audre Lorde, "The Uses of Anger," *Women's Studies Quarterly* 9: 3, 1981, 9.
3 WAR member Jacqueline Skiles once asked, "'Permanent revolution'—is it possible?" "Addendum: Some Notes on Our Founding and HerStory," in Women Artists in Revolution, *A Documentary HerStory of Women Artists in Revolution* (Pittsburgh: Women's Interart Center, 1973), 74. Reprinted by Primary Information (New York) in 2021.
4 Faith Ringgold, "The 1970s: Is There a Women's Art?," in *We Flew over the Bridge: The Memoirs of Faith Ringgold* (Durham, NC: Duke University Press, 2005), 167.
5 "Preserving Guerilla Television," University of California Berkeley Art Museum & Pacific Film Archive, guerrillatv.bampfa.berkeley.edu.
6 Lauren O'Neill-Butler, "Faith Ringgold on the Making of Her Retrospective," March 4, 2022, artforum.com.
7 Margaret Talbot, "Faces of an Epidemic," *New Yorker*, October 30, 2017.
8 Wojnarowicz interview in Laura Poitras (dir.), *All the Beauty and the Bloodshed* (Neon: 2022).
9 Nan Goldin interview with the author, February 11, 2020.
10 "Statement by X12, Group show of 12 women artists beginning Jan. 27 at Museum 729 Broadway," Sabra Moore NYC Women's Art Movement Collection, 1969–1996; Box 1 and Folder 1; Barnard Archives and Special Collections, Barnard College.

1. The Jacket

1 The former president was advised by Dr. Anthony Fauci, who became director of the National Institute of Allergy and Infectious Diseases in 1984. He encouraged Reagan to act swiftly.

2 For more on viral modes of cultural production and physical epidemic, see Gregg Bordowitz, *General Idea: Imagevirus* (Cambridge: Afterall Books, 2010).
3 Nan Goldin (curator), *Witnesses: Against Our Vanishing* (New York: Artists Space, 1989), 11.
4 Burroughs once compared Wojnarowicz to François Villon, poet of "the outcast, the thief, the whore."
5 Maddie Sofia, "Coronavirus and Racism Are Dual Public Health Emergencies, Interview with David R. Williams," Short Wave, National Public Radio, June 5, 2020.
6 Avram Finkelstein, Queer Social Spaces and COVID-19, UC Press Blog, June 5, 2020.
7 Deborah Solomon, "Lessons from Robert Gober, Anxious Homebody," *New York Times*, May 31, 2020.
8 Douglas Crimp, "Seize Control of the FDA," AIDS Demo Graphics (Seattle: Bay Press, 1990), 76.
9 Zoe Leonard, ACT UP Oral History Project, interview with Sarah Schulman, January 13, 2010.
10 Dr. Fauci's work on the regulation of the human immune system was credited with helping to reveal how the HIV virus destroys the body. He led clinical trials for zidovudine (aka AZT), the first antiretroviral drug to treat AIDS.
11 Paul Duggan, "1,000 Swarm FDA's Rockville Office to Demand Approval of AIDS Drugs," *Washington Post*, October 11, 1988.
12 Douglas Crimp, "Before Occupy: How AIDS Activists Seized Control of the FDA in 1988," *Atlantic*, December 6, 2011.

2. Women Artists in Revolution, 1969–71

1 Lucy R. Lippard, "Biting the Hand: Artists and Museums in New York since 1969," in *Alternative Art New York, 1965–1985*, ed. Julie Ault; published in collaboration with The Drawing Center, New York (Minneapolis: University of Minnesota Press, 2002), 95.
2 Women Students and Artists for Black Art Liberation (WSABAL) was formed in May 1970 in response to "Afro-American Artists: New York and Boston," curated by Edmund Barry Gaither for the Museum of Fine Arts, Boston, and School of the Museum of Fine Arts. It was a show of seventy-two artists, nine of which were women. WSABAL was involved with several more protests—notably against the Art Strike's *"Liberated" American Pavilion Venice Biennale* exhibition in 1970, and they also advocated for the creation of the Martin Luther King, Jr. Wing at the Museum of Modern Art.
3 See, for example, Julia Bryan-Wilson, *Art Workers: Radical Practice*

in the Vietnam War Era (Berkeley: University of California Press, 2009).

4 Lippard, "Biting the Hand," in *Alternative Art New York, 1965–1985*, 84.

5 Lucy R. Lippard, "The Art Workers' Coalition: Not a History," in *Get the Message? A Decade of Art for Social Change* (New York: E. P. Dutton, 1984), 11–12.

6 Jacqueline Skiles, "The National Art Workers' Community: Still Struggling," *Art Journal* 34: 4 (1975), 320. doi.org/10.2307/775913.

7 Julie Ault, "A Chronology of Selected Alternative Structures, Spaces, Artists' Groups, and Organizations in New York City, 1965–1985," in *Alternative Art New York*, 21.

8 Lippard, "Biting the Hand," in *Alternative Art New York, 1965–1985*, 98.

9 Juliette Gordon, "The History of Our WAR from Beginnings to Today or, Life Under Fire in the Art World Dear Workers, *Manhattan Tribune*, May 2, 1970, in *A Documentary HerStory of Women Artists in Revolution* (Pittsburgh: Women's Interart Center, 1973), 2. Reprinted by Primary Information (New York) in 2021.

10 Ibid.

11 Sabra Moore interview with the author, March 26, 2024.

12 Muriel Castanis, "Preface to the Revised Edition," in *A Documentary HerStory of Women Artists in Revolution*, iii.

13 A February 1970 solicitation flier by WAR, in *A Documentary HerStory of Women Artists in Revolution*, 4.

14 Gordon, "The History of Our WAR," in *A Documentary HerStory of Women Artists in Revolution*.

15 Sabra Moore interview with the author, March 26, 2024.

16 Betsy Jones and John Szarkowski, "Report on meeting with the Women's Committee of the AWC," in *A Documentary HerStory of Women Artists in Revolution*, 21.

17 Therese Schwartz, "Confusion to the Met!," *The New York Element*, November 1970, in *A Documentary HerStory of Women Artists in Revolution*, 62.

18 Gordon, "The History of Our WAR," in *A Documentary HerStory of Women Artists in Revolution*, 2.

19 Sabra Moore, *Openings: A Memoir from the Women's Art Movement, New York City, 1970–1992* (New York: New Village Press, 2016).

20 Letter from Stephen E. Weil to Dolores Holmes, June 18, 1970, in *A Documentary HerStory of Women Artists in Revolution*, 28.

21 Ibid.

22 Castanis, "Preface to the Revised Edition," in *A Documentary HerStory of Women Artists in Revolution*, iii.

23 Poppy Johnson interview with the author, July 24, 2023.

24 Therese Schwartz, "50%—No Joke," *New York Element*, November 1970, in *A Documentary HerStory of Women Artists in Revolution*, 29.
25 Letter from Stephen E. Weil to Lucy R. Lippard, October 19, 1970, in *A Documentary HerStory of Women Artists in Revolution*, 31.
26 Ibid.
27 Faith Ringgold, "The 1970s: Is There a Women's Art?," in *We Flew Over the Bridge: The Memoirs of Faith Ringgold* (Durham, NC: Duke University Press, 2005), 178.
28 Brenda Miller interview with the author, August 4, 2023.
29 Jan van Raay interview with the author, December 21, 2023.
30 Letter from Poppy Johnson, Lucy R. Lippard, Brenda Miller, and Faith Ringgold, For the Ad Hoc Committee of Women Artists to Stephen E. Weil, November 9, 1970, in *A Documentary HerStory of Women Artists in Revolution*, 33.
31 Poppy Johnson interview with the author, July 24, 2023.
32 Lucy R. Lippard, *Stuff: Instead of a Memoir* (New York: New Village Press, 2023), 65.
33 Schwartz, "50%—No Joke," in *A Documentary HerStory of Women Artists in Revolution*, 29.
34 Grace Glueck, "Women Artists Demonstrate at the Whitney," *New York Times*, December 12, 1970.
35 Lippard, *Stuff*, 64.
36 Ringgold, "The 1970s: Is There a Women's Art?," in *We Flew over the Bridge*, 180.
37 Glueck, "Women Artists Demonstrate at the Whitney."
38 Correspondence with Joyce Kozloff, June 24, 2024.
39 Julia Bryan-Wilson, *Art Workers: Radical Practice in the Vietnam War Era* (Berkeley: University of California Press, 2009), 160.
40 Brenda Miller interview with the author, August 4, 2023.
41 Julie Ault, "Chronology," in *Alternative Art New York*, 28.
42 Jacqueline Skiles interview with the author, July 25, 2023.
43 Ibid.
44 Laurie Johnston, "Women Activism Turns to Alternatives in Arts," *New York Times*, March 21, 1973.
45 Nathan Tempey, "Urban Removal: How a Utopian Vision for Hell's Kitchen Burned Out." *Gothamist*, September 20, 2016.
46 Adrienne Rich, "Living the Revolution," *The Women's Review of Books* 3: 12, September 1986, 3.
47 Howardena Pindell interview with the author. Published in *November* vol. 0, September 2020, novembermag.com.
48 Poppy Johnson interview with the author, July 24, 2023. For more on the FBI's infiltration, see Letty Cottin Pogrebin, "The FBI Was Watching You," *Ms.*, June 1977, 42.

49 Michele Wallace interviewed by Mary Lodu, *The Third Rail Quarterly* 9, November 2016.

3. The Black Emergency Cultural Coalition, 1969–82

1 Heather Ann Thompson, *Blood in the Water: The Attica Prison Uprising of 1971 and Its Legacy* (New York: Vintage Books, 2016), 28.

2 Donald Noble, Peter Butler, Frank Lott, Carl Jones-El, and Herbert Blyden X., "The Attica Liberation Faction Manifesto of Demands and Anti-Depression Platform (1971)," *Race and Class* 53: 2 (2011), 28–35.

3 Most accounts of the BECC focus on its work until 1971, including its protests of the Met's *Harlem on My Mind* and the Whitney Museum of American Art's *Contemporary Black Artists in America* from 1970 to 1971. To name a few examples: Bridget Cooks, *Exhibiting Blackness: African Americans and the American Art Museum* (Amherst: University of Massachusetts Press, 2011); Caroline V. Wallace, "Exhibiting Authenticity: The Black Emergency Cultural Coalition's Protests of the Whitney Museum of American Art, 1968–71," *Art Journal* 74: 2, Summer 2015, 5–23; Susan E. Cahan, *Mounting Frustration: The Art Museum in the Age of Black Power* (Durham, NC: Duke University Press, 2016); and Howard Singerman and Sarah Watson, *Acts of Art and Rebuttal in 1971* (New York: Hunter College Art Galleries, 2018). The latter is a catalog accompanying an excellent exhibition held at Hunter in 2018.

4 Aruna D'Souza, *Whitewalling: Art, Race & Protest in 3 Acts* (New York: Badlands Unlimited, 2018), 128.

5 Grace Glueck, "Art Notes: Into the Mainstream, Everybody," *New York Times*, D24, June 15, 1969.

6 Howard Singerman, "Rebuttal and Representation," in *Acts of Art and Rebuttal in 1971*, 11.

7 Black Emergency Cultural Coalition records, Schomburg Center for Research in Black Culture, The New York Public Library, box 2, folder 13.

8 Ibid.

9 Ibid.

10 Mimi Poser, "Art in the Prisons, 1973," interview with Mary Bardsley, Katherine Colin, Barbara Jakobson, Benny Andrews, and Cliff Joseph, Guggenheim Museum, New York: guggenheim.org/audio/track/art-in-the-prisons-1973. Last accessed September 13, 2023.

11 Ibid.

12 Richard F. Shepard, "Drawing Class at Tombs Eases Pent-Up Emotions," *New York Times*, November 16, 1971.
13 Jo Ann Whatley, "Art Lives in Tombs," *New York Amsterdam News*, January 22, 1971.
14 "May Stevens in Conversation" in Patricia Hill, *May Stevens* (Warwick: Pomegranate Europe, 2005), 33.
15 Michele Wallace, "A Women's Prison and the Movement," *Invisibility Blues* (New York: Verso, 1990), 45. See also Faith Ringgold, *For the Women's House, 1971*: faithringgold.com.
16 Michele Wallace interviewed by Mary Lodu, *The Third Rail Quarterly*, issue 9, November 2016.
17 Julie Ault, "A Chronology of Selected Alternative Structures, Spaces, Artists' Groups, and Organizations in New York City, 1965–1985," *Alternative Art New York, 1965–1985*, ed. Julie Ault; published in collaboration with The Drawing Center, New York (Minneapolis: University of Minnesota Press, 2002), 20.
18 Vivian Browne interview with James Hatch and Camille Billops. March 31, 1972. Oral History Interview with Vivian Browne (Part 1). Oral history, Archives & Special Collections at the City College of New York (CCNY).
19 Camille Billops interview with James Hatch, June 2, 1973. Oral History Interview with Camille Billops (Part 1). Oral history, Archives & Special Collections at the City College of New York (CCNY).
20 Benny Andrews studio journal, June 28, 1970, page 142, entry 894. Benny Andrews Estate.
21 "Camille Billops," Ryan Lee Gallery: ryanleegallery.com.
22 Vivian Browne interview with James Hatch and Camille Billops, March 31, 1972.
23 Ibid.
24 Benny Andrews and Rudolf Baranik, eds. *The Attica Book* (South Hackensack, NJ: Custom Communications System, 1972).
25 Ringgold, "The 1970s: Is There a Women's Art?," in *We Flew Over the Bridge: The Memoirs of Faith Ringgold* (Durham, NC: Duke University Press, 2005), 189.
26 E. C. Feiss, "The Contemporary Arts of Attica," Blank Forms, August 8, 2022: blankforms.org, last accessed September 13, 2023.
27 Joseph et al., "Letters," *Artforum International* 11: 10, 1972, 8–9: artforum.com/print/197306/letters-73439.
28 Ibid.
29 Nicole Fleetwood, *Marking Time: Art in the Age of Mass Incarceration* (Cambridge, MA: Harvard University Press, 2020), 163.
30 Ibid.

31 Poser, "Art in the Prisons, 1973."
32 Andrews quoted in "Black Emergency Coalition Teaches in Prisons," *Art Workers News* 5: 19, February–March, 1976.
33 Anna Riley-Hiscox, "Interview—Cliff Joseph: Art Therapist, Pioneer, Artist," *Art Therapy* 14: 4, 1997, 277.
34 Lee Bernstein, *America Is the Prison: Art and Politics in Prisons in the 1970s* (Chapel Hill: University of North Carolina Press, 2010), 7.
35 George Goodman Jr., "Tombs Art Show: Life and Fantasy," *New York Times*, February 8, 1973.
36 Mimi Poser, "Tombs Art Show, 1973," Guggenheim Museum, New York: guggenheim.org/finding-aids/file/tombs-art-show-mimi-poser-benny-andrews-2. Last accessed September 13, 2023.
37 Black Emergency Cultural Coalition records, Schomburg Center for Research in Black Culture, The New York Public Library, box 2, folder 9.
38 Ibid.
39 Black Emergency Cultural Coalition records, Schomburg Center for Research in Black Culture, The New York Public Library, box 2, folder 10.
40 Andrews quoted in "Forum: What's the Assessment of Prison Art Programs After a Decade?" *American Artist* 45: 464, March 1981, 73.
41 Ibid., 74.
42 Ronald G. King, "Art and the Ex-Con," *BECC Newsletter*, 1980, 18.
43 "Honor Roll of Teachers," *BECC Newsletter*, 1980, 23.
44 Nene Humphrey interview with the author, September 2, 2022.
45 Black Emergency Cultural Coalition records, Schomburg Center for Research in Black Culture, The New York Public Library, box 1, folder 18.
46 Alexandra C. Anderson, "Art from the Inside," *Art in America*, March 1973, 14.
47 Nene Humphrey interview with the author, September 2, 2022. The formal closure of the BECC is not documented in the Black Emergency Cultural Coalition records at the Schomburg Center for Research in Black Culture, The New York Public Library.
48 Tomie Arai in "Godzilla Roundtable," *November* magazine, no. 25, 2021.
49 Godzilla letter to David Ross, September 28, 1991, in *Godzilla: Asian American Arts Network, 1990–2001* (New York: Primary Information), 101.

4. Top Value Television, 1972–79

1 "Making the Scene," *Newsweek*, July 24, 1972.
2 See *Signals: How Video Transformed the World*, Museum of Modern Art, New York, March 5 to June 8, 2023.
3 Paul Goldsmith (dir.), *TVTV: Video Revolutionaries*, 2018.
4 Maureen Orth, "Guerilla Video: Days of Tape at the Conventions," *Rolling Stone*, July 20, 1972.
5 David Joselit, "An Allegory of Criticism," *October* 103, 2003, 8.
6 According to video curator Steve Seid, the group of twenty-eight included: Wendy Appel, Skip Blumberg, Nancy Cain, Frank Cavestani, Steve Christiansen, Michael Couzens, Bob Devine, Bart Friedman, Stanton Kaye, Chuck Kennedy, Anda Korsts, Joan Logue, Chip Lord, Andy Mann, Hudson Marquez, Doug Michels, Martha Miller, T. L. Morey, Jim Newman, Judy Newman, Maureen Orth, Allen Rucker, Ira Schneider, Curtis Schreier, Michael Shamberg, Jodi Sibert, Tom Weinberg, and Megan Williams—"a national sampling of Portapak politicos, ready to record." See Steve Seid, "Confrontation TV," Essays, Berkeley Art Museum & Pacific Film Archive, guerrillatv.bampfa.berkeley.edu.
7 Deirdre Boyle, *Subject to Change: Guerrilla Television Revisited.* (Oxford/New York: Oxford University Press, 1997), 38.
8 Skip Blumberg interview with the author, October 12, 2023.
9 TVTV, "Top Value Television Coverage of 1972 Political Conventions," *Radical Software* 2: 1, 1972.
10 Skip Blumberg interview with the author, October 12, 2023.
11 Richard Reeves, "Conventional Behavior," *New York Magazine*, August 28, 1972.
12 John J. O'Connor, "TV: A 'Scrapbook' of the Democratic Convention," *New York Times,* August 17, 1972.
13 Boyle, *Subject to Change*, 45.
14 Megan Williams interview with the author, May 29, 2024.
15 Boyle, *Subject to Change*, 55.
16 Hunter S. Thompson, "More Fear and Loathing in Miami," in *Fear and Loathing at Rolling Stone: The Essential Writing of Hunter S. Thompson* (London: Simon & Schuster, 2012), 253.
17 Boyle, *Subject to Change*, 61.
18 Ibid, 72.
19 Top Value Television, *The Prime Time Survey*, 1974.
20 Megan Williams interview with the author, May 29, 2024.
21 Lucy Lippard, "Too Political? Forget It!," in *Art Matters: How the Culture Wars Changed America* (New York: NYU Press, 1999), 60.
22 Tania Bruguera, "Notes on Political Timing Specificity," *Artforum* 57: 9, May, accessed October 14, 2023, artforum.com.

23 For more on *occasione*, see Machiavelli, *The Prince* (1532).
24 Boyle, *Subject to Change*, 41.
25 Claire Bishop, "Rise to the Occasion," *Artforum* 57: 9, May, accessed October 14, 2023, artforum.com.
26 Stuart Hall and Doreen Massey, "Interpreting the Crisis: Doreen Massey and Stuart Hall Discuss Ways of Understanding the Current Crisis," *Soundings* 44, 2010, 57.
27 Ibid.
28 Bishop, "Rise to the Occasion."
29 Renata Adler, "The Air: Who's Here? What Time Is It?," *New Yorker*, September 16, 1972, 116.

5. Agnes Denes, 1931–

1 Holland Cotter, "At 88, Agnes Denes Finally Gets the Retrospective She Deserves," *New York Times,* November 7, 2019.
2 Agnes Denes, *Book of Dust: The Beginning and the End of Time and Thereafter*, in *The Human Argument: The Writings of Agnes Denes* (Putnam, CT: Spring Publications, 2008), 71.
3 Agnes Denes, Lucy Lippard, et al., "Letters: Politics," *Artforum* 9: 4, December 1970, 37, artforum.com.
4 Ibid.
5 "Holding the Universe in the Palm of Your Hand: Hans Ulrich Obrist in Conversation with Agnes Denes," in *Agnes Denes: Absolutes and Intermediates* (New York: The Shed, 2019), 22.
6 Marina Hupfield and Jason Lujan, "Older Than the Dawn," in *Crossroads—New Views on Art and Environment*, ed. Ilari Laamanen (New York and Helsinki: Finnish Cultural Institute and University of the Arts, 2019), 84.
7 The exhibition catalog for *The International Art Show for the End of World Hunger* lists fifteen cities; eighteen cities are mentioned in the 1991 obituary for Bozzo, who was an art teacher at Hunter College High School. Eleanor Blau, "Ana Cristina Bozzo; Organizer of Show on Hunger Was 47," *New York Times*, May 3, 1991.
8 By the 1980s, the IMF's "structural adjustment programs" imposed on most of the former colonial world were devastating. It's odd the show took place here.
9 Rasheed Hislop, "Reaping Equity: A Survey of Food Justice Organizations in the U.S.A." (master's thesis, University of California, Davis, 2015), 24. See also Carole Counihan and Valeria Siniscalchi, "Ethnography of Food Activism: Introduction," in *Food Activism: Agency, Democracy and Economy*, ed. Carole Counihan and Valeria Siniscalchi (London, New York: Bloomsbury Academic, 2014).

10 James Nisbet, "Preface," *Second Site* (Princeton, NJ: Princeton University Press, 2021), 25.
11 Eero Yli-Vakkuri, "On Land and Environmental Art Conservation," eero.storijapan.net. Also published in *Crossroads—New Views on Art and Environment,* ed. Ilari Laamanen (New York and Helsinki: Finnish Cultural Institute and University of the Arts, 2019), 122. Yli-Vakkuri notes, "Our small restoration team included the gardener Minna Sihvonen and intern Joni Ahonen. In practice we were landscapers: we uprooted weeds, replanted trees, collected trash, and repaired structures."
12 Ibid, 123.
13 Eero Yli-Vakkuri interview with the author, October 30, 2023.
14 *The Living Pyramid* was recreated in Kassel, Germany, for documenta 14 in 2017, and in Istanbul, Turkey, in 2023, at the Sabancı University Sakıp Sabancı Museum.
15 Agnes Denes interview with the author, July 6, 2023.
16 "Entropy Made Visible: Robert Smithson interviewed by Alison Sky (1973)," in *Robert Smithson: Selected Writings* (Berkeley: University of California Press, 1996), 307.
17 Agnes Denes, "A Forest for New York," agnesdenesstudio.com.
18 Ibid.
19 Agnes Denes interview with the author, July 6, 2023.

6. fierce pussy, 1991–

1 Kate Eichhorn, *Adjusted Margin: Xerography, Art, and Activism in the Late Twentieth Century* (Cambridge, MA: MIT Press, 2016), 144. Eichhorn takes this quote from Jim Hubbard and Sarah Schulman's ACT UP Oral History project.
2 fierce pussy interview with the author, September 29, 2018.
3 For more see "Women and the AIDS Crisis," in *We Are Everywhere: Lesbians in the Archive*, Yale University Library online exhibits, onlineexhibits.library.yale.edu.
4 fierce pussy interview with the author, September 29, 2018.
5 Ibid.
6 Tara Burk, "The Use of Ephemera in Queer Visual Politics in New York City, 1991–1995," presented at the IFA-Frick Symposium on the History of Art, April 20, 2012, 11.
7 fierce pussy interview with the author, September 29, 2018.
8 Richard Rorty, "Feminism, Ideology, and Deconstruction: A Pragmatist View," *Hypatia* 8: 2, Spring 1993, 96.
9 Jo-ey Tang interview with author, September 13, 2018.

10 fierce pussy interview with Adrianne Ramsey, July 1, 2024: novembermag.com/content/fierce-pussy.
11 Ibid.
12 Michelle Alexander, "We Are Not the Resistance," *New York Times*, SR1, September 23, 2018.
13 fierce pussy interview with Adrianne Ramsey.
14 fierce pussy interview with the author, September 29, 2018.
15 fierce pussy interview with Adrianne Ramsey.
16 Ibid.

7. Dyke Action Machine!, 1991–2008

1 Carrie Moyer in Ian Berry, "Sensation Zone: A Dialogue with Carrie Moyer," in *Carrie Moyer: Pirate Jenny*, exhibition catalog (Saratoga Springs, NY: The Frances Young Tang Teaching Museum and Art Gallery, Skidmore College, 2013), 15.
2 Douglas Crimp, "Introduction," in "AIDS: Cultural Analysis/ Cultural Activism," ed. Douglas Crimp, special issue, *October* 43, Winter 1987, 7.
3 Lucy Lippard, "Too Political? Forget It!," in *Art Matters: How the Culture Wars Changed America*, eds. Brian Wallis, Marianne Weems, and Philip Yenawine (New York: New York University Press, 1999), 55.
4 Perhaps they had also learned from earlier Latin American artist-led groups fighting repression, such as the "No+" (No more) campaigns in Chile used by the Colectivo de Acciones de Arte (CADA) in the early 1980s.
5 Carrie Moyer, "Paintings, Posters, and Other Forms of Empowerment," *Carrie Moyer* (New York: Rizzoli, 2021), 248.
6 DAM! interview with the author, December 29, 2023.
7 Ibid.
8 G. J. Gates, "Discharges Under the Don't Ask, Don't Tell Policy: Women and Racial/Ethnic Minorities," The Williams Institute, UCLA School of Law, September 1, 2010.
9 Collier Schorr, "Poster Girls," *Artforum* 33: 2, October 1994, 14, artforum.com.
10 Moyer, "Paintings, Posters, and Other Forms of Empowerment," 248.
11 Ibid.
12 Carrie Moyer, "Street Appeal: Dyke Action Machine! and the Look of Gay Liberation in the 1990s," *Avantgarden und Politik. Künstlerischer Aktivismus von Dada bis zur Postmoderne*. Bielefeld, Germany: transcript 2009, 13.

13 Robert Atkins, "Girls with Wheatpaste and Webspace," *The Media Channel*, May 2001.
14 Dyke Action Machine!, *Dyke Action Machine INCORPORATED*, dykeactionmachine.com.
15 DAM! interview with the author, December 29, 2023.
16 Ibid.
17 Josh Kline, "Top Ten: The Best of 2023," *Artforum*, December 2023, artforum.com.

8. Hock E Aye Vi Edgar Heap of Birds, 1954–

1 Adam Fortunate Eagle, "Urban Indians and the Occupation of Alcatraz," in *American Indian Activism: Alcatraz to the Longest Walk*, Troy Johnson, Duane Champagne, and Joane Nagel, eds., (Chicago: University of Illinois Press, 1997), 61.
2 Johnson, Champagne, and Nagel, eds., *American Indian Activism*, 9.
3 The Vera List Center for Art and Politics, "On Country: Proppa NOW in Conversation with New Red Order."
4 Robin Wall Kimmerer, *Braiding Sweetgrass* (Minneapolis, MN: Milkweed Editions, 2015), 311.
5 The pipeline began transporting oil that June, under the insistence of President Donald Trump. At the time of this writing, it is undergoing an environmental and safety review by the US Army Corps of Engineers and there is an ongoing court fight determining whether the US government should cover the $38 million North Dakota spent responding to the protests.
6 Edgar Heap of Birds interview with the author, *Artforum*, April 25, 2017, artforum.com.
7 Bill Anthes, *Edgar Heap of Birds* (Durham, NC: Duke University Press, 2015), 13.
8 Ibid.
9 Vine Deloria Jr., "Indian Humor," in *Native American Literature: An Anthology*, ed. Lawana Trout (Chicago: NTC Publishing Group, 1999), 662.
10 New Red Order in conversation with Giampaolo Bianconi, *Artforum*, October 8, 2020, artforum.com.
11 Heap of Birds interview with the author, April 25, 2017.
12 Ibid.
13 Ibid.
14 William Smith, "In the Studio: Hock E Aye Vi Edgar Heap of Birds," *Art in America*, October 2017, artnews.com.
15 Edgar Heap of Birds, *Sharp Rocks* (Buffalo, NY: CEPA, 1986), n.p.

16 Robin Wall Kimmerer, *Braiding Sweetgrass*, 49–50.
17 Heap of Birds, *Sharp Rocks*.
18 "Does ve'ho'e Mean "Whiteman" or "Trickster"?," Cheyenne Language, cheyennelanguage.org/vehoe.htm.
19 Jenny Holzer interviewed by Kiki Smith, *Interview*, March 26, 2012, interviewmagazine.com/art/jenny-holzer.
20 Jean Fisher, "Edgar Heap of Birds," *Artforum* 26: 5, January 1988, 116–17.
21 Edgar Heap of Birds interview with the author, February 6, 2023.
22 Ibid.
23 Ibid.
24 Ibid.
25 Correspondence with the author, October 11, 2024.
26 Ibid.
27 Heap of Birds interview with the author, April 25, 2017.
28 Ibid.

9. Project Row Houses, 1994–

1 bell hooks, "House Art: Merging Public and Private," *Row: Trajectories Through the Shotgun House*, David Brown and William Williams, eds. (Houston: Rice University School of Architecture, 2004), 24.
2 Rick Lowe interview with the author, March 19, 2024.
3 Adam Bradley, "From Houston to Athens, Rick Lowe Takes His Social Sculpture Global," *New York Times Style Magazine*, June 7, 2023.
4 Rick Lowe interview with the author, March 19, 2024.
5 Andrew Garrison (dir.), *Third Ward, TX* Houston, TX: Welcome Home Productions, LLC, and Houston PBS: 2007), DVD.
6 Ibid.
7 Ibid.
8 "Social Vision and a Cooperative Community," an interview between Rick Lowe and Mark J. Stern, in Tom Finkelpearl, *What We Made: Conversations on Art and Social Cooperation* (Durham, NC: Duke University Press, 2013), 175.
9 hooks, "House Art: Merging Public and Private," 24.
10 Ibid.
11 Rick Lowe interview with the author, March 19, 2024.
12 Ryan N. Dennis, "Artists in Action," in *Collective Creative Actions: Project Row Houses at 25*, ed. Ryan N. Dennis (Houston: Project Row Houses, 2018), 15–16.

13 Rick Lowe interview with Folasade Ologundudu, Artnet, September 19, 2022.

14 "Project Profile," Project Row Houses application for the Rudy Bruner Award in Urban Excellence, 1996, rudybruneraward.org.

15 Board members include Terri Hamm, the owner and founder of Kindred Stories, a bookshop adjacent to a PRH building; Phillip Pyle III, an artist; Anita Smith, a community volunteer who has been on the board for decades; and Emily Rahbar-Daniels, a lawyer.

16 Israel McCloud interview with the author, October 15, 2024.

17 Marc Furi, "Israel McCloud: I Love 3rd Ward," vimeo.com/297841666.

18 Israel McCloud interview with the author, October 15, 2024.

19 Arts education programs at the time of this writing include an after-school program that serves more than fifty students in grades K-9 every year, and a summer program for sixty to eighty students in grades K-9, all taught by professional artists. The education program has maintained long-term, meaningful collaborations with several schools and organizations that include Houston Grand Opera, Houston Children's Museum, the Museum of Fine Arts Houston, Trinity United Methodist Church, and the Experiment in International Living Program.

20 After graduating from Penn State with a PhD and teaching at the University of Pittsburgh for three years, former YMRP member Assata Richards returned to PRH to direct the YRMP program. Former YMRP member Terena Molo, now a lawyer, has served on PRH's Board of Directors.

21 Michael Kimmelman, "In Houston, Art Is Where the Home Is," *New York Times*, December 16, 2006.

22 National Low Income Housing Association, "The Gap: A Shortage of Affordable Rental Homes," nlihc.org/gap.

23 Willie Jamaal Wright and Cameron Khalfani Herman, "No 'Blank Canvas': Public Art and Gentrification in Houston's Third Ward," *City & Society* 30 (2018), 89–116.

24 Rick Lowe interview with the author, March 19, 2024.

25 Row House CDC, "About Row House CDC," rowhousecdc.org.

26 Row House CDC, "Properties," rowhousecdc.org/property.

27 Ibid.

28 Quianta Moore, Christopher F. Kulesza, Assata Richards, *Third Ward Comprehensive Needs Assessment Data Report*, Rice University's Baker Institute for Public Policy, October 2019.

29 Wright and Khalfani Herman, "No 'Blank Canvas.' Census data shows that the white population in the Third Ward rose about 170 percent, from 1,283 residents in 2010 to 3,465 in 2020.

30 Garrison, *Third Ward, TX*.

31 Rick Lowe interview with the author, March 19, 2024.
32 Row House CDC, "About Row House CDC."
33 Ben Davis, "A Critique of Social Practice Art: What Does It Mean to Be a Political Artist?," *International Socialist Review*, 2013, isreview.org.
34 Rick Lowe interview with the author, March 19, 2024.
35 Marshella Abrams interview with the author, April 22, 2024.

10. Prescription Addiction Intervention Now, 2017–

1 Nan Goldin interview with the author, February 11, 2020.
2 Patrick Radden Keefe, "The Family that Built an Empire of Pain," *New Yorker*, October 23, 2017.
3 Joanna Walters, "Tate Art Galleries Will No Longer Accept Donations from the Sackler Family," *Guardian*, March 22, 2019. See also Laura Raicovich, *Culture Strike: Art and Museums in an Age of Protest* (Verso, 2021) for a detailed account of PAIN's beginnings.
4 Nan Goldin interview with the author, February 11, 2020.
5 "Nan Goldin on the Intertwining of Art and Activism and *All the Beauty and the Bloodshed*," a conversation moderated by Rachael Rakes, New York Film Festival.
6 Harry Cullen interview with the author, May 9, 2024.
7 Wall label, *Zoe Leonard: Survey*, Whitney Museum of American Art, 2018.
8 Ibid.
9 Harry Cullen interview with the author, May 9, 2024.
10 Other early examples include a People Against Nerve Gas demo in Seattle (then a hub for transporting the chemicals) in May 1970 and a large-scale Women Strike for Peace protest in New York in 1972.
11 "Ecology Action Plans 'Earth Day' for April Environmental Teach-In," *Harvard Crimson*, March 6, 1970.
12 Jeremy S. Bluhm, "Peaceful Earth Day Ends with Conflict at Airport," *Harvard Crimson*, April 23, 1970.
13 José Medina, *The Epistemology of Protest: Silencing, Epistemic Activism, and the Communicative Life of Resistance* (United Kingdom: Oxford University Press, 2023), 257.
14 Daniel Ross, "The Die-In: A Short History," Active History, June 29, 2015, activehistory.ca.
15 Harry Cullen interview with the author, May 9, 2024.
16 Yates McKee, *Strike Art* (New York and London: Verso, 2016), 3–4.

17 Patrick Radden Keefe, "An Astounding List of Artists Helped Persuade the Met to Remove the Sackler Name," *New Yorker*, December 10, 2021.

18 Hakim Bishara, "In Surprise 'Die-In,' Protesters Demand Harvard Take Down Sackler Name," *Hyperallergic*, April 20, 2023.

19 Harrington, United States Trustee, region 2 v. Purdue Pharma L.P. et al. 603 (2024).

20 PAIN, "We've Shamed the Sacklers. Who's Next?," *Flash Art* 341, Winter 2022–23.

21 Wojnarowicz interview in Laura Poitras, *All the Beauty and the Bloodshed* (Neon: 2022).

Index

INDEX